STANI

Standing in the Shadow of Giants: Plagiarists, Authors, Collaborators

Perspectives on Writing:
Theory, Research, Practice

Kathleen Blake Yancey and Brian Huot
Series Editors

Standing in the Shadow of Giants:
Plagiarists, Authors, Collaborators

by
Rebecca Moore Howard
Texas Christian University

Ablex Publishing Corporation
Stamford, Connecticut

Printed in the United States of America

Library of Congress Cataloging-in-Publication Data

Howard, Rebecca Moore.
    Standing in the shadow of giants : plagiarists, authors, collaborators /
by Rebecca Moore Howard.
        p. cm. — (Perspectives on writing ; v. 2)
    Includes bibliographical references and index.
    ISBN 1-56750-436-1 (cloth) — ISBN 1-56750-437-X (pbk.)
    1. Plagiarism.   2. Literary ethics.   3. Authorship.   4. Creation
(Literary, artistic, etc).   I. Title.   II. Series.
PN167.H69   1999
808—dc21   99-49978
                                                              CIP

Ablex Publishing Corporation
100 Prospect Street
P.O. Box 811
Stamford, CT 06904-0811

For

Tim Garten

Contents

III.   Collaborators: How Can We Get Out of this Mess?

Preface

My interest in plagiarism began in 1986, when fully one third of the students in my General Education course committed what at that time I regarded as heinous plagiarism. The "solutions" to which I resorted did not seem to solve the problem, nor could I find satisfying alternatives. I began reading the literature on plagiarism available in composition studies; I talked with deans, colleagues, and students about the quandary; and as these discussions progressed, I became increasingly dissatisfied with my own ideas about plagiarism—and everybody else's, too. Eventually I began reading theory of authorship and relevant intellectual history, and I have now come to a moment in the inquiry when I am ready to share my thoughts with readers. These thoughts are considerably different from my beliefs when I began this inquiry.

The changes that my beliefs have undergone are the result of dialogue with far more people than I can name here, but I would like to credit a few who would not otherwise receive bibliographic citation in the text. Peter Elbow has taken the time to talk with me about the representations of the gatekeeper in Chapter 2. The Foucaudian argument in that chapter was presented as a conference paper first at the 1992 Penn State Conference on Rhetoric and Composition, where Jack Selzer's supportive response gave me heart to continue working with the controversial material; and then, revised and expanded, at the Modern Language Association in 1992 and 1993, thanks to Deborah Tannen's receptivity to my ideas. Dennis Baron carefully read a later draft and helped me avert errors in reasoning to which I was falling prey, as did anonymous reviewers for *College English*. In a generous E-mail exchange, John Schilb helped me ponder the implications of the word "resistance" as I use it in Chapter 3. The members of SHARP-L, the electronic discussion group sponsored by the Society for the History of Authorship, Reading, and Publishing—and especially Raymond G. McInnis—helped me gather and interpret expressions of the metaphor "standing on the shoulders of giants" that are detailed in Chapter 4. Also in Chapter 4, Andrew Keller advised me as I considered the differences between ancient and medieval authorship. My account of 19th-century American attitudes is substantially indebted to conversations with Tom Howard, and Sarah Wider gave me important leads in 19th-century American literary theory. Portions of the article "Cryoauthorship: The Mummy Walks!" (Howard, 1995a) appear, in a revised form, in Chapter 5 and elsewhere. Also, portions of "A Plagiarism Pentimento," published in the *Journal of Teaching Writing* (Howard, 1993), appear, in a revised form, in Chapter 9 and elsewhere. As a reviewer for that journal, Joseph Harris offered invaluable advice for interpreting the issue of patchwriting. Sandra Jamieson's perspectives on pedagogy, which I absorbed as we collaborated on *The Bedford Guide to Teaching Writing in the Disciplines* (Howard & Jamieson, 1995), have substantially influenced not just my ideas but my very voice, especially in Chapter 8. Dozens of Colgate University students in successive offerings of General Education 327, "Talent, Society, and the State: Defining and Regulating Intellectual Property," have made helpful responses to my ideas about plagiarism and authorship, especially with reference to the policy questions that appear in Chapter 9. One of those students, Cade Beerman, also reminded me of the difficulties I might have in engaging a readership for *Standing in the Shadow of Giants*. When I told him I would like to quote students' opinions in this book, he approved of the plan—but not for reasons I had considered: "You're going to need student comments to quote if you're going to have enough material to fill a book on plagiarism. Not that many people find this a fascinating subject, you know." Revised excerpts from the article "Plagiarisms, Authorships, and the Academic Death Penalty," published in *College English* (Howard, 1995b), appear in Chapter 9 and elsewhere. As respondents to that article, Peter Schroeder (1996) and Barbara Welch (1996) pushed me to realize that I had to articulate a position on patchwriting that could not readily be absorbed into established thinking on the subject.

Alan Glos, Linda Murphy, Lynn Waldman, and Keith D. Miller have helped me recognize the practical issues involved in adjudicating plagiarism. Frederick Luciani's and Elayne Zorn's readings of interim drafts substantially improved the text. Martha Dietz not only read and commented upon portions of this book but also listened to it as together, summer and winter, we bicycled along thousands of miles of rural New York roads. Hers has always been a voice of reason in my ear. David

Hughes helped me track down obscure sources and also took it upon himself to keep me abreast of new publications on the topic of plagiarism. Paul Amore applied his considerable store of authorship theory to reading a late draft of the manuscript and offering valuable suggestions. And my editors at Ablex, Kathleen Blake Yancey and Brian Huot, have been unflaggingly supportive—not only by being willing to publish this book in the first place but also by pushing me forward when I flagged. Tom Howard gets the Oscar for his unfailing enthusiasm for this project, his willingness to read, respond to, and proofread innumerable drafts, his skill in teaching these materials with me, the cultural capital with which he has broadened my understanding of authorships' roles in Western culture, and his willingness to carry the load on the frequent occasions when I am one.

Most recently, I have had the good fortune to be part of the (In)Citers, a Texas Christian University scholarly collaborative that is developing some important theories of authorship. The ongoing work of Paul Amore, Mary Lamb, Thomas Reedy, Amy Rupiper, Kurt Schick, and Patricia Tallakson has deepened my understanding of theory of authorship. Among the many traces of our work apparent in this volume is "(re)formative composition," a term that rescues me from a lexical abyss.

Throughout this volume, I am indebted to the theoretical work of Martha Woodmansee. In her various publications and in her work at conferences and in professional organizations she has, I believe, made theory of authorship a recognized field of inquiry in print culture studies. When we think of authorship we tend to think most readily of Foucault (1977b) and Barthes (1977); but it is Martha Woodmansee (often with copyright attorney Peter Jaszi) who is accomplishing the aetiological work of connecting the 18th-century birth of modern authorship to our present circumstances (see Jaszi & Woodmansee, 1994, 1996; Woodmansee, 1984, 1994a, 1994b; Woodmansee & Jaszi, 1994a, 1994b, 1995).

The contribution that this book endeavors to make to the field of composition studies is centrally indebted to a single article written in 1989 by Glynda Hull and Mike Rose. As Chapter 8 explains, the implications of that article on my own thinking have been far reaching; they have made the thesis of this book both possible and plausible. In that article, Hull and Rose have done composition studies a great service, for they have provided, in research and theory, a fresh way of thinking about writer-text collaboration. The courage of their stance on writer-text collaboration has emboldened me, and, I hope, others, to think again about what we believe to be "true" and "right."

The work that most informs *Standing in the Shadow of Giants* is that of Andrea Lunsford and Lisa Ede (Ede & Lunsford, 1983; Lunsford & Ede, 1990, 1994), who have, under the rubric of collaboration theory, made theory of authorship a recognized field of inquiry in composition and rhetoric. Their *Singular Texts/Plural Authors* (Lunsford & Ede, 1990) demands that teachers and scholars of composition consider the indissoluble link between theories and pedagogies of collaboration. My book endeavors to open up the writer-text collaborations that are customarily hidden or outlawed in pedagogy, though acknowledged and even celebrated in theory. Hence, the work at hand may be seen as making explicit one set of implications in *Singular Texts*. Lunsford and Ede's work is the primary intertext for *Standing in the Shadow of Giants,* and their insistence on the mutual constitution of theory and practice is a guiding principle for this book.

I have asked for and accepted a lot of help from my friends (whose shoulders must by now be mighty sore), and I have made many new friends as this project unfolded. Though I can't begin to name and thank them all individually, they are all in here.

Exergue: Standing On and Climbing Down from the Shoulders of Giants

Imitation is natural to man from childhood, one of his advantages over the lower animals being this, that he is the most imitative creature in the world, and learns at first by imitation.

Aristotle

We are as dwarfs mounted on the shoulders of giants, so that although we perceive many more things than they, it is not because our vision is more piercing or our stature higher, but because we are carried and elevated higher thanks to their gigantic size.

Bernard of Chartres

We are like dwarfs on the shoulders of giants...by whose kindness we see further than they do, when we adhere to the works of the ancients and arouse into some newness of being their more elegant sentences, which age and human neglect have let decay and become almost lifeless.

Peter of Blois

It is silly to trust only the ancients. The early discoverers were men too. If we should be discouraged by perceiving too many tracks of our predecessors, we should be ashamed.... And we should not be moved by that trite, vulgar saying that there is nothing new, and nothing new can be said.

Petrarch

I say with Didacus Stella, a dwarf standing on the shoulders of a giant may see farther than a giant himself.

Robert Burton

Imitari is nothing. So doth the hound his master, the ape his keeper, the tired horse his rider.

Love's Labor Lost

But hee is worst, who (beggarly) doth chaw
Others wits fruits, and in his ravenous maw
Rankly digested, doth those things out-spue,
As his owne things....

John Donne

It is true they open'd the gates, and made the way, that went before us; but as Guides, not Commanders.

Ben Jonson

If I have seen further it is by standing upon the shoulders of Giants.

Isaac Newton

It was widely believed in the eighteenth century, even by defenders of the Ancients, that modern philosophy had made remarkable strides beyond that of the past.

George A. Kennedy

Invention builds on a foundation of knowledge accumulated from previous generations, knowledge that constitutes a social legacy of ideas, forms, and ways of thinking.

Karen Burke LeFevre

My title [Giants and Dwarfs] emphatically does not refer to the old saw "We are dwarfs, but we stand on the shoulders of giants." This expresses, in the guise of humility, too much self-satisfaction. Do giants let themselves be climbed so easily? Is it their function to carry dwarfs on their shoulders? Perhaps they were once so gracious but now have set us down on the earth and quietly stolen away, leaving us with an illusion of broader perspectives. The groundless assumption of intimacy with greatness soon gives way for a new generation which denies that there ever were giants and asserts that the whole story is a lie made up by their teachers to empower themselves. The giants are, I presume, looking down on this little comedy and laughing.

Allan Bloom

We may not always be able to claim that we see far because we stand on the shoulders of giants; we do, however, stand on the shoulders of thousands of good-willed teachers and writers surprisingly like us, who faced in 1870 or 1930 problems amazingly similar to those we confront each time we enter the classroom.

Robert J. Connors

Two different acts are considered plagiarism: (1) borrowing someone's ideas, information, or language without documenting the source and (2) documenting the source but paraphrasing the source's language too closely, without using quotation marks to indicate that words and phrases have been borrowed.

Diana Hacker

Introduction: Toward a Pedagogy of (Re)Formative Composition

Finding one's language, one's voice…is not finding something which is out there, or in here, but is forged dialogically in response to the already written and in anticipation of the hearer's responsive word—it is forged on the borderline.

George L. Dillon (1988)

In 1986, one third of the students in my General Education class at a prestigious liberal arts college plagiarized an assigned paper. The sort of plagiarism they committed is what I have come to call "patchwriting": copying from a source text and then deleting some words, altering grammatical structures, or plugging in one synonym for another. The practice is uniformly banned in composition handbooks and in colleges' academic codes. Even when patchwriting is accompanied by citation and documentation, our standard academic rules label it a transgression subject to punishment.

When the patchwriting occurred in my 1986 class, I responded in what I then thought was a generous way: I gave all the plagiarists an "F" on the paper, lectured them on quotation, citation, and plagiarism, and invited them to revise. I now regard that response not only as inappropriate, but as detrimental to the students' learning. The immediate results, for one thing, were unsatisfactory: two of the students *still* plagiarized, even on the revision. Deeply disturbed by their seemingly irremediable failure to observe basic rules of academic discourse, I searched for answers. Why had so many well-prepared students, at a prestigious university with high admissions standards, plagiarized the paper in the first place? Why was it that two of those students didn't seem to respond to instruction, didn't seem able to stop plagiarizing? Was there something wrong with those students' ethics? With their academic preparation? With their willingness or ability to learn? With the university's admissions procedures? Or was there something wrong with my teaching? Had I offered inadequate explanation? Had I overlooked something that I should have explained?

Or, I finally came to ask, were there problems with my notion of plagiarism and academic ethics? I now answer this question with a "yes." My "generous" response was ineffective because it proceeded from erroneous premises. I was wrong to believe that the students had plagiarized; I was wrong to believe that they patchwrote either because they were unethical or because they did not know how to quote and cite. Those students were *learning*, not cheating, and there was nothing wrong with their willingness or ability to learn.

But there *was* something wrong with my teaching. My zeal to socialize them into the avowed conventions of academic writing was actually preventing their learning. Patchwriting was for them—as it is for us all—a primary means of understanding difficult texts, of expanding one's lexical, stylistic, and conceptual repertoires, of finding and trying out new voices in which to speak.

Patchwriting is a form of *imitatio,* of *mimesis.* It is a process of evaluating a source text, selecting passages pertinent to the patchwriter's purposes, and transporting those passages to the patchwriter's new context. Patchwriting accomplishes a (re)formation of a source text by providing a new locale and thus new meaning for source material.[1] It is a form of verbal sculpture, molding new shapes from preexisting materials. It is a form of *pentimento,* in which one writer reshapes the work of another while leaving traces of the earlier writer's thought and intentions.[2] It is something that all academic writers do. Patchwriting belongs not in a category with cheating on exams and purchasing term papers, but in a category with the ancient tradition of learning through apprenticeship and mimicry.

THE MEAN CASE OF PLAGIARISM

To make these assertions is to advance a theory of authorship, focusing on the field of textual behaviors currently labeled plagiarism. To bring theory to bear on this field is an unusual move. Plagiarism is an undertheorized field, commonly regarded as a distasteful, instrumental, necessary function of pedagogy, unrelated to theory. Until very recently, scholarly discussion of plagiarism assumed it to be a natural (though loathsome) category, not a constructed one; hence, these discussions did not undertake causal and evaluative arguments about the construction of plagiarism and the cultural work that this construction performs. Instead, most scholarship on plagiarism either reported the incidence of plagiarism, described students' or teachers' attitudes toward it, or offered policy proposals for preventing, catching, or punishing it. Such studies are often cited in composition and rhetoric: Doris R. Dant's 1986 research into the incidence of plagiarism, published in the *English Journal*, reports that among the high school students she surveyed, 80 percent confessed to having plagiarized. Barry Kroll's article "How College Freshmen View Plagiarism" (1988) describes students' and teachers' attitudes toward it. Thomas Mallon offers a book-length policy proposal: his popular *Stolen Words* (1989) argues that plagiarism is rampant, that it constitutes a threat to text production, and that we all must therefore accept the responsibility of punishing plagiarists.

The theoretical silence on plagiarism, the absence of causal arguments about the construction of the category and evaluative arguments about the cultural work it performs, is itself semiotic. It is no accident that the Platonic dialogue *Crito* (trans. 1969/1994) is structured such that the eponymous character Crito serves the rhetorical function of providing Plato's Socrates with counterevidence, and that by the end of the dialogue, Socrates has rendered Crito speechless. Counterargument must be silenced; yet the silence continues to mark the place of counterargument. The reasons for counterargument's being silenced rather than honored are always worth investigating; to recognize and explore absence is to deepen our understanding of an issue. Why could Crito not be left with a voice and a plausible opinion at the end of the dialogue? Why are theoretical discussions of plagiarism too distasteful to be held?

Textual scholars have, from time to time, explained and justified the silencing of theoretical considerations of plagiarism. Augustus Kolich (1983) offers his rationale:

> ...I doubt whether many textbook writers or journal authors would boast
> that their approach to composition improves student writing while reducing
> the incidents of plagiarism. This is hardly a claim that anyone would want to
> attach to a writing program and hardly something positive to boast about.
> So the issue of plagiarism is usually pushed to the appendix of any discus
> sion of the teaching of writing. (p. 142)

Plagiarism, in other words, exemplifies what Cicero would deem a "mean" case, "unworthy of serious attention (trans. 1968, p. 20; see also Crowley, 1994, p. 174). Writing in the same decade as Kolich, Thomas McFarland's 1985 book *Originality and Imagination* asserts that we are ambivalent not only about accusing others of plagiarism but also about theorizing it:

> Plagiarism is a cultural occurrence about which there has been remarkably little theoretical discussion. The reason is not far to seek: the practice occupies a gray area, encroaching in many instances on clearly defined standards of propriety and ethics. Although plagiarism must surely be—one can hardly doubt the fact—a variant form of the phenomenon of imitation and influence, it brings the conception of individuality into conflict with itself and thereby tends to be rather uneasily dismissed from cultural consciousness. (p. 22)

In 1994, when the topic of plagiarism was introduced in WPA-L and WAC-L E-mail discussion groups (for writing program administrators and writing-across-the-curriculum practitioners), some commentators urged silence, charging that plagiarism did not offer a suitable topic for the group to investigate. The discussion—which did, in truncated form, ensue—included expressions of distaste for the topic, as well as assertions that the dead horse of plagiarism had already been unduly flogged; implications that plagiarism is a matter of instrumentalist practice rather than theoretical exploration; and contradictory assertions that the theoretical import of plagiarism needs further exploration.

Dant, Kroll, Mallon, and Kolich were writing in the 1980s, in a time when the theoretical silence on plagiarism still dominated composition studies. The silencing impulses in the WPA-L and WAC-L on-line discussions are an artifact of the 1980s status quo.

But that status quo changed in the 1990s. Composition studies at century's end includes fresh inquiry into theory of authorship and its cohort, plagiarism. Glynda Hull and Mike Rose (1989), Andrea Lunsford and Susan West (1996), Mary Minock (1995), Martha Woodmansee and Peter Jaszi (1995), and many others are advancing causal and evaluative arguments about our received notions of the author—arguments that, in the 1990s, have gained a wider audience.

Drawing on their work, *Standing in the Shadow of Giants* ventures an evaluative argument about the author's supposed opposite, the plagiarist. Part I argues that the term "plagiarism" has come to describe disparate textual behaviors and that the inclusion of patchwriting in the category of plagiarism denies students opportunities to become scholars. In my evaluation, patchwriting has positive rather than negative value.

Yet the prospect of decriminalizing patchwriting causes seismic disturbances in composition studies. Labeling patchwriting as a form of plagiarism is far more than a simple categorical error that, once recognized, can be readily remedied. Even when we acknowledge that we all patchwrite (with varying degrees of sophistication), we persist, paradoxically, in associating patchwriting with academic dishonesty. Apparently that association accomplishes cultural work so important that patchwriting must continue to be criminalized, despite overwhelming evidence that this criminalization is arbitrary, unnecessary, illogical, and counterproductive.

Part II of this book amounts to an archaeology of the cultural work accomplished by the criminalization of patchwriting: The criminalization of patchwriting seems necessary and natural *because* it denies students means of joining the academy. When pedagogy treats students as criminals for practicing one of the important means by which scholars write, it closes the gate to the academy, locking students out. It serves what James Berlin (1996) would call the purposes of the liberal culturalists or what Pierre Bourdieu and Jean-Claude Passeron (1977/1990) would call the protection of the power of the dominant culture. The educational system can appear to be a meritocracy, facilitating students' entry to power, while the criminalizing of patchwriting surreptitiously blocks that entry and maintains the hierarchical status quo.

Richard Leo Enos's 1993 book, *Greek Rhetoric before Aristotle*, establishes that rhetoric's origins are more political than intellectual. *Standing in the Shadow of Giants* essays a similar task for the representations of plagiarism in composition pedagogy: despite appearances, their impetus is more ideological than philosophical. These representations are so embedded in academic culture that teachers of widely divergent ideological orientations come together to affirm patchwriting as plagiarism, unaware that this affirmation serves liberal culture ideology.

Most contemporary scholars of composition and rhetoric do not endorse the hierarchical ideals of liberal culture. As a discipline, we more readily align ourselves with what Berlin (1987) describes as social-democratic rhetoric. We see ourselves, in Peter Elbow's terms (1983), as facilitators, enablers. We describe ourselves, in Paolo Freire's terms (1968), as engaged in liberatory pedagogy. How, then, can we reconcile ourselves to the continuing criminalization of patchwriting? My answer is that we cannot. Even though patchwriting's complex imbrication in our hierarchical culture prevents its ready transformation into an authorized classroom practice, we must undertake the hard work of that transformation. Part III of this book surveys rhetorical practices on which that transformation might draw, and then it offers my own policy arguments for a positive pedagogy of patchwriting and for supportive institutional structures.

WRITING HISTORIES OF COMPOSITION STUDIES

This is a history of composition studies. Many histories precede it. James Berlin (1984, 1987, 1996) provides the model for the genre; John Brereton (1995) offers primary documents; David Russell (1988) and Susan Miller (1991) reveal the operation of ideology in composition curricula;

and Maxine Hairston (1982) and Richard Ohmann (1976) take a teleological perspective. Miriam Brody (1993) traces the politics of gender in
the development of the discipline, and Sharon Crowley (1990) undertakes an aetiology of the emphasis on correctness.

This history is like Brody's (1993) and Crowley's (1990), inasmuch as it
follows a single strand: plagiarism. The problem it addresses is the contradictions between what composition scholars now collectively believe
about reading and writing, and what composition teachers—including
many of those same composition scholars—actually put into practice in
their classroom representations of authorship and plagiarism. Like Hairston (1982) and Ohmann (1976), this history is teleological: I conclude
this volume with recommendations for how those contradictions might be
reduced or at least addressed. Like Russell (1988) and Miller (1991), this
history expends a great deal of ink in the task of connecting the development of the notion of plagiarism—and the development of the discrep-
ancy between current belief and practice—to ideology. Unlike Brereton
(1995), it does not include primary documents. But in the spirit of Brereton, it endeavors to include a wide range of perspectives, and to allow
commentators their own voices.

The composition history that this book offers is a history of how patchwriting came to fall outside the category of mimesis and into the category
of cheating. Its ideological task is to identify the cultural work that this
criminalization of patchwriting serves. And its teleology is an effort to
restore patchwriting to the category of mimesis.

This history asserts that patchwriting has a legitimate and valuable
place in literacy instruction. I am prepared to take a further step and recommend that the category of plagiarism be redefined by educational
institutions: that authorial intention become a component in determining
what is and is not plagiarism, and that patchwriting qualify as plagiarism
and thus as transgression only if the author's intention is fraudulent—
only if the author, the student, appears to have been trying to deceive his
or her readers. Absent any evidence of unethical authorial intention, the
default category for patchwriting should be learning rather than cheating. This is not to advocate a "more lenient attitude" toward plagiarism;
rather, it is to enlarge the range of imagined motivations for textual practices traditionally labeled plagiarism, which in turn enlarges the range of
appropriate responses, redefining and recategorizing the very word *plagiarism*. Consigning patchwriting to the category of cheating serves liberal
culture gatekeeping purposes: it is a means of determining who is *already
possessed* of high literacy. It brands those who are still acquiring high literacy not as learners but as criminals, thereby fettering their acquisition of
high literacy.

NOTES

[1]The scholarly group (In)Citers, of which I am a member, has generated the term "(re)formation" to describe what authors do when they cite sources. The term derives from Jerome McGann's (1998) "deformative criticism," in which the action of criticism includes making new texts.

[2]Pentimento, in Lynn Worsham's (1991) description of Lillian Hellman's metaphor, amounts to "a form of repentance that occurs when a painter changes his or her mind and redraws the lines expressing an artistic conception. When the paint ages and becomes transparent, it is sometimes possible to see the original lines and the initial conception still etched in the memory of paint and canvas. Pentimento is 'a way of seeing,' Hellman writes, 'and then seeing again'" (p. 85).

1

Plagiarists: What a Mess!

1

The Problems of Plagiarism

Repetition in Butler's poststructuralist model is not necessarily repetition of the same; instead, repetition or citation is always potentially repetition with a difference—hence the possibility for resignifying and subverting identities.

Tim Dean (1994)

Some of the problems of plagiarism are well known among teachers. There's the problem of catching plagiarists—the legendary hunt through the library in the (usually vain) hope of finding the plagiarist's sources. "The burden of plagiarism," says Edith Skom (1986), "falls less (maybe never) on the criminal than on the one who has to follow through on the crime" (p. 5). Whereas Skom describes the triumphs of her own library detective work, Thomas Mallon (1989) alludes to his frustrations in the fruitless faculty search through the library "while Heather's back in Wyatt Hall blowing a joint and watching a Billy Idol video" (p. 96).

There's also the problem of punishing plagiarists. Mallon (1989) again offers an evocative description, this time of the plagiarist who has been suspended from school and who, far from wallowing in shame, will "only go to Aspen for a couple of weeks" (p. 98).

Then there's the very basic problem of defining plagiarism. The *Council Chronicle*, distributed to members of the National Council of Teachers of English, heads an article with the title, "We Want to Know: How Do You Define Plagiarism?" (1993). The article compiles responses to a previous issue's invitation for readers to contribute their definitions of plagiarism. The irony is profound, even startling: College teachers engage in energetic searches for library sources; feel "tentative" and "embarrassed" about accusing students of the crime (Skom, 1986, p. 5); feel angry when the plagiarist isn't ashamed of the crime; worry that lax attitudes toward plagiarism threaten civilization (Navrozov, 1993); yet cannot define the term that causes so much anxiety—and, if the rhetoric of the *Council Chronicle* is any gauge, take for granted that no commonly held definition of plagiarism exists. Nothing in the issue that calls for reader contributions (nor in the issue that compiles them) suggests any individual or collective embarrassment about the elusiveness of a definition for an act that, if committed, can be punished with the academic death penalty—expulsion from college.

In that milieu, I offer my own contribution to definition: I assert that patchwriting does not belong in the category of plagiarism. In that sense, I am working toward reducing the problems of plagiarism.

But in another sense, I wish to increase them. To the preceding list I would add another problem of plagiarism: the variation not only in how we define it, but also in how we respond to it. Two case studies will illustrate the extent of that variation and will also suggest patterns within it.

UNDERGRADUATE STUDENTS AND ROBERT DAVIDSON

Illustrating sanctioned, standard responses to plagiarism, my first case study comes from my own class. In Spring 1986, while engaged in the familiar task of responding to students' papers, I encountered the loathsome apparition of plagiarism—or what at that time I categorized with plagiarism. I believed, too, that I knew the best way to deal with it. In General Education 101, a core course required of all first-year students at Colgate University, I had asked the students to read a brief excerpt from Robert L. Davidson's *Genesis 1-11* (1973) and to consider its implications not only for a reading of Genesis, but also of Plato's *Phaedo* (trans. 1981). The following sentence in one student's paper, though, violated the textual ethics described in writers' handbooks and in the college's academic honesty policy:

> Specifically, story myths are not for entertainment purposes, rather they serve as answers to questions people ask about life, about society and about the world in which they live. [Student 3]

The similarity of this passage to the original text, Davidson's *Genesis 1-11* (1973), was too close to be acceptable:

Such 'story myths' are not told for their entertainment value. They provide answers to questions people ask about life, about society and about the world in which they live. (p. 10)

The student writer, I assumed, had been insufficiently educated in the handling of sources. But then I read another paper whose author had the same problem:

Story myths provide answers to philosophical questions about life, society and the world. [Student 6]

As I read through the stack of papers, I was faced with a veritable flood of plagiarism. Some of the students had documented the source and some had not; but 9 of the 26 writers in my class had failed to summarize, paraphrase, or quote from the Davidson text. Instead, they had appropriated Davidson's (1973) words wholesale:

Davidson explains that story myths answer questions people ask about life, about society and about the world that we live in. [Student 8]

The first type of story myths, which are used to explain a principle or answer a question about life, society, and the world. [Student 4]

It provides answers to questions people ask about life, about society, and about the world in which they live. [Student 9]

He says it can either answer questions people ask about life, society and the world in which they live or it can be the literary creation of a teacher to help others learn the meaning of life. [Student 5]

The story myth will be discussed in the following context: story myths provide answers to questions people ask about life, society, and the world in which they live; these stories can be handed down within the community or by a conscious literary creation of a teacher whose concern is to help others share his insight of the meaning of life. [Student 7]

When recapitulating the source material, these writers appropriated phrases, patched together into new sentences; they appropriated whole sentences, deleting what they consider irrelevant words and phrases; and they appropriated phrases and sentences in which they changed grammar and syntax, substituting synonyms straight from *Roget's Thesaurus*. Some provided footnotes, attributing the source; others did not. The samples reproduced above represent only a portion of the patchwriting that characterized the prose of one third of the class.

After consulting with the Dean of Students, I gave the patchwriters "F's," delivered a lecture on citation and documentation, and invited them to revise. All nine did; seven of the revisions contained no obvious patchwriting.

GERHARD JOSEPH AND THOMAS MCFARLAND

Our responses to the appearance of patchwriting in colleagues' texts are not always of a kind with our responses to the patchwriting of students. Consider, for example, Gerhard Joseph's patchwriting from Thomas McFarland's *Originality and Imagination* (1985):

> Because it *brings the bourgeois conception of individual identity into conflict with itself,* plagiarism *tends to be easily dismissed from our cultural consciousness* and has occasioned *relatively little theoretical discussion....* (emphasis added; Joseph, 1994, p. 267)

This quotation appears in the middle of an extended summary of and commentary on McFarland's book. Whereas McFarland is advancing general theories of authorship, Joseph is applying them to the question of Charles Dickens' complex relationship with international copyright. Both in signal phrases and in footnotes, Joseph acknowledges McFarland as his source. However, his patchwriting from McFarland is apparent when one compares the preceding quotation from Joseph with the following from McFarland:

> Plagiarism is a cultural occurrence about which there has been *remarkably little theoretical discussion.* The reason is not far to seek: the practice occupies a gray area, encroaching in many instances on clearly defined standards of propriety and ethics. Although plagiarism must surely be—one can hardly doubt the fact—a variant form of the phenomenon of imitation and influence, it *brings the conception of individuality into conflict with itself* and thereby tends to be rather *uneasily dismissed from cultural consciousness.* (emphasis added, p. 22)

Joseph's collaboration with McFarland's text offers some interesting variations. Joseph changes McFarland's adverb *uneasily* to *easily,* and he elides all mention of propriety and ethics. His insertion of the adjective *bourgeois* to describe the "concept of individuality" may constitute his own summary of McFarland's discussion of propriety and ethics. Joseph may, in other words, be identifying propriety and ethics as bourgeois constructs.

If Gerhard Joseph had been in my General Education class in 1986, he would have received an "F," a lecture on citation, and an invitation to revise. Instead, he is a theorist of authorship who, in a brief passage, allowed his patchwriting from an acknowledged source to be apparent rather than erased. Does anyone think he should be punished or censured? Not likely. In fact, in order to write about the case, I have to fend off the feeling of being mean-spirited; I respect Gerhard Joseph as a scholar. He doesn't deserve the punishment of an "F" on the essay—and neither did my students.

The passage in question is, I believe, best described as a momentary lapse from the smooth erasure of patchwriting that he, as a professional academic writer, customarily accomplishes. It's not that Joseph usually doesn't patchwrite but did in this instance; it's that all of us patchwrite all the time, but we usually cover the trail. Traces sometimes crop up, as they do in the Joseph passage and as they no doubt do from time to time in this book. Erasing the trail is not a matter of hiding guilty evidence; it's a matter of good prose style. When the trail is obvious, we call it plagiarism; when it is erased, we call it synthesis or even original writing.

PATCHWRITING AS LEARNING

Although neither my pedagogy of 1986 nor most of today's college plagiarism policies acknowledge it, students' patchwriting is often a move toward membership in a discourse community, a means of learning unfamiliar language and ideas. Far from indicating a lack of respect for a source text, their patchwriting is a gesture of reverence. The patchwriter recognizes the profundity of the source and strives to join the conversation in which the source participates. To join this conversation, the patchwriter employs the language of the target community.

Patchwriting occurs on the borders of texts—an image that derives from Bakhtinian notions of polyphony and dialogism that have wide currency in composition studies. Kathryn T. Flannery (1991) states, "Students are always caught 'intertextually'—they are never inventing a new language out of nothing, but patch together fragments of the multiple texts, the multiple voices (as Bakhtin would put it) that are already available to them" (p. 707). Bakhtin's (1981) theory of dialogism denies the possibility of anyone's owning language. Composition studies' appropriations of Bakhtin's theory assert that learning happens in the sharing of language.

WRITING AS PATCHWRITING

Patchwriting is not only a means of students' learning; it is at the heart of writing itself. It is a means whereby experienced writers like Gerhard

Joseph interpret and build upon the ideas and words encountered in their sources. George Dillon (1988) speaks not just of students, but of all writers: "Finding one's voice is...not just an emptying and purifying oneself of other's words...but also an admitting, an adopting, an embracing of filiations, communities, and discourses" (p. 71). David R. Russell (1993) agrees:

> Learning is at bottom acquiring habits from other people, habits of activity, including communicating and thinking, which are, in the deepest sense, kinds of activity, since there is no real division between mind and body, thinking and doing. (1993, p. 183)

Corroborating the example of Joseph's (1994) patchwriting from McFarland (1985) is an extensive literature cataloguing professional writers' visible border writing, which in this literature are usually labeled "plagiarism" (see, for example, Fruman, 1971; Lindey, 1952; Mallon, 1989; Miller, 1990, 1992). Most of these catalogues describe incidents of patchwriting in order to "expose" plagiarists. The plagiarists of whom they speak typically include those who appropriate entire texts, as well as those who engage in visible patchwriting. Thomas Mallon (1989) is perhaps the most energetic of these commentators; his project is to persuade his readers that plagiarists and those who do not expose them must be denounced and punished, in order to preserve writing itself. A few, however—Keith D. Miller (1990, 1992, 1993) most notable among them—endeavor to challenge the notion of plagiarism as a unified, criminal category.

The many catalogues of professional writers' unmarked appropriations from texts demonstrate how persistent the practice is—which to some will prompt the observation that we are living in a degraded age. To me, though, it suggests that patchwriting might not be so much a sin into which writers lapse as it is a fundamental part of the writing process. Even Harold Bloom (1973), as he yearns for a time now passed, a time in which poets could participate in the "primordial chaos" that is the fountainhead of poetic creativity (p. 60), acknowledges that all writing today is "influenced." We do not write alone, and often it is texts, not people, with whom we collaborate.

PATCHWRITING AS TRANSGRESSION

Yet college writers' handbooks describe patchwriting not as learning nor as a natural part of writing, but as cheating. (Handbook discussions of plagiarism usually address patchwriting and citation; they do not include enjoinders against buying term papers. It is in college academic codes that the three are grouped together.) These handbook discussions deserve careful consideration: By definition, handbooks speak for the textual status quo, and their representations are concise. They are not the place where cutting-edge theory is put into practice; they are the place where standard practice is explained. Their representations provide essential data for exploring yet another problem of plagiarism: the cultural work accomplished by the criminalization of patchwriting.

Contemporary writers' handbooks severely constrain students' collaboration with source texts. One may *respond to* source texts or use them as *evidence of* one's own assertions, or one may *learn from* source texts. All of these uses, the handbooks tell students, must be scrupulously marked (cited). The instructions for citing sources are extensive; the fifth edition of *The Bedford Handbook* (Hacker, 1998), for example, devotes seven pages to "integrating sources" and then 28 pages to MLA and APA documentation.

All handbooks' instructions on handling sources proceed from the assumption that ideas and words can be differentiated according to source—that they can be attributed, cited, documented. The *St. Martin's Handbook* (Lunsford & Connors, 1992) is unusual in its recognition of the ambiguities involved, when it observes that citing "every idea you build on…is an impossible task. In practical terms, where do you draw the line" (p. 577)? Such statements accord with the contemporary theory from which literary theorist Susan Stewart speaks when she declares that scrupulous citation would amount to "a full (and necessarily impossible) history of the writer's subjectivity" (1991, p. 25). However, writers' handbook representations of authorship seldom speak from contemporary theory, but instead from a point of view that might variously be associated with modernism, Romanticism, or current-traditionalism.

In handbook representations of patchwriting, ambiguities are not acknowledged but resolved. One key to that resolution is ethical discourse: handbooks tell students that ethical writers mark all their influenced words and ideas and that they do not patchwrite.

The combination of suppressing ambiguity and calling upon ethical principles results in a sort of covenant theology for composition.[1] Although covenant rhetoric derives from the Hebrew Testament, it has met with a variety of secular applications. An important part of American Puritan literature, for example, was "federal exhortations couched in the vocabulary of the covenant of grace" (Bercovitch, 1974, p. 8). To describe the individual's relationship with the New World community, the Puritans drew upon the Hebrew Testament language that described humans' relationships with God.

To unify and legislate the writer's relationship with source texts, contemporary writers' handbooks employ a similar rhetoric. Kennedy (1980) describes a tripartite "general pattern" of Hebrew Testament covenant rhetoric, and this pattern echoes audibly in contemporary writer's handbooks' enjoinders against patchwriting:

1. "[S]trengthen the authority of the Lord by reminding the audience of what he has done";
2. "[A]dd new commandments";
3. Warn of "what will happen if the commandments are disregarded." (p. 123)

In writers' handbooks, the reinforced authority is that of the source text; the new commandments forbid patchwriting; and the warnings are of punishments for plagiarism. This covenant rhetoric operates in a particular context: the injunctions against plagiarism are usually situated in the research section of the handbook. Students are first taught techniques for reading sources and taking notes. This instruction modernizes and secularizes the first step in covenant rhetoric, establishing the authority—and sanctity—not of the Lord but of the source text. The *Prentice Hall Handbook for Writers* (Leggett, Mead, & Kramer, 1991), for example, first presents sections titled "Recording Exact Bibliographic Information for each Source" and "Taking Careful Notes: Summary, Paraphrase, and Direct Quotation," and then follows them with a section titled "Drafting the Paper: Do Not Plagiarize the Work of Others, either by Accident or by Design."

The second part of covenant rhetoric, new commandments, emerges in injunctions against patchwriting. To be effective, these injunctions must, of course, include one or more examples of patchwriting. The examples provided in Anson and Schwegler's *Longman Handbook for Writers and Readers* (1996) are a characteristic part of handbooks' covenant rhetoric. (The headings and citations in the following quotations are Anson and Schwegler's.)

ORIGINAL PASSAGE

We have used two emotionally charged films in our studies. One is a medical teaching film showing the birth of a baby; the other is an anthropological documentary of a subincision initiation rite practiced by a primitive Australian group. Both films are capable of arousing a range of strong reactions. The material in both is sexually exciting. Both show mutilation of or injury to the body, particularly the sexual organs, thereby arousing feelings about physical aggression. They also provide opportunities for "looking" at usually forbidden sights. Previous studies of the subincision film by Lazarus *et al.* (1962) have found strong physiological reactions to it. (From Herman

Witkin and Helen Lewis, "Presleep Experiences and Dream," in *Experimental Studies of Dreaming*, Ed. Herman A. Witkin, p. 153.)

PLAGIARIZED VERSION
Herman A. Witkin describes an experiment using presleep hypotheses where the subjects watch films before they go to sleep. To get good results, the researchers needed films that were emotionally charged. They showed two films to the subjects. One was a medical teaching film showing the birth of a baby; the other was an anthropological documentary of a subincision initiation rite practiced by a primitive Australian group. Both of these films were said to be able to arouse a variety of strong reactions, especially since both of the films contain material that is sexually exciting. Both show injury to the sexual organs, which arouses feelings about physical aggression. The experiment produces good results because of the strong psychological reactions to the film (Witkin 153). (Anson & Schwegler, 1996, pp. 634–635)

Whether injunctions against patchwriting are a new commandment for college students is a matter of debate; one often hears teachers growl, "They all know they shouldn't plagiarize and so when they do, they should be punished." However, over the years, I have watched students' faces as I explain patchwriting and its illegality to them, and I can say with confidence that it amounts to a new commandment. What they thought was good scholarship and good writing—or at least what they thought was necessary to their conducting scholarship—is *cheating!* College seniors, honors students, are stunned when confronted with the specificity of injunctions against patchwriting. Once I was invited to talk about plagiarism with a college's judicial board. Faculty and student board members alike were scandalized when I took them through their own college's student handbook policy on patchwriting, the policy that they themselves had been enforcing when adjudicating plagiarism cases: every member of that board was taken aback to realize that cited but unquoted phrasing from a printed source was forbidden. Certainly they all knew that one should mark quotations, and certainly they knew that sources should be cited. But they hadn't thought that phrases could not be incorporated into one's own sentences without benefit of quotation marks, especially if those phrases were grammatically or syntactically altered. These were neither stupid, ill-intentioned, nor ill-informed people; they were highly respected faculty and students charged with and experienced in one of the academy's most solemn tasks. Yet when they realized the implications of the policy they had been enforcing, one student member observed that the entire university would have to be academically dismissed. The rest of the student members of the board (the faculty were circumspectly quiet at this juncture) ruefully agreed, readily admitting that they themselves were "guilty" of regular practices of patchwriting.

Students' being provided with guidance for avoiding patchwriting doesn't offer much immediate relief. A section in Hacker's *Bedford Handbook* (1998) sketches what appears to be a sound strategy for avoiding patchwriting:

> To avoid plagiarizing an author's wording, close the book, write from memory, and then open the book to check for accuracy. This technique prevents you from being captivated by the words on the page; it encourages you to write naturally, in your own voice, without plagiarizing. (p. 479)

Hacker follows this passage with samples of paraphrases written without recourse to the source text—and hence not patchwritten. Her advice accords with some of the pedagogies that I describe in Chapter 8. However, these pedagogies offer little immediate succor to students confronted with the new commandment against patchwriting; students readily recognize that what is being offered them is a lot more work than patchwriting was. It is work that is monumentally challenging for them, because it asks them to write like members of disciplines to which they are outsiders. It is a task in which, even after great effort, they may very well not be able to succeed—as demonstrated by the two patchwriters in my General Education class whose revisions still contained visible patchwriting.

The third part of covenant rhetoric comes in the form of threats of punishment, which in this case typically include the admonition that ignorance is no excuse. A section in Troyka's *Simon & Schuster Handbook for Writers* (1996), for example, warns students:

> To **plagiarize** is to present another person's words or ideas as if they were your own. Plagiarism is like stealing. The word *plagiarize* comes from the Latin word for kidnapper and literary thief. Plagiarism is a serious offense that can be grounds for failing a course or expulsion from a college. Plagiarism can be intentional, as when you submit as your own work a paper you did not write. Plagiarism is also intentional when you deliberately incorporate the work of other people into your writing without acknowledging those sources and the use you have made of them. Plagiarism can also be unintentional—but no less serious an offense—if you are unaware of what must be acknowledged and how to do it. College students are expected to know what plagiarism is and how to avoid it. (p. 519)

The paratactic style of this passage invites analysis.[2] Why do so many of these sentences begin with the word *plagiarism* plus a copula verb? What caused the violation of parallel structure in the fourth sentence? The overall effect is sermonic—or awkward and unformed, depending upon the reading. According to the general rules of the same handbook, it is awkward and unformed:

> Your writing will have more impact when you choose VERBS that are strong because they directly convey an action. *Be* and *have* are not strong verbs, and they tend to create wordy structures. When you revise weak verbs to strong ones, often you can reduce the number of words in your sentences. (p. 334)

Thus goes standard handbook wisdom on use of the copula. But in another interpretation, the *Simon and Schuster Handbook* (1996) passage on plagiarism is not awkward and unformed but sermonic and authoritative. C. Jan Swearingen's (1991) history of rhetoric supplies this perspective when she identifies the emergence of the copula with the emergence of *logos*. "*Logos* is order and orders things; it is binding and binds" (p. 34). Similarly, the copula establishes (apparently) neat equations through "a logosophical discourse directed at finding, defining, testing, and proving concepts rather than at representing events" (p. 38). Viewed in this interpretive framework, a handbook injunction against plagiarism, when expressed in successive short sentences hinged by the copula verb, achieves the effect of stone-tablet commandments.

THE CULTURAL WORK OF CRIMINALIZED PATCHWRITING

Apparently students and teachers are treated differently when they patchwrite. Why can't we either change our pedagogy so that it is less punitive, or else start cracking down on the patchwriting professors? Why can't we simply agree that patchwriting has been inaccurately categorized?

The difficulty is that neither the question nor its answer is that easy. It is no casual error that writers' handbooks enjoin students against the appropriation and manipulation of language from source texts that professional writers—indeed, all writers—do. Including patchwriting in the category of plagiarism and labeling plagiarism as academic dishonesty accomplishes cultural work that became important to the liberal cultural rhetoric of Anglo-American letters in the late 19th century.[3] Even though compositionists may today espouse a social democratic rhetoric, they continue to do the work of liberal culture—the work of protecting a hierarchical status quo—when they continue to criminalize patchwriting in their pedagogy.

Undergraduate students are punished for their appropriations from a source text; professional writers seldom are. According to Mallon (1989), that is a mistake. We should collectively denounce and punish all plagiarists alike, whether they are students or professional writers. Mallon's assumption is that a lack of will prevents the even application of foundational textual ethics.

I would offer a different interpretation of the discrepancies. First, I would assert that all the writing that we all do all the time is patchwriting. Second, I would suggest that at some level we all know or at least suspect that all writing is patchwriting. Third, I would suggest that even though plagiarism is represented as part of natural, neutral, impartial, foundational textual ethics, the cultural work that it accomplishes is anything but natural, neutral, impartial, or foundational. Patchwriting is a decidedly modernist construct, and modernism "constructs borders framed in the language of universals and oppositions" (Giroux, 1991, p. 22). The textual ethics that have dominated the 20th century are an invention of the 19th century, and the purpose they serve is hierarchical. Our construction of plagiarism is designed to bar the Great Unwashed from membership in the intellectual elite. Standards applied to undergraduate students simply aren't applicable to professional writers, because those standards are designed to prevent students from writing in precisely the ways that professional academic writers do. Hence, we do not pursue professional writers for occasional textual indiscretions—not because, as Mallon (1989) would have it, we are faint of heart, but because what they have done is only to make obvious the manner in which all of us necessarily write. On the other hand, it seems virtuous to prosecute students for the same indiscretions, however occasional, because what they have done is to make obvious their absence of professional writing skills.

PLAGIARISM AS CULTURAL INDEX

What constitutes acceptable and unacceptable textual practices changes from one era to another. Plagiarism and forgery, says historian Giles Constable (1983), are cases in point. Today, all forms of unattributed incorporation of another's words or ideas, as well as all forms of attributing one's own writing to another, are considered immoral and even criminal. But within the categories currently labeled "plagiarism" and "forgery" are textual practices that in the Middle Ages were quite acceptable. Practices that we might today prosecute as forgery include what was to the medieval cleric a fine way of furthering the divine purpose on Earth. In the Middle Ages, truth could be found not in propositions, but in the mind of God.

For the medieval writer, practices that we now excoriate as plagiarism and forgery could provide ethical, sensible means for establishing one's authorial credibility and advancing God's Truth. As a historian, Constable

(1983) finds medieval forgeries and plagiarisms useful for understanding the era:

> Forgeries and plagiarisms...follow rather than create fashion and can without paradox be considered among the most authentic products of their time. They therefore deserve attention not only in order to distinguish them from those works which are considered original and authentic but also to assess their own value as historical sources. (p. 2)

Constable's (1983) assertion that textual ethics and practices provide indices to their society can be applied not just to the Middle Ages but to the present as well. In the Modern era, plagiarism causes excitement and uncertainty among academics. For many years, that animation was occasioned mainly by difficulties in ascertaining and punishing plagiarism. Familiar features of academic discourse are the assertions that plagiarism is on the rise (the phrase "Internet plagiarism" quickens the professorial blood); that students are increasingly indifferent to textual ethics; and that teachers must take vigorous punitive action in order to protect public morals, text production, or civilization itself.[4]

Recent work in textual studies has created excitement and uncertainty of another sort, as increasing numbers of scholars challenge received definitions and categories of plagiarism, as they raise disturbing questions about the cultural motivations for sustaining these categories, and as they describe alternative economies of authorship (for example, among African American preachers, or in hypertext composition) that are sustained by markedly different notions of authorship. Contemporary scholarship asserts that the premises upon which the modern notion of plagiarism is based—the premises that a writer can and should be autonomous and original, and that as a result the writer can also be deemed moral and should be accorded ownership of his or her writing—are a fiction, produced by and for a capitalistic, patriarchal society. That we are pursuing plagiarism with increased vigor while at the same time doubting the validity of the very concept is only one of the many contradictions in our economy of authorship.

If these textual values and practices are indices to our society, they certainly point to an age of shifting, conflicting opinions about textual ethics. These shifting, conflicting opinions do not, however, indicate a moral uncertainty. Textual ethics describe rather than guide a society; they derive from social conditions. Unifying our textual ethics would not guide us toward more moral practices; our beliefs about plagiarism demonstrate rather than cause change in the social organism.

Instead, we should identify our textual beliefs and make sure that our practices regarding plagiarism are in accord with them. And we have some work to do: By including patchwriting in the category of plagia-rism—which is the customary practice today—composition teachers are not only contradicting contemporary textual scholarship, but they are also undercutting the social-democratic motivations that prevail in the discipline of composition.

NOTES

[1] George A. Kennedy (1980) calls covenant speech "the most characteristic" type of Hebrew Testament rhetoric. "In a general way the Old Testament as a whole constitutes a vast covenant speech.... A characteristic of the covenant speech is that whatever the specific occasion, the basic message of Judaism—the covenant with God—is incorporated in the speech" (pp. 123–124).

[2] Sondra Perl and Arthur Egendorf (1986) offer a useful review of scholarship on parataxis, which has long been associated with orality (in contrast to hypotaxis, which has been associated with written discourse). The distinction between parataxis and hypotaxis has, in the hands of some scholars (see Thomas J. Far-rell's "environmental hypothesis"), been marshaled in the cause of associating higher IQ with hypotaxis. Here, I am participating in none of the hierarchical purposes to which the linguistic distinction between parataxis and hypotaxis has been put, but am only asserting that the paratactic features of this handbook pas-sage diverge from customary handbook discourse and from Troyka's (1996) own style elsewhere in the *Simon & Schuster Handbook*.

[3] Although James A. Berlin's taxonomies of composition theories have been criticized as overdetermined, they do help identify trends in the discipline. In *Rhetorics, Poetics, and Cultures* (1996), he describes three paradigms in composition pedagogy: current-traditionalist, in which arrangement *(dispositio)* and grammati-cal correctness *(elocutio)* are the focus of instruction (p. 29); liberal culturalist, in which writing is a "product of genius," a "manifestation of one's spiritual nature (p. 31); and social-democratic, which is "most committed to egalitarianism in mat-ters of race, gender, and class—an objective to be encouraged through education" (p. 33). Berlin's descriptions of the three paradigms, together with an arrange-ment that suggests chronological progress, encourages readers to identify with social-democratic rhetoric. To that extent is his historical account prescriptive. His own clear identification with social-democratic rhetoric is also descriptive; James Berlin's allegiances are those of a great many composition scholars.

[4] The very fact that plagiarism is customarily categorized within the scope of "academic honesty" illustrates the moral issues that for many people are at stake in the punishment of plagiarists. Thomas McFarland (1985) regards the morality issue as a means whereby plagiarism "is dismissed from our cultural consider-ations," a task accomplished "by treating each instance, as it comes into our awareness, as a special case, and invoking ethical censures to isolate it still further" (p. 22). Thomas Mallon (1989) is one who makes the claim that text production will be injured if plagiarism is not prosecuted, and Andrei Navrozov (1993), that civilization itself will be injured.

2

The Anxieties of Authorship and Pedagogy

...in th[e] debate on The White Hotel *I believe we are viewing only an overt version of a contemporary critical muddle regarding the status and, more significantly, the locus of textual appropriation. On the one hand, we are dealing with authorial intent and with the historical issue of sources and influences; on the other, it is a question of reader interpretation whereby visible sources become signs of plagiarism, and influences yield to "intertextual" echoes.*

Linda Hutcheon (1986)

Many composition pedagogies describe writing as a way to discover and develop one's immanent beliefs. Therefore, composition instruction aims to teach writing as discovery and to help writers express themselves in their own, authentic language. By honoring the individual voice and legislating autonomous writing, composition studies offers textual validation of individualism. The binary opposite of this notion—necessary, it would seem, for the notion to have meaning— is the plagiarist, the writer who would purloin the thoughts and expressions of others.[1] However, even when teachers believe they are enacting "humane" attitudes toward plagiarism, they may actually be participating in a juridical gatekeeping function. Composition pedagogy maintains a juridical stance toward all the textual strategies that have come to be labeled as plagiarism.

We cannot find a neat solution to the terminological and conceptual muddle that is plagiarism. I hope to bring considerable clarity to the issues, but that clarity will include what I believe to be a fact: cultural notions of plagiarism are by their nature shifting and indeterminate. Fixed, inflexible definitions of and policies for plagiarism cannot alter that fact. Definitions of plagiarism are a form of political language, and political language is itself by definition contested. All definitions of plagiarism will therefore always be contested. "Political developments and the language that describes them," Murray Edelman (1988) explains, "are ambiguous because the aspects of events, leaders, and policies that most decisively affect current and future well-being are uncertain, unknowable, and the focus of disputed claims and competing symbols" (p. 104). Plagiarism is deeply implicated in intellectual politics; hence it is irresolvably indeterminate and unknowable. Plagiarism can never be remedied; it can never be fixed.

THE ELUSIVE DEFINITION

Consider the definitions offered by historian Giles Constable (1983) and literary theorist Susan Stewart (1991). In defining *plagiarism,* both Constable and Stewart differentiate it from its cousin, forgery. Yet despite this apparent similarity, their approaches to defining the term are markedly different. Constable offers definitions of *plagiarism* and *forgery* that are generally familiar to academic culture: whereas forgery involves the "fabrication of documents," plagiarism is the "stealing of words and ideas" (p. 26). These definitions differ in their apparent victims: forgery, with its fabrication of documents, is a crime against the reader, whereas plagiarism, with its stealing of words and ideas, is a crime against the writer (or text) from whom one has stolen. In Constable's modernist definition, plagiarism transgresses against the author(s) of its source(s).

Stewart, however, differentiates forgery and plagiarism on the basis of the claims that the transgressor makes. Whereas forgers make claims for the authenticity of the document, the plagiarist makes claims "for the authenticity of himself or herself as a site of production" (1991, p. 24). Implicit in Stewart's definitions is the postmodern view that plagiarism is a social construct. She does not differentiate forgery and plagiarism on the basis of their victims but on the basis of discursive claims. Discourse involves not just a speaker, but also listeners, interlocutors who participate in meaning-making. Since plagiarism is a discursive formation, it is "made" not just by the supposed transgressor but by the other discourse participants as well.

Demonstrating that plagiarism is a politically implicated signifier, modern and postmodern debates about plagiarism are characterized by rancorous exchanges. Postmodern critics charge that those who adhere to received modern textual values "close...down the complexity of the problem" (Stewart, 1991, p. 30, n. 44), and defenders of textual purity dismiss redefinitions of plagiarism as "sophistry and drivel" (Pappas, 1993, p. 27). Both the modernist and postmodern representations, though, can be deemed "correct" if one differentiates types of plagiarism and if one accounts for social context. Too much of the discussion of plagiarism (both modern and postmodern) treats it as a unified phenomenon, whereas in fact the term encompasses a heterogeneous range of textual practices.

Because Constable's (1983) victim-based definition of *plagiarism* is taken to be valid in all contexts, patchwriting is treated as a pedagogical evil that students must be cured of and even punished for. Writing for a business communications journal, Michael T. O'Neill (1980) regards patchwriting as "the most common (and most serious) error that writers make...." (p. 34). Robert Palmer Saalbach (1970) contends that a simple experiment demonstrates the nature of plagiarism: assign two themes on the same source. Call one of them a summary and the other a critical evaluation; they will be differentiated by their plagiarism:

> [T]he summary will be plainly marked as such and the only possible plagiarism will come from copying too closely without quotation marks, a technical fault rather easily cleared up with adequate instruction. But the second, masquerading as a critical evaluation of an author's point-of-view, will be found to be almost wholly plagiarized. Since he is writing his own theme, it will not occur to the student to use footnotes and quotations, and he will often say or imply that certain of the author's facts he dug up for himself and that the opinions of the author are, without qualification, his own. (p. 45)

To regard patchwriting as a "masquerade," a crime against the author of the source, is to obscure the discursive operation that it often represents: a discursive operation aimed not *against* the source author but *toward* the context in which the operation occurs.

Institutional policies describe student plagiarism—including patchwriting—solely in transgressive terms. These policies are not easily revised, for they take on what Wittgenstein (1972) calls the super-hardness of the law: once installed, they give the appearance of foundational, immutable principles. Still, unlike copyright laws, which are legislated by the state, plagiarism falls into the purview of society, where it is adjudicated by local standards. Plagiarism policies can therefore be revised more readily than can copyright law; plagiarism policies have the potential to more readily reflect the changing values of society, and specifically the academic community's changing notions of what an author is.

The difficulty of plagiarism policies is that they attempt to make visible that which does not exist: the line between what is textually "mine" and that which is "theirs." All discussions of plagiarism are therefore vexed by problems in defining the term. Having interviewed directors of university communications, who report that plagiarizing from other institutions' viewbooks is commonplace, John Shea (1987) concludes, "Simply put, there's some uncertainty about what constitutes plagiarism...." (p. 39). College senior Robert Metz (1994) expresses the sentiments of many students when he says he doesn't understand exactly what is and is not plagiarism:

> I am having difficulty writing about this whole issue because everything about plagiarism seems so vague. There are no strict guidelines about plagiarism, and there are so many exceptions. (n.p.)

Jerry Chaney and Tom Duncan's 1985 survey of journalism schools and departments reveals that there, too, faculty are not agreed as to what constitutes plagiarism nor what its punishments should be. A survey in the *Council Chronicle* asks composition teachers to define plagiarism ("We Want to Know: How Do You Define Plagiarism?," 1993). A follow-up article in a subsequent issue interviews composition scholars who agree that plagiarism is hard to define (Flanagan, 1994). It is indeed an irony that a concept so apparently fundamental to the teaching of composition, a concept about which teachers become so animated and for which students have been reprimanded and even ejected from the academy, should remain an undefined, and perhaps indefinable, term.

In the *Council Chronicle*, as elsewhere, the problems of defining plagiarism are described as problems of consensus. It is not plagiarism that is indeterminate but commentators who are truculent or ill-informed. According to this logic, we all simply need to endorse identical definitions of and punishments for plagiarism; that will resolve the ambiguity (see, for example, McCormick, 1989). Letter-writers responding to Keith Miller's 1993 editorial in the *Chronicle of Higher Education* take him to task for a "relativistic" representation of plagiarism. Yet, implicitly acknowledging the impossibility of a foundational definition of plagiarism, the *Council Chronicle* initiates its series on the topic with a 1993 article entitled, "We Want to Know: How Do You Define Plagiarism?" Asking composition teachers for their personal definitions of plagiarism plainly acknowledges that the definition and treatment of plagiarism is socially constructed, and thus subject to change.

Professor Amy Newman was accused of plagiarism and found guilty by a University of Massachusetts departmental personnel committee. The committee found that "although Newman had 'no conscious intent to deceive,' her 'scholarship had been negligent and contained an objective instance of plagiarism'" (Weeks, 1994, p. 7). The committee made its findings public and barred Newman from administrative work and from membership on "various academic boards." Newman sued, saying that her right to due process had been violated. "[S]ince definitions of plagiarism differ significantly, for the university to sanction her based on one particular definition was to act arbitrarily...." Newman cited definitions of plagiarism that specified intent to plagiarize as a necessary cause, whereas the university was attributing her plagiarism not to intent but to negligence. The federal court upheld the university's right to choose its own definition of plagiarism, affirming that the defining of plagiarism is a local affair.

What exactly *is* the "locality" that should define plagiarism? In the federal court's decision, the locality was the university. But even within the university, instructors are often given the task of devising their own definitions of and punishments for plagiarism. Augustus Kolich (1983) champions this practice, saying that the adjudication of plagiarism should rest with the instructor, for university regulations cannot govern "moral standards" (p. 148). The adjudication of plagiarism, then, would amount to the imposition of a teacher's moral standards—which vary from one teacher to another—upon the students in his or her charge. And plagiarism would be not so much a crime against a victim nor a discursive operation as it would be the plagiarist's violations of the teacher's personal code of ethics.

Many commentators agree that plagiarism, in at least some of its forms, is cheating and is thus a moral choice behavior. Elizabeth M. Nuss (1984), for example, lists "fourteen forms of academic dishonesty." Her list includes two types of student plagiarism: "paying someone to write a paper to submit as your own work" and "copying a few sentences without footnoting in a paper" (pp. 140–141). While Nuss differentiates among types of plagiarism, she simultaneously asserts their unity under the rubric of academic dishonesty. She does not feel a need to defend this unifying principle; plagiarism as a subset of academic dishonesty is an established, "natural" precept that needs no explanation. Richard A. Fass (1986), too, replicates common wisdom when he places plagiarism within the purview of cheating—not only the plagiarism of purchased term papers, one of the "blatant forms of cheating" that "do not require description or elaboration," but also writing tutors' assistance in the "style and structure of a paper" (pp. 33–34).[2]

Most attempts to define plagiarism are taxonomic. That plagiarism belongs to the larger set of cheating (academic dishonesty) is a cultural precept that apparently needs no arguing. The subsets within plagiarism, on the other hand, garner considerable attention. High school teacher Hildegarde Bender (1994) defines plagiarism by identifying five types, and writing program administrator Dorothy Wells (1993) names four. The "Official Guidelines" for *The Glatt Plagiarism Teaching Program* (1988), which by virtue of being computer software would mechanize and regularize definitions and interpretations of plagiarism, says that composition textbooks commonly differentiate "direct" and "indirect" plagiarism—verbatim copying and "'quasi' paraphrasing" (n.p.).

In most discussions, the subsets of plagiarism are presented as coordinate lists. Seldom are they ranked according to the severity of the "crime"; according to the difficulty that one might have in classifying and labeling any given incident; or according to mitigating factors such as authorial intention. Plagiarism is typically described as a unified, stable category of transgression in which subsets may be identified—but only to provide detail in the definition of the overall category. Many times, no subsets are mentioned—or if they are, they are conflated. Just as commentators do not feel a need to provide evidence for calling the unitary phenomenon of plagiarism a form of academic dishonesty, so they feel no compulsion to make distinctions among its types. For example, at the beginning of a discussion of how "outrageous" plagiarism is, Edward M. White (1993) focuses on the term papers purchased from "research assistance" companies. He then segues into a discussion of students who don't know "how to use sources properly"—a segue that conflates two very different activities and which thereby brands the two equally "outrageous." But even those who do differentiate among subsets of plagiarism then typically assert the unity of the overall category. After Bender (1994) lists her five different types of plagiarism, she declares that they all should be treated the same, with "F's."

The unity of the subsets of plagiarism is sustained by eliminating from consideration any factors that recognize heterogeneity. Bender (1994), for example, is specific in excluding authorial intention from consideration when labeling an incident "plagiarism." Such suppression of complexity is also typical in published discussions of student plagiarism, which are dominated by juridical language that presents plagiarism as a transgression against common morals. Most intractable of such commentary is that which defines plagiarism solely according to formalist characteristics of texts, excluding consideration of context, the reader's role in making meaning, or authorial intention.

FEAR OF PLAGIARISM

The economy of plagiarism that has for the past century governed student writing postulates three tiers of writers: those who are original; those who are derivative but have the intellect and decency to acknowledge it; and those who are derivative and either don't know it or won't acknowledge it. The label *plagiarist* marks and criminalizes this third category, a textual "Other" that is widely feared in contemporary Western culture. Writers fear they will succumb to "influence" that will stifle their creativity. They worry, too, that others will plagiarize their work. Not only writers but everyone fears the plagiarists, fears their contaminating influence, fears the threat that they pose to the values of print culture. When Newman was barred from administrative duties and committee membership, she was allowed to remain in the academic community, but only as a marginalized and disempowered member.

Contemporary composition scholarship participates in this general fear of plagiarism and plagiarists. Many of the scholars who endorse collaborative composition pedagogy feel a need to limit their purview to interactions among writers or between writer and audience. To include writer-text collaboration in the realm of collaborative composition theory would be to contaminate that field, to render it illegitimate.

Understanding the excluded plagiarist and his or her moral beliefs takes a prominent place in the scholarship of plagiarism. Like the scientific model of anthropology that is now in eclipse, this approach to plagiarism sets up a textual "Us" and "Them," in which the civilized, researching "Us" endeavors to understand the native, pagan "Them." These questions are often answered quantitatively. Fred Schab (1980) conducted research in 1969 that he replicated in 1979, leading him to conclude,

> A significant increase in plagiarism was revealed, as indicated by the change from an admission in 1969 of 63.5 percent of those going to college to 78.7 percent in 1979. Among the others, the 1969 group's figure was 70.1 percent while in 1979 it had increased to 81.1 percent. (p. 379)

Plagiarism statistics take on the aura of crime statistics; they report rising rates and describe shocking moral turpitude. Almost all agree that plagiarism is widespread, though the reported numbers vary (see, for example, Dant, 1986; Fass, 1986; Hawley, 1984; Schab, 1980). One scholar, Charlotte Allen (1994), disagrees:

> Most studies of college cheating indicate that the percentage of cribbers has not changed much over the past twenty or thirty years: About 60 to 80 per-

cent of college students admit, as they did during the Sixties and Seventies, to having fudged an exam, term paper, or problem set at least once during their four years. (p. 61)

Not only the difficulty in defining plagiarism but also the difficulty in adducing reliable statistics about its incidence raise the anxiety level of those who regard plagiarism as a threat. And a threat it is widely perceived to be. Constable remarks, "Today, plagiarism far more than forgery threatens our most cherished values...." (1983, p. 26). The values to which he refers surely include individualism. In their textual application, these values attribute autonomy and originality to the "true" author. The author who is autonomous and original has the right to own his or her literary product. The author who is derivative, on the other hand, demonstrates not just a lack of intellect but even a lack of character—and is not an individual, as demonstrated by his or her having participated in illegitimate collaborative writing. Hence a rising rate of plagiarism is often believed to correlate with a decline in respect for the values of high literacy. The menace to print culture that is plagiarism would, if left to run amok, destroy that culture. Andrei Navrozov (1993), for example, identifies American writers' and journalists' cavalier and even hostile attitudes toward literary originality as a symptom of the "eclipse of American civilization" (p. 40).

Plagiarism threatens not only civilization in general, but the academy in particular. College teacher Edna Maye Loveless (1994) calls it "the cardinal sin of academe" (p. 10), and White (1993) explains precisely how it threatens the academy:

> Plagiarism is outrageous, because it undermines the whole purpose of education itself: Instead of becoming more of an individual thinker, the plagiarist denies the self and the possibility of learning. *Someone who will not, or cannot, distinguish his or her ideas from those of others offends the most basic principles of learning.* (emphasis added, p. A44)

The fight against plagiarism and plagiarists is not infrequently described as an essential academic battle. Drummond Rennie, an editor of *The Journal of the American Medical Association*, articulates how important are the values that plagiarism transgresses: "The bottom line is, if we don't take a stand on plagiarism, what the hell *do* we take a stand on?" (Mooney, 1992, p. A13). The prosecution of plagiarism, in his description, is the last line of defense for academic standards. Writing for *The American Scholar*, Peter Shaw (1982) would go so far as to measure "the literary conscience of the period" by the energy with which plagiarists are brought to justice (p. 326). Leslie Fishbein (1993) characterizes the current textual situation as one of "moral decline" (p. A52). The very title of Fishbein's article—"Curbing Cheating and Restoring Academic Integrity"—assumes that academia was once characterized by higher textual morals—a state that might, given the proper correctives, be recaptured. The proper correctives, says Fass (1986), are to define and enforce codes of academic honesty; that might stem the decline in students' ethical behavior that he believes has been occurring since the 1960s.

The issue of enforcement is a frequent theme in commentary on plagiarism. Speaking in a university context, David L. Ison (1994) declares, "[W]hen we lose our sense of outrage (or responsibility), we're doomed" (p. 11). Speaking from the K-12 perspective, Margaret S. Geosits and William R. Kirk (1983) concur: "For the school administrator, plagiarism is a clear and present danger. If it is suspected, the principal must act decisively to attack the problem" (p. 38). In *Stolen Words: Forays into the Origins and Ravages of Plagiarism* (a trade book very popular in the academy), novelist Thomas Mallon (1989) gives quarter neither to plagiarists nor to those who are unwilling to name the crime when they discover it—the "apologists for plagiarists" whom he accuses of cowardice (p. 35). Jerold Hale (1990), too, believes that action must be taken: "The problem is that people don't see [plagiarism] as a problem so nobody has done anything to remedy it" (p. 37). Fishbein (1993) attributes the inaction to excessively cumbersome institutional procedures for adjudication: "[S]o few cases of cheating are prosecuted that any enforcement of disciplinary codes that does occur seems arbitrary and capricious and, therefore, inherently inequitable and unjust." White (1993) agrees that universities make strong policy statements but effect weak punishments. Ruefully acknowledging how uneven society's response to plagiarism is, Mallon asks,

> So why don't we give up worrying about an offense that leaves many of us feeling amused or ambivalent? Because ceasing to care about plagiarism would not mean that writers had experienced a rise in wisdom and generosity; it would mean that they had permitted themselves a loss of self-respect. And if ego stopped mattering, then, very likely, writers would stop writing— or at least stop writing so frequently and well. Which means that, finally, plagiarism would be a crime against the reader. (pp. 237–238)

Plagiarism, in his account, transgresses not just against the original source, but against the reader and eventually against writing itself. If plagiarism is not punished, writing will cease. Small wonder that theorists of imitation and collaboration strive to distance their work from any association with the textual activities labeled plagiarism.

To adjudicate plagiarism means that the plagiarist must be caught, a task approached by a variety of methods. Some commentators focus upon the difficulty of the task: it can involve the teacher in distasteful, often fruitless detective work. Edith Skom (1986) explains, "The burden of plagiarism falls less (maybe never) on the criminal than on the one who has to follow through on the crime." She describes with delight her own triumphs in library detective work. But for others, that search can make of the teacher a persecutor and the student a victim. Kolich (1983) recounts, from a Bernard Malamud novel, the story of a teacher's library search for the plagiarist's sources: Malamud's reader is inexorably drawn into regarding the teacher as persecutor, even though the student plagiarist is hardly an admirable character. Compounding teachers' distaste for assuming the role of accuser is their fear of making false accusations. Sandra Jamieson and I advise teachers of writing across the curriculum that noncriminal motivations may lie behind every supposedly telltale textual sign of plagiarism (Howard & Jamieson, 1995), and Richard Murphy's (1990) story of his charging two students with plagiarism reveals the anguish of a teacher who has made an unjust accusation. Moreover, teachers are often hesitant to prosecute plagiarism for fear of themselves becoming victims in the judicial process. Allen (1994) cautions that outraged professors "should know that their own lives may be made miserable by disciplinary proceedings that drag on and by threats of lawsuits" (p. 65).

The fear of plagiarism is only compounded by the widespread suspicion that there is no such thing as originality—that all "originality" is actually "influenced." If plagiarism is immoral, transgressive—a threat to culture, the academy, and writing—and if its binary opposite, originality, does not exist, then all writers are plagiarists. This can lead to a peculiar form of existential despair.

From the depths of this despair, when teachers lecture to their classes, they, too, are plagiarists. Literary theorist Neil Hertz (1982) goes so far as to describe teachers' prosecution of student plagiarism as a self-righteous displacement of their anxieties about their own classroom practices. Those anxieties derive from their giving lectures that synthesize unattributed sources in such a way that the students assume they are hearing the lecturer's own ideas. "[T]he teacher's position is experienced (by the teacher as well as by his class) not as a middle ground somewhere between his author and his students, but as a dramatic occupation, more or less earned, of the position of authority itself" (pp. 66–67). By excoriating student plagiarists, teachers assuage their anxieties about their own classroom impersonations. Writing teacher and novelist Edith Skom (1986) offers a constructive remedy: she recommends that professors credit the sources of their lectures. Such a practice, she says, would set a good example and thus discourage students from plagiarizing.

In Hertz's (1982) and Skom's (1986) scenarios, the teacher is a class-room appropriator of the ideas of others. The figure is a familiar one from Virginia Woolf's fiction: In the 1923 book *Jacob's Room*, pedagogues Erasmus Cowan and Miss Umphelby act as classroom mirror to the revered source, Virgil. In Miss Umphelby's case, the mirror would break if the teacher were faced "with the image of the taught." But Cowan strives to surmount the source, to become not just the representative of Virgil, but "the builder, assessor, surveyor" (p. 42). Lester Faigley (1992) describes modernist, essentialist pedagogy as having the desired outcome of a student who achieves "rationality and unity by characterizing former selves as objects for analysis" (p. 129). Similarly, Virginia Woolf's Erasmus Cowan, the classroom impersonator of Virgil, achieves his own subjectivity by adopting a rational, analytic stance toward his former self, his source. Only in this manner can he overcome the anxiety of influence.

Undergraduate Denise DiBacco (1994) is bothered by teachers' class-room impersonations, but she compares the situation to the oral tradition that Keith D. Miller (1992) attributes to Martin Luther King, Jr. A version of that oral tradition, she says,

> ...is prevalent in college classrooms. Professors talk about a topic, present it as their own—although it's understood that it obviously comes from some-where else (which is hardly mentioned)—and we take the notes down, not knowing the source. Now, if we were to write on that topic, using ideas from class—what is that? Those ideas shape what we think. Then if we build upon them, how could that be plagiarizing, when what we learn is mostly plagia-rized text? (n.p.)

Jennifer Markson (1994), a college senior, does see it as an issue of pla-giarism: "I write down word for word what the professor says—and that's a sort of plagiarism" (n.p.). From Markson's perspective, both professor and student are plagiarizing when they participate in the familiar aca-demic ritual of lecturing and note-taking. Writing to the *Council Chronicle*, teacher Linda S. Bergmann (1994) would agree:

> I used to tell students that whenever you submit someone else's words or ideas as your own, it is plagiarism. But that is exactly what most faculty ask students to do when they take tests—to repeat, usually without attribution, the ideas they have learned from the textbook and class lectures.... (p. 15)

College junior Andrew Dunkle (1994) says he used to write his papers in this manner, but he does not consider it a desirable system. "The day before a paper was due, I would look at my notes, see what my professor thought about a subject, and just copy his thoughts nearly word for word. As I said before, this sort of plagiarism always worked" (n.p.).

In a different vocabulary, the process that Dunkle describes might be called "learning." Despite the criticism that many scholars, including C. H. Knoblauch and Lil Brannon (1983), have visited upon the lecture method, it continues to be a prominent mode of college instruction. But although students like Markson, DiBacco, and Dunkle are being asked to learn through the lecture method, they are also being taught textual values that attach a sense of shame to that learning.

GATEKEEPING IN COMPOSITION PEDAGOGY

Two competing definitions of the individual are advanced in composition studies: "the subject of high modernism: a coherent consciousness capable of knowing oneself and the world" and "the postmodern 'free' individual" who can choose identities by choosing consumer goods (Faigley, 1992, pp. 16–17).

But composition teachers cannot themselves freely choose the student subjectivities that their pedagogies will represent, for, as Faigley (1992) acknowledges, the discipline is accountable to lay notions of what constitutes responsible literacy education. We might expect a strong, negative public reaction if composition pedagogy were to declare the autonomous author defunct and thus abolish strictures against plagiarism. The notion of plagiarism, Constable (1983) says, expresses core values of our society. Composition instruction is charged with upholding and replicating these core values.

Susan Miller (1991) describes composition studies as the guardian of textual purity—specifically, the guardian of the perfection of literary texts. Composition studies and literary studies labor side by side (though not equally) in English departments, two sides of the textual studies coin, because the "low" function of composition—to offer grotesque,[3] imperfect students instruction by adjunct composition teachers—contrasts with, and therefore further elevates, the classical beauty and perfection of the literary texts taught to talented students by tenured literature professors (the elect). The origins of composition, says Miller, should be ascribed to the need for maintaining a high and a low. That task is accomplished by a gatekeeper who examines the credentials of applicants for membership in the ranks of the elect.

In Miller's (1991) account, the gatekeeper is hardly a desirable role. In other accounts, though, the gatekeeper is a positive force, a beneficent guardian. It is in such terms that Peter Elbow (1983, 1986) describes gatekeeping and facilitating as two opposing functions of pedagogy. The gatekeeper makes sure that the standards of the academy—and hence the academy itself—are preserved; teachers disposed toward gatekeeping are concerned that students be certified only when they have demonstrated the necessary qualifications. Teachers disposed toward facilitation, in contrast, make sure that students have every chance to meet those qualifications: facilitating teachers are student- rather than discipline-oriented, striving to provide students with the tools requisite to success. Elbow says that every teacher plays both roles, but that each of us is more highly invested in one than the other. He believes, moreover, that both roles are necessary to the successful operation of the educational system. He does not advise that teachers try to strike an even balance between the two; rather, he recommends that they recognize and nurture both impulses, "mak[ing] peace between opposites by alternating between them so that you are never trying to do contrary things at any one moment. One opposite leads naturally to the other...." (1983, p. 334).[4]

Gatekeepers, from an anthropologist's point of view, "may...attempt to exercise some degree of surveillance and control" (Hammersley & Atkinson, 1983, p. 65). It is in such a framework of surveillance and control that educational theorists Pierre Bourdieu and Jean-Claude Passeron (1977/1990) interpret gatekeeping. They believe that gatekeeping is the fundamental function of pedagogy, and that the gate in question is not to the academy, but to the society that sponsors the academy. The function of education, in their account, is to make sure that the dominated remain under control; that only the dominant are able, as a result of education, to walk through the gates of power; and that all—dominated and dominant alike—accept this dynamic as "natural" and believe that the success of the dominant derives from their superior abilities,[5] not from their social advantages. The educational system, according to Bourdieu and Passeron, is one of those social advantages. The facilitator role is an ideal that enables teachers to feel good about the gatekeeping function that is the reality of their pedagogic work. The two are not contraries toward which teachers variously tend; rather, all teachers are engaged in one—gatekeeping—while optionally comforting themselves with the illusion of the other—facilitating.

Cynthia Haynes-Burton (1995) describes the ways in which representations of student authorship allow composition studies to accomplish its gatekeeping function. In the face of "new modes of intelligibility"—notions of authorship that do not entail autonomy, originality, proprietorship, and morality—compositionists defend the old order. Haynes-Burton declares,

> We must examine what is at stake in our position as gatekeepers of an outdated system of scholarship that is at odds with the digitotalitarian state in which we now live. It is time to question our complicity in the punitive economy of plagiarism. (p. 86)

The adjudication of plagiarism takes its place among the gatekeeping events described by linguists John J. Gumperz and Jenny Cook-Gumperz (1981): "...interviews, counseling sessions, committee meetings, interrogations. The ability to be effective in such gate-keeping events is crucial to economic success in modern societies" (p. 433). Like interviews, counseling sessions, and committee meetings, the adjudication of plagiarism seems innocuous and "normal," especially since it provides the options of "harsh" and "humane" punishments. But "harsh" and "humane" punishments for plagiarism are not opposites, gatekeeper and facilitator. Rather, both are functions of the gatekeeping impulse: both affirm the cultural system of textual purity. The purpose of both is to assure the continuation of that cultural system. The "humane" approach reproduces a juridical economy of authorship just as surely as does the "harsh"; both apply to plagiarists the sort of discipline described by Michel Foucault (1979). This discipline differentiates subjects so that they may be controlled and manipulated. The composition teacher confronted with plagiarism can elect the harsh response and turn the matter over to the campus judiciary, or she can opt for the humane response, choosing prevention and education. Exercising the humane response, she supplies plagiarists, including patchwriters, with correct information about acknowledging one's sources—subjecting her students to a discipline that will, in Foucault's terms, differentiate in order to control and manipulate. This "humane" approach is still reproducing the individualistic textual values of the modern economy of authorship; it facilitates students' learning only in the most shallow sense. Both the "harsh" and "humane" responses to plagiarism differentiate student plagiarists from ethical, knowledgeable academics, and both responses encourage those students to see their plagiarism as a mark of their outsiderness. The teacher then uses the written essay as the examination that combines hierarchical observation and normalizing judgment, scrutinizing the students' subsequent finished texts to ascertain whether the proper conventions of documentation are now being applied. Finally, if a patchwriter fails this examination, the teacher will regretfully but righteously punish him or her for plagiarism, a punishment that marks the student as an outsider to the academic community and simultaneously reproduces composition studies' established place as gatekeeper to that community.

Elbow (1983, 1986) is certainly right in his assertion that the gatekeeper and facilitator are opposing impulses, impossible to sustain simultaneously. But contemporary pedagogy's representations of student plagiarism allow no room for the facilitator. Because the discursive formation of student plagiarism allows only for gatekeeping, it thwarts the egalitarian pedagogy in which many teachers believe themselves engaged. It privileges the well-prepared student writers whose education and family background have made them comfortable with academic discourse. And it deters the awkward student, the one who feels uncomfortable with the texts he or she reads and who feels unable to find a voice in which to respond to them, from entering the inner circle of academic discourse.

NOTES

[1] Binaries have a bad name in academic culture today; all dichotomies are suspected of being false dichotomies. Patricia Harkin (1989) specifically associates them with falsification: "I decline to use the word 'opposition' here because I'd like to think that I don't argue in a patriarchal way. That is, I try not to force difference into binary oppositions. I don't attempt to falsify" (p. 59). Teresa L. Ebert (1991) explains how the falsification occurs: Binary oppositions, such as male/female, gain meaning by suppressing recognition of difference within, the relation of supplementation, and instead attributing it to a difference between, the relation of identity. The second term in the binary opposition is always subordinated to the first, which is always phallogocentric, privileging qualities associated with the male (p. 893). Chapter 1, "Subjects of Sex/Gender/Desire," in Judith Butler's book, *Gender Trouble* (1990), sketches a variety of feminist objections to binaries.

But Walter Kaufman (1974/1995), Nietzsche's translator, notes that Nietzsche believes that binaries are necessary in the making of meaning. Working with the theories of Jacques Derrida, William B. Stanley (1992) reaches a similar conclusion: Undecidability is "always a *determinate* oscillation between possibilities [that] are themselves highly *determined*" in their context (rhetorical, political, etc.). The product of this oscillation is "relations or differences of force." Nor should we resist bipolarity, for there must be poles between which we can play (p. 178). Stanley's is not the unanimously received reading of Derrida on this topic, though; Sharon Crowley (1990) says that Derrida identifies an "internal-external dichotomy...as central to Western thought. He argues that Western culture is built on a series of hierarchical dichotomies in which a term is paired with, and privileged over, an opposing term. Such dichotomies authorize the creation of entire discursive practices" (p. xiv).

I am inclined to think that both points of view are accurate. I do not identify all dichotomies as false dichotomies; rather, I believe that meaning can be made through binaries, as long as we remember that meaning is actually made in the relay between the poles. When that caveat is forgotten or obscured, falsification occurs. Such a falsification obtains, I believe, in the binary opposition of plagiarism and authenticity. The result is an overdetermined opposition in which neither pole can be verified, but in which the meaning created in the relays between the poles is condemned as compromise or faint-heartedness.

[2] Irene L. Clark (1988, 1993) has worked hard to challenge this image of plagiarism. Yet, in an extreme manifestation of the valorization of the autonomous author, the notion persists that tutoring, even in its most "innocuous" forms, amounts to plagiarism.

[3] "Grotesque" refers here to the Bakhtinian sense described by Peter Stallybrass and Allon White (1986): it contrasts with the classical body. The classical body is characterized by its smooth surfaces; the grotesque body by its gaping orifices, its absences.

[4] In 1986, Elbow expanded these notions in a book-length exploration of pedagogy with *Embracing Contraries: Explorations in Learning and Teaching*.

[5] In "The Forms of Capital," Bourdieu (1983/1986) explores the notion of "ability" in some detail. Differentiating cultural capital, symbolic capital, and social capital, he asserts that cultural capital sometimes masquerades as symbolic capital, which means that it is seen not as capital but as "legitimate competence." When it translates into academic success, the commonsense view regards it as a "natural aptitude." Aptitude, Bourdieu says, should be examined in terms of its unequal distribution among the classes (pp. 243–245).

3

Autonomous Collaboration

We know now that a text is not a line of words releasing a single "theological" meaning (the "message" of the Author-God) but a multi-dimensional space in which a variety of writings, none of them original, blend and clash. The text is a tissue of quotations drawn from the innumerable centres of culture…. Succeeding the Author, the scriptor no longer bears within him passions, humours, feelings, impressions, but rather this immense dictionary from which he draws a writing that can know no halt; life never does more than imitate the book, and the book itself is only a tissue of signs, an imitation that is lost, infinitely deferred.
Roland Barthes (1977)

P atchwriting is categorized as a form of plagiarism, which is in turn categorized as a form of academic misconduct. Patchwriting is, by the usual laws and procedures of the academy, criminalized. But to criminalize patchwriting is to criminalize collaboration.

The academy is certainly not accustomed to thinking of patchwriting as collaborative writing. In the received model of collaborative writing, two or more people gather together to accomplish a common task. Sometimes that task is accomplished dialogically, with the participants working on the entire project together, sharing more or less equally in the work and the credit. At other times, the collaboration is hierarchical, with the component tasks divided among the participants, perhaps with some people taking greater responsibility and more credit for the process.

In the case of patchwriting, it is a text and a person who "gather together." The collaboration may seem to be too hierarchical to qualify as collaboration at all: The person—the patchwriter—clearly determines task and outcome, and clearly takes all the credit.

Or does she? To make this assumption is to assert agency in the (patch)writer. If, however, the writer is actually the written, it is in part the source text that does the writing. Patchwriting *is* a form of collaboration— it is writer-text collaboration based on mimesis—and the agency does not necessarily accrue entirely to the patchwriter. The text does not have to have a consciousness and volition in order to exert some control over the outcome of the collaboration. In fact, when readers complain about patchwriting, it is usually because the text has exerted *too much* control over the outcome: The patchwriter's words and phrases are too obviously indebted to the source text. Even when the patchwriting is invisible, though—even when its traces have been stylistically erased—the source text plays a role in determining the possible meanings of the patchwritten text.

Yet the writer-text collaboration that is patchwriting has an entirely negative role in received composition pedagogy. If it is to be recovered— rehabilitated—for positive uses in the classroom, those uses must be identified afresh; they do not presently exist in composition textbooks. In search of models that might be adapted to a positive pedagogy of writer-text collaboration, one might logically turn to the theory and pedagogy of collaborative writing.

One would be disappointed. Deriving from the early work of Kenneth A. Bruffee (1984a), very little of the available composition scholarship on collaboration is compatible with writer-text collaboration, because most of it, even as it describes writers working together, assumes a normative solitary author. Most of the scholarship on collaborative writing demonstrates how powerful is the modern notion of the autonomous author, how conflicted are the representations of agency in composition studies, and how reluctant is contemporary culture to appreciate mimesis of any kind. Indeed, the scholarship of collaboration speaks almost exclusively of writers' collaborating with readers and other writers. Only rarely does it allude to writers' collaborating with texts—and usually for the purpose of outlawing writer-text collaboration. At the intersection of expressionist and collaborative scholarship, the difficulty becomes acute. Composition theories of collaboration are therefore of limited value to a pedagogy of mimesis—not only because they predicate the possibility of autonomous writing on the notion of individual agency and focus on writer-to-writer rather than writer-text collaboration, but also because they often secure the legitimacy of writer-to-writer collaboration by stipulating the illegitimacy of writer-text collaboration.

This does not mean that collaborative theory has nothing to offer a pedagogy of writer-text collaboration. But without an understanding of the ways in which writer-text collaboration accords with and diverges from the larger category of collaborative theory, a new pedagogy may very well undercut its own purposes (as collaborative theory does) by retaining an underlying model of an originary, autonomous author.

Although much of collaborative theory identifies itself as antihierarchical, the autonomous author that persists in collaborative theory is a legacy of 19th- and 20th-century intellectual hierarchy. The "hierarchy" of which I speak here is not Lunsford and Ede's (1990) hierarchical collaboration, in which writers divide tasks, but the hierarchy that the rhetoric of liberal culture strives to sustain: the hierarchy that assumes that some writers are born with "the gift." The others can only be socialized not to make fools of themselves when writing—and to revere the writing of the truly gifted.

Pedagogy associated with the rhetoric of liberal culture leans heavily toward gatekeeping rather than liberatory agenda. It is to the adherents of liberal culture that Bruce Horner (1997) no doubt alludes when he speaks darkly of "powerful others committed to the use of composition courses to police and exclude students from higher education" (p. 526).

To declare that all writing is collaborative yet to retain the normative autonomous author is to contribute significantly to the reproduction of this hierarchy. Classroom collaboration then becomes not a form of genuine resistance, but rather what John Schilb would call "opposition that merely reinforces what it opposes" (1988, p. 25).[1] A positive pedagogy of writer-text collaboration, on the other hand, could offer genuine opposition to liberal-culture hierarchy, because criminalized patchwriting is an important means of maintaining that hierarchy. Criminalized patchwriting prevents students from writing in precisely the ways that the "naturally gifted" do, even while those gifted pose as "originary" writers. Coleridge and Wordsworth, major players in the development of the regulatory fiction of the gifted, originary writer, were anything but autonomous in their own writing (see Fruman, 1971; Jaszi & Woodmansee, 1996).

AUTONOMY IN COLLABORATIVE THEORY

Martha Woodmansee declares that research since Foucault (1977b) "suggests not only that the author in this modern sense [the autonomous author] is a relatively recent invention, but that it does not closely reflect contemporary writing practices" (1994b, p. 15).[2] She questions whether solitary, originary authorship has ever described how any writer composes; instead, she characterizes authorial autonomy as an ideal constructed and promulgated for economic purposes. Woodmansee is working in theory of authorship, not in composition theory of collaboration; but a range of compositionists including David Bleich (1988), Linda Brodkey (1987), Lester Faigley (1992), Karen Burke LeFevre (1987), Andrea Lunsford and Lisa Ede (1990), and Susan Miller (1989) also question the autonomous author. Creating a tension in collaborative theory are the representation of the writer as autonomous and capable of independent action, and the representation of the writer as always collaborative and incapable of independent action. James Porter (1986) labels these two poles "Romantic" and "intertextual." Porter locates himself at the intertextual pole:

> Writing is an attempt to exercise the will, to identify the self within the constraints of some discourse community. We are constrained insofar as we must inevitably borrow the traces, codes, and signs which we inherit and which our discourse community imposes. We are free insofar as we do what we can to encounter and learn new codes, to intertwine codes in new ways, and to expand our semiotic potential—with our goal being to effect change and establish our identities within the discourse communities we choose to enter. (p. 41)

The Romantic vision of the writer, Porter says, must give way to the intertextual vision, for its presentation of heroic writers—"that writers are born, not made"—is at heart antirhetorical (p. 41). But to examine the ways in which the community constrains writers would take us "outside the prevailing episteme of composition pedagogy, which presupposes the autonomous status of the writer as independent *cogito*" (p. 42).

That "prevailing episteme" of the independent *cogito* holds sway even in collaborative theory. Whether it is to build upon or argue with his precepts, most composition scholarship on collaboration derives from the early work of Kenneth A. Bruffee (1984). And thus collaborative theory in composition has, from its inception, been fettered by a persistent underlying model of autonomous authorship.

In his landmark essay, "Collaborative Learning and the 'Conversation of Mankind,'" Bruffee (1984) sketches the history of collaborative learning in American pedagogy. Collaborative learning, he says, arose as a pedagogical technique in response to educational needs in the early 1970s, when teachers observed that the rising numbers of nontraditional students were not responsive to traditional forms of academic help. One of the notable products of collaborative learning pedagogy, he says, is peer tutoring (pp. 636–638).

Bruffee's (1984) focus is not on collaborative writing but on collaborative learning. For him, writing is a component of learning, and techniques of collaborative learning produce better writing. His principles are just as applicable to a class in sociology as they are to a college composition class. Hence, in his formulation, collaborative learning functions in a metadisciplinary way:

> [Collaborative learning] is viewed as a way of engaging students more deeply with the text and also as an aspect of professors' engagement with the professional community.... In both these contexts collaborative learning is discussed sometimes as a process that constitutes fields or disciplines of study and sometimes as a pedagogical tool that "works" in teaching composition and literature. (p. 635)

It is in Bruffee's (1984) valorization of peer tutoring that collaborative theory falls prey to the underlying model of autonomous authorship. Peer tutoring typically involves a text that the writer brings to the writing center. The tutor reads and responds to that text. Certainly, tutors can help students with invention, but the *model* for tutoring involves a text to be improved upon. LeFevre (1987) calls this an "interactive" model of collaboration and says that it is prevalent in composition studies:

> What I term an "interactive" type of collaboration occurs often in composition. A writer interacts with others (teachers, peers, colleagues, editors) in the course of writing and revising. Generally in this type of relationship, one person (writer, teacher, boss) has the right to make final decisions about which ideas are to be kept or changed or omitted. The principal role of others is to help the individual to generate and evaluate ideas and information.... Underlying this model are the assumptions that there is something valuable and original and unspoiled in the writer, and that the reader can help to cut through stereotyped or irrelevant language and ideas so that the real writer can be heard. (p. 68)

This interactive collaboration, representing an autonomous writer assisted by readers, underlies many composition pedagogies of peer response. LeFevre deems such pedagogies inadequate, for they do not help students with their invention tasks. She notes but does not directly challenge the constituent assumption of the individual who is possessed of agency sufficient for invention (pp. 69–70). Her indirect challenge to interactive collaboration comes a few pages later, when she calls joint invention "true" collaboration (p. 72).

A great many composition scholars now espouse the belief that all writing is collaborative. Yet peer response to work in progress has become so firmly entrenched in composition pedagogy that few recognize LeFevre's (1987) key point: Peer group work that *begins* with a draft in hand is a "collaborative" pedagogy that may very well assume in the invention stage an autonomous writer.

The focus on peer response to drafts in progress is strongly associated with social constructionist theory. Suzanne Clark and Lisa Ede (1990) note that the "major theoretical formulations" of Bruffee, LeFevre, and Anne Ruggles Gere are based on social constructionism (p. 276). Gere explains why social construction is valuable to a theory of collaborative learning:

> Knowledge conceived as socially constructed or generated validates the "learning" part of collaborative learning because it assumes that the interactions of collaboration can lead to new knowledge or learning. A fixed and hierarchical view of knowledge, in contrast, assumes that learning can occur only when a designated "knower" imparts wisdom to those less well informed. (1987, pp. 72–73)

But the shortcoming of a social constructionist approach to collaboration, say Clark and Ede, is that it works toward a unified, autonomous classroom, rather than accounting for "culture, politics, and ideology" (pp. 277–278).

Social constructionism celebrates multiple authorship and portrays a subject who is constructed in the social environment, yet in composition pedagogy it also portrays subjects as capable of exercising control over the social environment and thus over their selves. In social constructionism, the subject is in dialogue with the social environment but is still an autonomous agent, capable of individual action—and solitary writing. Social constructionism and its collaborative pedagogies leave open the possibility of autonomy in the subject, and as long as that autonomy is left unchallenged, so is the notion of plagiarism: The possibility of solitary, autonomous authorship is the most essential tenet of our culture's representations of plagiarism.

Linda Flower (1996) is one of the scholars who have challenged Bruffee's (1984) social constructionism, but the "negotiated construction"[3] that she offers as an alternative also imagines an autonomous writer. Flower's objection to conversation theory is that it produces one meaning from conversation, the meaning rendered in consensus.[4] The negotiated construction that she advocates would, in contrast, place conflict in the foreground and acknowledge that each participant takes away his own meaning from the conversation. How the participant might himself be a product of the conversation is not, however, part of Flower's account. "Collaboration...depends on more than conversation; it demands the construction of a new negotiated meaning, an invention attuned in a particular, provisional way to...competing, conflicting voices" (pp. 50–51). Rather than avoiding conflict, intercultural collaboration must embrace it. "Conflict, embedded in a spirit of stubborn generosity, is not only generative but necessary because it acknowledges the undeniable—the social and economic substructures of power, of racism, of identity that will not be erased by goodwill" (p. 51). It is in conflict that Flower believes that collaboration produces knowledge—but that knowledge is the product and possession of each individual member of the collaboration, and the knowledge will differ from one individual to another.

> [C]onflict calls for more than an *awareness* of difference. It calls for the extended, ultimately individual process of *constructing* a negotiated meaning—a new representation of ideas and issues that makes a new (if necessarily provisional) sense out of competing, and often hard to grasp, ways of seeing. (original emphasis, p. 60)

In another example of the autonomous writer within collaborative theory, composition scholar Charlotte Thralls (1992) unequivocally declares all writing to be collaborative. Yet the language of her essay reveals slippage in her position, evidence of the multiple allegiances that typify contemporary thought, especially with regard to the writing of poetry and fiction. She acknowledges a coercive dimension to the collaborative nature of writing when she repeatedly refers to the "demands" that "collaborative partners" make upon writers (pp. 70, 77). Writers, Thralls says, struggle against these demands. If they are working for corporations, she advises them to relinquish the struggle; but if they are writing a novel or a poem, they "may find that...authorship requires a writer to engage in conflict, mediating, and even writing against, collaborative voices" (p. 77). The collaborative nature of all writing is, in other words, a handicap for writers of poetry and fiction. They must struggle against influence.

Middle school teacher Mary K. Simpson-Esper (1988) not only "starts" collaboration at the revision stage, but also judges the writers in her peer revision groups as autonomous agents. She offers "a list of specific behaviors to look for as the students share...their writing in revision groups—specific changes in my students and their writing that would suggest that I [am] on the right track" (p. 93). The "right track," it turns out, is her students' maintaining their individual autonomy and proprietorship, even while working in groups. Simpson-Esper specifies the following three evaluative criteria:

[1] maintaining individual identity within the group, approaching the group with self-confidence, and establishing ownership of the written piece;

[2] using the advice/suggestions of the group wisely to improve one's writing; and

[3] developing the skills of group interaction (for example, helping and supporting fellow authors). (p. 94)

Simpson-Esper's (1988) concerns are widely shared. William Condon and Liz Hamp-Lyons (1991), for example, report on the difficulties of maintaining individual authorship in composition portfolios. To prevent ghostwritten entries in the portfolio, they say, students must be prohibited from including anything that wasn't assigned in the course. These concerns focus not on writer-text collaboration but on what I would call "real" plagiarism—submitting a paper written by someone else.

It is worth my pausing here to assure readers that the writer-text collaboration that I am advocating does not include the "substitute authorship" of ghostwritten papers.[5] Certainly, some textual strategies that are labeled plagiarism—purchased term papers, for example—call for a juridical response. But other types may not signify immorality or ignorance of attribution systems, but what Suzanne Clark and Lisa Ede (1990) call "moments of possibility" (p. 280) that reveal the multiple communities in which learners simultaneously participate—and the strategies they employ to gain and maintain memberships in those communities, as well as their resistances to them. Having recognized these types of "plagiarism" as membership strategies, teachers might respond with appropriate pedagogy that supports students in their membership bids instead of penalizing or preventing the attempt.

In addition to the issue of ghostwriting in portfolios, Condon and Hamp-Lyons (1991) also contemplate means for excluding unattributed writer-text collaboration, in the form of essays initiated by the putative author but subsequently contributed to by others. The policy of allowing only assigned work from the course safeguards against ghostwritten texts but does not settle the question of solitary authorship in a revised essay. This question, as Condon and Hamp-Lyons point out, isn't created by portfolios but is only brought out into the open (p. 242).

In giving examples of the autonomous writer in scholars' accounts of pedagogy, I should pause for two additional words of caution. First, I have encountered no commentator, including myself, who articulates a unified position on either collaborative or solitary authorship. All of our images of authorship are traversed and destabilized by traces of that which we would deny. As I work on the final draft of this book, I see traces of beliefs about plagiarism, authorship, and collaboration that I no longer hold. I seriously doubt that when *Standing in the Shadow of Giants* goes to press, it will express only my current thinking on the subject; rather, it will probably express various stages of my thinking, with the current beliefs dominant. The vanguard reader will no doubt be able to detect contradictions that reveal the quandaries with which I have struggled and the succession of solutions that I have postulated for those quandaries. The question for me, then, is not whether traces of that which we would deny can be detected in text—for they almost always can; rather, it is the question of which one provides the premises for the argument.

A second caveat is that in my own teaching, I have so far found it impossible to persuade all students that all writing is collaborative. Whether that "persuasion" is undertaken directly or indirectly, many students have a lifetime of schooling that has convinced them otherwise. I have read and heard assertions that some teachers have succeeded in the endeavor, have developed fully collaborative classrooms—but I am not, so far, one of those teachers. I have found, on the contrary, that pushing an unwilling student too far into intentional collaboration can result in a full-scale revolt, resulting in frustration for me and no learning for her. For the present, therefore, my writer-to-writer collaborative pedagogy provides some escape routes for the recalcitrant student who is convinced that she is not learning to write unless she is learning to write autonomously. I prefer sanctioning her learning within a model that I do not myself endorse than her not learning at all. Meanwhile, hoping that she will, even after the end of the course, come around to the model that I endorse, I strive to keep that model the active, dominant mode in my classroom.

The exceptions to the normative autonomous author in composition pedagogy are not plentiful, but they are refreshing. Second grade teacher Sharon E. Tsujimoto (1988) describes a collaborative curriculum in which her students work together *from invention* through publication. Tsujimoto offers no "justification" for her pedagogy, instead she seems to regard it as "natural." I agree; but a great many other teachers and scholars apparently do not. In many pedagogies, collaboration means assembling groups of writers to work together on drafts that the individual members have produced on their own. *Peer response*, in other words, is often considered synonymous with, rather than a subset of, *collaboration*.

One of the negative products of a normative autonomous authorship is the possibility of a hierarchy of authorship. If writers can be separated from each other and their texts, they can be arranged into a qualitative hierarchy—as so much testing of writing attempts to do—according to who is best and who is worst. If they are possessed of agency, writers can be held responsible for their "skills" (which include the skill of not plagiarizing, of keeping oneself free of influence, and of acknowledging that influence when one does fall prey to it)—or lack thereof; and they can be instructed in such a way as to hold them individually responsible for the acquisition of skills. Moreover, if students are autonomous agents, so are teachers; and if the students are to be arranged hierarchically, the teacher must perforce function at the summit of that hierarchy.

Collaborative theory and pedagogy would seem to challenge these hierarchical notions, and indeed, many practitioners have made such claims.

Bruffee says that collaborative learning seems a comfortable pedagogy until we recognize that it is "not merely a better pedagogy" but also a model of "how knowledge is generated, how it changes and grows" (1984, p. 647). That change, he says, comes in part through its challenge to traditional, hierarchical authority structures—chiefly the teacher. Taking a page from Bruffee, John Schilb (1992) says that in the discipline of composition, collaboration is valued for its challenge to "the teacher's authority and the misleading image of the isolated writer" (p. 107). Lunsford and Ede (1990) concur: "At least potentially, we would argue, collaborative writing holds out the promise for a plurality of power and of authority among teacher and students, what Ohmann calls an 'opening up' of the classroom" (p. 120). And Johanna W. Atwood (1992) celebrates the potential of collaborative writing "as a way to correct the philosophy of competition and to show the falsity of individualism in writing" (p. 20).

What's so bad about an authoritative teacher? Isn't it foolish—not to mention impossible—for a teacher to surrender authority? Donald C. Jones (1996) charges that Lester Faigley, by "abrogating his authority" as a teacher, "denies his own agency" (p. 84). But Robert Brooke, Judith Levin, and Joy Ritchie (1994) offer a Lacanian rationale for eschewing the teacher-controlled classroom:

> Seeing learning as guided by transference—that is, by a person's projecting onto another person the authority of a "subject supposed to know," one who can give answers to fundamental life questions—has helped us understand our own and our students' learning. Similarly, seeing learning as threatened by countertransference—by an authority's naive belief that he or she can decide life questions for another, can accept the role of the subject who is supposed to know, even though the authority is only human—has helped us understand some of the mistakes we continue to make as teachers. (p. 159)

In the pedagogical framework adapted from Lacan, the student is not in a position to learn as long as he is depending upon the authority of the teacher. And the teacher is always in danger of succumbing to the desire to be an authority, the desire to be desired. When the teacher is the center of the classroom, desiring to be desired, community—the community in which students learn how to learn from each other and write together—is thwarted.[6]

Mary Minock (1995) asserts that the dynamic extends to students' relationships with their texts. Lacan makes obvious the paradox that students learn best when teachers are not the repositories of knowledge and "when we defer the assumption that texts are instruments of consumable knowledge." Instead, says Minock, students should be led to "engage in dialogues with texts, dialogues that are often based on unconscious desires."

She describes the product of such dialogues as *"irrational* responses," which she values as part of "a temporary suspension of the usual academic business." These irrational responses "inspire in students a great attention to texts, a willingness to read and respond to them over and over again, and an *unpredictably* high incidence of imitation" (original emphasis, p. 499).

Lacanian theory mistrusts hierarchy for its subordination of student to both teacher and text, thereby fettering the student's learning. In *Discipline and Punish,* Foucault (1979) offers a different but equally compelling warning of the dangers of hierarchy. It functions, he says, for the purpose of differentiating individuals who can be arranged taxonomically and who can thus be controlled. Discipline—including the discipline in which teaching is inevitably involved—"'makes' individuals; it is the specific technique of a power that regards individuals both as objects and as instruments of its exercise." It utilizes "hierarchical observation, normalizing judgment and their combination in a procedure that is specific to it, the examination" (p. 170). Discipline makes use of a double system of punishments and rewards, setting up two poles between which all behavior falls. The activity that occurs between those two poles is that of punishment (a student's placement in developmental composition provides an example of the punishment that Foucault describes), which hierarchizes subjects in relation to each other, effecting individuation. Rank ordering, part of the system of discipline and punishment, accomplishes the twofold task of ordering and judging. When employed in an educational institution, it would order students according to their value even after they leave school.

Going one step further, Pierre Bourdieu and Jean-Claude Passeron (1977/1990) declare hierarchical control an unavoidable outcome of schooling. Whereas Foucault's (1979) focus is on the prison, Bourdieu and Passeron's is on the educational establishment, which they say necessarily and inescapably functions to reproduce hierarchical social power. All pedagogic action constitutes symbolic violence, because it imposes meaning while hiding the power relations that enable that imposition— and because it reproduces its arbitrary selection process. Whereas both Karen Burke LeFevre (1987) and Anne Ruggles Gere (1987) look to sociologist Emile Durkheim for principles that would inform collective collaboration, Bourdieu and Passeron find Durkheim inadequate, because his theories portray cultural capital as the common property of all members of the culture. Durkheim does not recognize the structures that distribute the cultural capital unequally, a process which reproduces the power relationships among the classes. Schooling, in Bourdieu and Passeron's analysis, would function in much the same way as does the physical coercion of Foucault's prison, producing a "misrecognition" of the "arbitrariness" of pedagogic action. One of the products of schooling is the naturalization of its own processes, so that these appear to be not cultural arbitraries, but accurate representations of a foundational reality—the reality of students' "abilities" and teachers' "authority."

Hence, a student judged inadequate (or extraordinary, or plagiaristic), believing that his abilities and actions have been accurately measured by value-free, objective mechanisms, strives to improve or fulfill his lot. If he is angry about the judgment, that anger is usually directed at one or more persons who did not ethically or competently enact either their role in implementing the objective mechanism of evaluation or their role in aiding the student to improve his "abilities." One of schooling's most effective products is to deter any of its participants from challenging the system itself. The "system" here is not *how* schooling is effected, but *that* it is effected. For, according to Bourdieu and Passeron (1977/1990), the purpose of schooling is to naturalize hierarchy. Once subjects have been persuaded that hierarchy is natural and egalitarian, they strive to improve their lot within the hierarchy rather than to challenge the hierarchy itself as a cultural arbitrary.[7]

Lunsford and Ede (1994) caution that some of the resistance attributed to collaborative pedagogy is illusory, leaving traditional textual and interpersonal power structures intact. They charge that models for collaboration have "failed to challenge traditional concepts of radical individualism and ownership of ideas and [have] operated primarily in a traditional and largely hierarchical way" (p. 431).

Regardless of what principles we operate upon (Lacanian, Foucaudian, etc.), whatever we are doing to redistribute power in the classroom (for example, the distribution of traditionally professorial authority among all the members of the class) functions in exactly the way that Bourdieu and Passeron (1977/1990) describe—it functions to naturalize the very hierarchy it claims to undo—*as long as we are leaving other mechanisms of pedagogical hierarchy intact and hidden.* And the cultural arbitrary of a writer who need not and may not collaborate with texts is, I believe, a profoundly powerful—and hidden—mechanism of pedagogical hierarchy. It belittles students, constructing and naturalizing their low status in comparison to both professional writers and the texts that students are asked to read and write about.

There are undoubtedly more—perhaps many more—of these generative, invisible mechanisms of hierarchy functioning in composition pedagogy. This book explores only one of those mechanisms, the criminalization (and, I hope, subsequent recovery) of writer-text collaboration. We must be alert, though, to the potential of others; and we must always be critiquing our own theories and practices for their adequacy. We can readily endorse an agenda like Stuart Greene's (1995): to see "beginning writers as authors" and thus "to read their work as we might any other author's text, not as the 'emerging' or 'failed' work of 'outsiders'" (p. 189). But can we effect the changes in our practices that will actually make this laudable goal possible? Can we effect changes not just in one sector of our practice but in all of them? Without comprehensive changes, pedagogy will continue to function in the chillingly hegemonic terms that Bourdieu and Passeron (1977/1990) so relentlessly describe. Change just one sector—such as peer group rather than solitary revisions—and the teacher has merely comforted himself with the illusion of empowering students; for the hierarchy, like mercury, simply slips into another compartment—for example, the one in which that same teacher forbids students to engage in the writer-text collaboration by which they learn and become members of a discipline. And the students still go away from the classroom with a clear sense of their place in the academic hierarchy, along with the clear belief that their own accomplishments or inadequacies account for that place.

Authorizing writer-text collaboration has the potential to rehabilitate what has functioned as an important support mechanism of hierarchy in composition instruction.

AGENCY IN COLLABORATIVE THEORY

Jeanne Fahnestock and Marie Secor's 1990 textbook *A Rhetoric of Argument* defines *agency* as "the connection between cause and effect" (p. 175). In terms of critical theory, though, the question of agency is a question of whether the writer is herself the connection between cause and effect, whether she can, by an independent act of volition, precipitate effect—or whether she is herself an effect, not writer but written. As Séan Burke (1995) puts it, "Is the author the producer of the text or its product?" (p. xv). Postmodern theory approaches with great skepticism the proposition that a writer is possessed of agency.

Students believe the tropes of "ability" and "skills" because pedagogy represents them to themselves as subjects possessed of agency. They have the capability of defining themselves and directing their own lives; hence it is they who are responsible for their failures. They believe they are born with a certain IQ, and they also believe that they must "live up to their potential." Composition scholars such as Kathryn T. Flannery (1991), Susan Miller (1991), David R. Russell (1993), and Lynn Worsham (1991) undertake not only to revise cultural traditions of authorship, but also to trace their effects upon composition studies. These scholars interrogate the agency, autonomy, unity, and stability that composition pedagogy ascribes to authors, and they point out that social constructionism, a major theoretical framework for composition studies, does not alter those presuppositions.

The difficulty is that agency and autonomy almost always go hand in hand. Social constructionist composition theories characteristically postulate a writer who, though perhaps working collaboratively with others, is possessed of both agency and autonomy. And, as the example of Flower (1996) demonstrates, so do some of its critiques. It is the belief in autonomy that makes of writer-text collaboration a crime, a failure to work independently, free of influence. And it is the attribution of agency to the writer that holds the patchwriter writer personally responsible for the failure.

This is not the same thing as saying that the writer is not autonomous. *Autonomy* and *agency* are not synonymous terms. The issue of autonomy is an issue of whether the writer acts alone, whereas the issue of agency is one of whether the writer acts or is an action.

If the writer acts alone, the constituent assumption is that the writer acts. If, on the other hand, the writer is incapable of acting alone, the whole verb-noun dyad of acting and action is thrown into indeterminacy. Working backwards through these enthymemes, one might readily suppose, in the absence of counterevidence, that a theorist who believes that the writer is capable of acting also believes that the writer is capable of acting alone. Hence, the issue of agency matters to the present discussion, for collaborative theory that assumes agency instead of interrogating it is, very possibly, theory that assumes collaboration to be an option for writers rather than a definition of writing. Agency and autonomy, though not synonymous, are not fully separable issues; hence Séan Burke speaks of the "autonomous agency" of the modernist author (p. xxviii).

That autonomous agency is, of course, a basic precept of expressionistic rhetoric.[8] When expressionism is criticized in composition studies, much of that critique speaks from the death of the author. The "author," who in this sense "dies," is that autonomous individual of expressionism whose inner soul is possessed of truth and knowledge and who can produce unaided written drafts in which those truths are discovered and articulated. The radical version of collaborative theory, in which collaboration is not merely an option available to a writer but is the very definition of writing and the locus of truth and knowledge, entails the death of this author. But, like the assertion that writing equals learning, the declaration of the death of the author is anything but a straightforward, unified assertion.

If the author is dead, who assumes responsibility for the text? To whom do we attribute agency? Lunsford and Ede (1990) succinctly describe the options usually chosen: it is the reader, the text, or the context that appropriates the agency formerly attributed to the author; and these positions can be identified, respectively, with Roland Barthes, Michel Foucault, and Mikhail Bakhtin (Lunsford & Ede, 1990, pp. 87–92). Both Foucault and Barthes associate the rise of the hegemony of the author with the rise of individualism. Barthes calls for the death of the author in order to give primacy to the reader, whereas Foucault focuses on the text as a "contested site." For Bakhtin, the emphasis is on context and the polyphonic self, from whose options the writer at any given time chooses a representative self.

ORIGINALITY IN COLLABORATIVE THEORY

Along with autonomy, originality is one of the fundamental properties of post-Enlightenment authorship. It is a precept informing most of collaborative theory—which is why it is no surprise that expressionistic rhetoric and collaborative theory work so well together.

One might even go so far as to say that expressionism is the prevailing model of writing in our culture. It emerges, for example, in the 1985 Report of the Association of American Colleges, which White quotes in his 1989 book, *Developing Successful College Writing Programs:* The report defines writing as "an active means of thought and learning, a way to discover what one means and who one is" (p. 4). Evocations of the expressionistic model dance through Jamaica Kincaid's account of reading her own published work for the first time—an account which Leslie Garis (1990), writing for the *New York Times,* describes. In the selection that follows, Garis begins by quoting Kincaid:

> "When I saw it, and it was just what I had put on paper, that is when I realized what my writing was." [Kincaid's] voice takes on a strange tone, as if she is listening to the echo of her words. "My writing," she says dreamily, "was the thing that I thought. Not something else. Just what I thought." (p. 78)

Jeanette Harris (1990) traces in some detail expressionism's origins in Romanticism. Though her aetiology goes back as far as the Enlightenment (which established the premises for expressionism by asserting that truth can be apprehended through individual sensory experience),[9] Harris's emphasis is on Romanticism, which she identifies as "an important, possibly an indispensable, influence on the development of the concept of expressive discourse" (p. 8). Although, as she points out, the term *expressive* was not associated with Romanticism until M. H. Abrams's 1958 book *The Mirror and the Lamp,* it is not hard to find examples of Abrams's and Harris's assertions in 19th-century literary theory. One need look no further than Ralph Waldo Emerson (1950), whose *Nature* describes writing in terms that accord precisely with the expressionistic rhetoric familiar to us today: The concluding section to his essay makes it plain that the purpose of writing is to articulate previously undiscovered thought.

Plato, of course, can be seen as a precursor to both Enlightenment and Romantic contributions to expressionism. *Phaedrus* (1914/1990) describes speech as superior to writing: as the language of the soul, speech is the language of Truth itself. Truth for Plato can only be accessed by the soul; information from the material world is misleading—an obstruction, rather than contribution, to knowledge. Writing, in contrast to speech, is material. Because it is responsive to social phenomena, it is less valuable, less an avenue to Truth:

> [T]he man who thinks that in the written word there is necessarily much that is playful, and that no written discourse, whether in meter or in prose, deserves to be treated very seriously...but that the best of them really serve only to remind us of what we know; and who thinks that only in words about justice and beauty and goodness spoken by teachers for the sake of instruction and really written in a soul is clearness and perfection and serious value, that such words should be considered the speaker's own legitimate offspring, first the word within himself, if it be found there, and secondly its descendants or brothers which may have sprung up in worthy manner in the souls of others, and who pays no attention to the other words—that man, Phaedrus, is likely to be such as you and I might pray that we ourselves may become. (p. 142)

This primacy afforded speech in the ancient world is hardly limited to Plato. And, as Sharon Crowley (1994) explains, for ancient culture it had a rhetorical as well as epistemological rationale: "For ancient rhetors and rhetoricians, spoken discourse was infinitely more powerful and persuasive than was written composition" (p. 233). This importance was based partly on the "scarcity of writing ability" and also on how small were the public gatherings.

> Ancient rhetoricians would be very surprised by the modern association of intelligence and education with literacy—the ability to read and write. For them, writing was an accessory technology, a support for memory as a way of storing information. (p. 234)

In the context of the ancient valorization of speech over writing, modern theories of expressionism might be regarded as an attempt to establish for writing the stature of speech—to make not only speech but writing an expression of the soul's truth.[10] In such a project, truth (knowledge) remains the property of the soul, but it can be discovered and expressed not only through speech but also through writing. Thus, as

Lunsford and Ede (1990), following LeFevre (1987), have noted, expressionistic collaboration typically involves peer groups *after* the individual writer has accomplished solo invention.

Bruffee's (1984) model of collaboration endorses or at least allows for an immanent, internal source of writing, notwithstanding his allegiance to social construction and a conversational definition of writing. He makes sweeping claims for the function of conversation: "The place of conversation in learning, especially in the humanities, is the largest context in which we must see collaborative learning" (p. 645). Collaboration is not an option that the learner chooses; it is a description of how learning takes place.

So far, Bruffee's (1984) positing knowledge in society rather than the individual seems plain. But he has not, in this assertion, defined *knowledge*. The equation of writing with learning is a familiar one in the discipline of composition studies—but it is by no means a unified notion. "Writing equals learning" actually means very different things, depending on who is talking. For expressionists, the learning that takes place in writing is a discovery of one's inner (hence, original) beliefs. That model of writing is also commonplace in contemporary culture. Erwin R. Steinberg (1995) recounts David Kaufer and Richard Young's assertion that one of the assumptions about composing that prevails in English departments is that "writing and thinking are inseparable," which Steinberg attributes to the belief that writing proceeds from inspiration—from genius—the "traditional romantic view of composing" (pp. 271–272).

LeFevre (1987) identifies Kenneth A. Bruffee, Peter Elbow, Donald Murray, and Ken Macrorie as proponents of what she calls "interactive collaboration," a model that allows for autonomous invention. Writing three years after LeFevre, Lunsford and Ede (1990) identify another problematic connection between expressionism and collaborative theory. Not only is the autonomous author still the agent of invention, but, in an assertion of the authorial property of originality, what is "invented" is actually *discovered*—within the writer. Lunsford and Ede associate Peter Elbow, Donald Murray, and James Moffett with this version of collaborative writing,[11] in which collaboration occurs as the writer's option, one that helps her discover and articulate her inner beliefs and personal voice.

Expressionism has long been the target for vitriol in composition studies. James Berlin (1987) describes Berthoff's historical perspective:

Ann Berthoff has [argued] that the Dartmouth Conference supported a bifurcation of language use into the communicative and the expressive, the communicative being identified with the public, rational, and empirical, and the expressive with the private and emotional. The result, she argues, is

that expressive writing—including art—has been divorced from the world
of practical affairs, becoming powerless and ineffective, a trivial discourse of
cathartic but ineffectual emoting. (p. 149)

Séan Burke (1995) demonstrates the outcome of this bifurcation:
"Twentieth-century discussions of the author have debated the role of
intentionality, rejected expressivist theories, and shifted the focus from
the author to the reader, a shift "from creative aesthetic to critical theory"
(p. 65). I do not join in this rejection of expressionism. In fact, Bruffee's
and Elbow's work has had great positive effect on my thinking and my
pedagogy. Elizabeth Rankin (1994) aptly characterizes their contributions:

[F]or those pioneers in composition studies now labeled "romantics" or
"expressivists," the real role of the writing teacher is to motivate, to inspire,
to help students overcome fears and writing blocks and develop confidence
in themselves as writers. (p. 63)

However, I do have reservations. My criticisms of expressionism, like
my criticisms of collaborative theory, are not aimed at the entire field, but
at some of its specific assumptions or consequences.

Lunsford and Ede (1990) characterize Bruffee's later scholarship as his
attempt to dissociate himself from the expressionism that would make
collaboration optional, secondary to autonomous invention. The emphasis on conversation in Bruffee's later scholarship (1984), they assert, is his
means of resolving the paradox of his earlier work, in which all writing is
collaborative yet in which writing expresses the immanent individual.
LeFevre's (1987) four types of invention, which she arranges on a contin-
uum rather than in mutually exclusive categories, illuminate the shift in
Bruffee's work that Lunsford and Ede detect: a shift away from the Platonic invention of the expressionists and toward what LeFevre calls the
"internal dialogic" model of invention:

[T]he internal dialogic view holds that the individual invents by carrying on
an inner conversation or dialectic with another "self" that also functions as
a bridge to the rest of the social world.... Even though the agent of invention is an individual, invention according to this view is affected and indeed
made possible by an "otherness" that is dynamically present in each. (p.
54)[12]

But how different is Bruffee's (1984) "internalized conversation" from
the "stranger within" described in Edward Young's (1759/1966) paean to
the originary author? In Bruffee's formulation, the "internalized conversation" is the writer's hypothesized engagement in a conversation with

others; in Young's formulation, the "stranger within" is (in Séan Burke's [1995] interpretation), "a kind of 'inner God' who dictates to the imagination from a darkling region of the poetic self" (p. 8). Both Bruffee and Young are describing writing as a sort of transcription, but with the writer entirely in charge; the difference is that for Young (as for his Romantic successors), the source of inspiration is an inner God, whereas for Bruffee it is a whole set of internalized gods—the community. In both cases, what is produced is necessarily original. And that valorization of originality is antithetical to the notion of writer-text collaboration.

NOTES

[1] William Spanos's book, *The End of Education: Toward Posthumanism* (1993), follows a similar argument in greater detail. According to Spanos, liberal educational reform, characterized by "the renewed appeal to disinterested inquiry," which is "grounded in metaphysics," furthers a conservative agenda, in that it seeks accommodation "to the humanist core or center" (pp. xiv–xv). From my own perspective, that "humanist core" embraces an autonomous author as a means of maintaining intellectual hierarchy. Schilb (1992) and Spanos voice caution about revision. Does it *change* that humanist core? Is it genuine reform, or does it merely offer the illusion of change while maintaining the status quo?

[2] Woodmansee (1994a) describes authorship with the phrase "relatively recent invention" in at least two of her other publications:

> The "author" in the modern sense is a relatively recent invention, a product of the development we have been exploring—the emergence in the eighteenth century of writers who sought to earn their livelihood from the sale of their writings to the new and rapidly expanding reading public. (p. 36)

> In my view the "author" in its modern sense is a relatively recent invention. (1984, p. 426)

I should note that the 1994a selection is a rewriting of the 1984 publication; her 1994b article, however, is not. I must therefore regard this phrase as a metathesis in Woodmansee's work. While her contributions to contemporary theory of authorship are legion, this particular assertion is debatable, given the extent to which the history of ancient philosophy of authorship contradicts it. Séan Burke's book, *Authorship: From Plato to the Postmodern* (1995), treats the matter in considerably more detail, offering selections from ancient primary texts that support his contention that the "modern" author can be dated at least as early as the 13th century and that the originary property of authorship has its genesis in the hieratic inspiration of the Homeric poet. In fact, in *Authorship*, Burke seems to be directly taking on Woodmansee (p. 7). That she is nowhere cited or mentioned in *Authorship*, or in Burke's earlier book, *The Death and Return of the Author* (1992), even though Woodmansee's acclaimed article "The Genius and the Copyright" was published on this side of the water in 1984, only makes the case more interesting. In *Authorship*, Burke says, "[A. J.] Minnis provides compelling evidence against the assumption that the author is a relatively modern category of thought and locates its emergence in the thirteenth-century shift from an allegorical to a literal interpretation of the Bible" (p. 7). Burke's phrase, "the author is a relatively modern category of thought" constitutes an intertextual trail for what Ellen McCracken (1991) calls the "vanguard reader," recalling as it does Woodmansee's metathesis, "the 'author' in its modern sense is a relatively recent invention." Burke's intentionality is not what is at stake here, for intertextuality, Linda Hutcheon (1986) tells us, is in the reader. And this reader finds an unmistakable trail in Burke's *Authorship*, one that denies Woodmansee's metathesis first by Burke's omitting any mention of her from his text and then by his refuting the validity of his patchwritten version of her signature phrase. Woodmansee's assertion, however, is widely endorsed among theorists of authorship, for example, in James E. Porter's 1996 entry for "author" in the *Encyclopedia of Rhetoric and Composition:* "The author is a fairly recent concept historically...." (p. 55) and his 1993 "Selected Bibliography," which notes that Foucault describes the "relatively recent emergence" of the author (p. 71). For Porter, the phrase functions as a commonplace upon which arguments can be built.

[3] In explaining this negotiation, Flower (1996) demonstrates her own interesting move away from the learner-centered cognitivism for which she is famous. Her article, "Negotiating the Meaning of Difference," negotiates between the audience- and context-based social constructionism and poststructuralism that have characterized recent composition scholarship, and the cognitivism of Flower's 1979 article, "A Cognitive Process Theory of Writing," or her 1981 article, "Writer-Based Prose" (co-authored with John R. Hayes).

[4] James Sosnoski (1991), by way of illustration, describes collaborative inquiry as seeking concurrence, which means "joining intellectual forces to get something done," focusing on people's similarities rather than erasing their differences (pp. 52–53). In this very quality of collaboration, though, many commentators sense danger. John Trimbur and Lundy A. Braun (1992) warn, "One of the complications of collaboration in contemporary science that teachers and theorists of written communications have largely overlooked is its tendency to consolidate the reputations of leading figures and to reproduce a scientific elite" (p. 33). And John Schilb (1992) identifies both the positive (composition pedagogy) and negative (de Man's collaboration with the Nazis in his native Belgium) uses of the word *collaboration* (p. 106). Schilb takes LeFevre to task for not considering the ethical dimensions of the dilemmas facing the professional writers whom she describes. He charges that LeFevre, dismissing these dilemmas as occasions that call for diplomacy, in effect endorses the writers' acceding to what they may consider unethical situations. She does not, Schilb says, consider the options open to them, which include refusing to write what they do not believe in; collaborating with co-workers to protest; or resigning their jobs (pp. 111–115).

[5] Ghostwriting is, of course, an accepted practice in public life. Two writers who explore the ethical issues involved in ghostwriting for public figures are Keith Miller (1992) and Thomas Mallon (1989). Chapter 8, "The Divorce Between

Speech and Thought," of Kathleen Hall Jamieson's book, *Eloquence in an Electronic Age* (1988), offers persuasive reasons for the practice of political speechwriting. A consideration of how those rationales might be applied to students' writing would constitute a provocative rhetorical exercise.

[6]For an extended argument against the teacher-as-savior, the teacher whose need to be loved is the rationale of pedagogy, see Bauer (1998).

[7]I use the term *cultural arbitrary* not in the lay sense in which *arbitrary* means *capricious*, but in a critical sense derived from the work of Pierre Bourdieu (Bourdieu & Passeron, 1977/1990). A cultural arbitrary is a historically bound construct that advances the interests of the powerful members of the community, while offering the appearance of a timeless moral principle. Nietzsche's (1967a) aetiology of the notions of "good" and "bad" is pertinent here.

[8]Jeanette Harris (1990) offers a definition of the term: "A review of composition textbooks published since 1980 reveals that the term is variously applied to writing that focuses on the writer, is based on experience, is personal or private, or communicates emotions or feelings" (p. 53). And of the two synonyms, Harris deems *expressionist* more apt than *expressivist*.

[9]Henry Louis Gates, Jr. (1986), articulates the sinister implications that have been drawn from this Enlightenment model: "...after Rene Descartes, *reason* was privileged, or valorized, above all other human characteristics. Writing, especially after the printing press became so widespread, was taken to be the *visible* sign of reason" (p. 8). Reason was the distinguishing characteristic of the human species; hence humanity was attributed to Blacks based on whether they were literate. And literacy, therefore, was legally denied Blacks in order to justify their enslavement on the basis of their nonliterate—therefore nonrational—therefore nonhuman—status. It is such politics of literacy as these that postmodern ethnographer Stephen A. Tyler (1986) may have in mind when he declares, "The true historical significance of writing is that it has increased our capacity to create totalistic illusions with which to have power over things or over others as if they were things. The whole ideology of representational signification is an ideology of power" (p. 131).

However, the literacy theories of French feminism make the expressionistic model of writing a principle of liberation. Writing, says Hélène Cixous (1991), comes not from "sources" and "grounds," but from a physical act from within that is its own source, from letting oneself float out of the boat, down the river, to the rapids:

> I don't "begin" by "writing": I don't write. Life becomes text starting out from my body. I am already text. History, love, violence, time, work, desire inscribe it in my body, I go where the "fundamental language" is spoken, the body language into which all the tongues of things, acts, and beings translate themselves, in my own breast, the whole of reality worked upon in my flesh, intercepted by my nerves, by my senses, by the labor of all my cells, projected, analyzed, recomposed into a book. (p. 52)

Lynn Worsham (1991) shapes such interpretations to the purposes of composition instruction when she says that what may seem an impossible desire, "to teach an unteachable relation to language," may actually become a practice of teaching how to recognize hegemony in its process of making itself appear natural. Worsham explains,

> Our emphasis should shift from the notion of writing as a mode of learning to that of writing as a strategy, without tactics or techniques, whose progress yields "unlearning." This result does not mean that writing produces ignorance; rather, it produces a sense of defamiliarization vis-à-vis unquestioned forms of knowledge. (p. 101–102)

[10] In *Dora,* Sigmund Freud (1963) casts writing in this role. Writing, in the case of Dora's aphonia, becomes a "physiological substitutive function"—a substitute for speech (p. 56).

[11] See *Singular Texts/Plural Authors* (Lunsford & Ede, 1990), pp. 7, 113–115, as well as the later "Collaborative Authorship and the Teaching of Writing" (1994), pp. 426–427.

[12] The other two types of invention that LeFevre describes are "collaborative," which asserts that "[s]omething new comes about because of the ways people act with each other; inventions do not occur solely in the mind of an independent actor" (p. 63); and "collective," in which "invention is influenced by a social collective, a supra-individual entity whose rules and conventions may enable or inhibit the invention of certain ideas" (p. 80).

II

Authors: How Did we Get into this Mess?

4

Historical Models

Tell me, Muse....
Homer (trans. 1967)

The normative model of the inspired, autonomous author so pervades contemporary pedagogy that it even informs models for classroom collaboration. Its influence serves as a powerful negation of the possibility of writer/text collaboration. It makes impossible a positive pedagogy for patchwriting, which, far from being celebrated or even tolerated, is instead criminalized. The autonomous, originary author is so naturalized that replacing criminalized patchwriting with a positive pedagogy of writer/text collaboration seems to menace not just the classroom, but society in general.

It has not always been so. This normal, necessary, natural model of authorship is, according to Martha Woodmansee (1984, 1994a, 1994b), a "relatively recent invention." Prior to that invention, Western letters readily embraced a variety of models for writer/text collaboration. Nor is the modern invention of the autonomous, originary author a function of intellectual "progress," a move from an unenlightened state toward some sort of foundational truth about authorship. Instead, the autonomous, originary author derives from economic and technological change and participates in maintaining hierarchical social relations that are potentially threatened by those changes.

In its role as academic gatekeeper, composition pedagogy must privilege and reproduce community values. For the past century and more, academic textual values have been relatively unified, ascribing four properties to the "true" author: autonomy, originality, proprietorship, and morality. Composition pedagogy therefore reproduces these properties: the author is or can be autonomous and should be original. The autonomous, original writer deserves property rights to his or her work. The writer who is not autonomous and original demonstrates an absence of morality, earns the label "plagiarist," and deserves punishment.

These four properties of authorship have long been regarded as "facts" of authorship; they are normal, natural, and incontestable. However, the textual values of the ancient world and the Middle Ages—and even of some modern communities—suggest that these are not foundational facts, but cultural arbitraries. Though the competing poles in the mimesis/originality and collaboration/autonomy binaries are evident at all times in the history of Western letters, social circumstances at any given moment determine which of these values is in the ascendant. In the medieval West, the collaborative author—or, more accurately, the accretive author—dominated, while the individual, autonomous author, though present, was a subordinate discourse. Then the technological and thus economic conditions of literacy shifted, and with them textual theory. The autonomous author assumed the dominant role, bolstered by literary theory derived from the philosophies of Thomas Hobbes and John Locke. The printing press, an expanded readership, and a need to differentiate "high" and "low" literacy have all been plausibly advanced as causal factors in the prevalence of the autonomous, originary author in the modern era.

The ongoing, simultaneous competition of mimesis with originality and collaboration with autonomy suggests that in any age, representations of authorship are indeterminate, conflicted, and heterogeneous. Binary accounts of medieval and modern cultures of authorship—accounts in which medieval authorship is depicted as collaborative, modern authorship individualistic—are worse than reductive and simplistic; they are inaccurate. So, too, are single-cause, deterministic accounts of the shift from the medieval author to the modern. With representations of authorship it is not a matter of "inventing" the autonomous author in the 18th century, nor "killing" her in the 20th; both have always been with us and presumably always will.[1] It is a question of which is given more credence at any given moment. And that question is variously resolved, in different eras and localities, according to social need. As culture changes, so do the properties of authorship.

This chapter offers thumbnail sketches of the history of Western authorship. While I cannot provide a comprehensive overview of that history, I can point to a few familiar authors and invoke moments in their work that illustrate some of the competing forces in authorship that always have been and presumably always will be informing our culture. I can also show how the history of a single metaphor—the commonplace that we are all standing on the shoulders of giants—suggests ways in which these competing forces become cultural trends.

HOMER, PLATO, AND THE AUTHORSHIP BINARIES

Western writers' thinking of themselves as individual authors can be traced as far back as the 8th century B.C. Hesiod (trans. 1993) names himself in his text, emphasizing that *a person* wrote the text, a person who is himself a presence in the texts. But he goes further: He names himself in two separate works, *Works and Days* and *Theogony,* inviting his readers to think of him not only as an individual but also as an author, whose texts constitute a corpus.

That the individual author was a familiar part of early Western letters is attested by Homer's depiction of the singer Demodokos:

> The herald came near, bringing with him the excellent singer
> whom the Muse had loved greatly, and gave him both good and evil.
> She reft him of his eyes, but she gave him the sweet singing
> art. Pontonoös set a silver-studded chair out for him
> in the middle of the feasters, propping it against a tall column,
> and the herald hung the clear lyre on a peg placed over
> his head, and showed him how to reach up with his hands and take it
> down, and set beside him a table and a fine basket,
> and beside him a cup to drink whenever his spirit desired it.
> They put forth their hands to the good things that lay ready before them.
> But when they had put away their desire for eating and drinking,
> the Muse stirred the singer to sing the famous actions
> of men on that venture, whose fame goes up into the wide heaven.... (trans.
> 1967, VIII.62–74)

We have in this portrait the singer/author who, though relating traditional materials in oral formulaic mode, is personally honored among the company whom he entertains. While it is the warriors whose fame goes up into the wide heaven, it is clear in this passage that honor is being paid to the singer as well—the singer, and not just the song. Nor is the singer merely (I use the word with some discomfort) a craftsman manipulating traditional materials; he is individually inspired by the Muse. However, within that individual inspiration lurks a sense of collaboration, of mimesis. "Tell me, Muse," begins the *Odyssey* (I.i), and the Muse does, indeed, tell; she tells the entire story, apparently to the swineherd Eumaios, who is suddenly addressed in the second person by the storyteller (XVII.311). Where does this leave the singer who recounts to one audience after another the story of what is now written down as the *Odyssey?* The singer is not an inventor but a reteller, an actor. He is engaged not in originality but in repetition, mimesis. Nevertheless, he is special; he is divinely inspired.

Some two to four centuries elapsed between the time of Homer and the time of Plato, but throughout Plato's works, Homer is a vivid character, one with whom Plato wrestles. The word that Plato uses to identify what he objects to in Homer is the word *mimesis*. The collegiate activity—the collaboration—and the mimesis of Homeric society and textuality speak to socially constructed and communally held truth; the truth that Plato pursues, though it can be approached through dialectic, can only be known through the individual experience of death. Yet even as he rejects the poets and their leading representative, Homer, he is indebted to them.

It is commonplace to think of Plato's quarrel with Homer in terms of a larger quarrel with poets and poetry. Sidney (1995) describes and endeavors to reconcile Plato's sometimes contradictory statements: Plato, he says, "banished [poets] out of his commonwealth" (p. 34), but Sidney counsels us to look at Plato's reasons. As a philosopher, Plato is a natural enemy of poets. He accuses poets of fostering "wrong opinions of the gods," but Sidney describes Homeric singing as a mimetic rather than originary activity: "the poets did not induce such opinions, but did imitate those opinions already induced" (p. 35). To resolve the contradictions in Plato's attitude toward the poets, Sidney points out that in the *Ion* (1995), Plato "giveth high and rightly divine commendation to Poetry" (Sidney, 1995, p. 36).

Basing his conclusions on the *Ion* (Plato, 1995), Sidney chooses to reconcile Plato's conflicting statements in favor of the poet. The choice, however, is a willful one: *Ion* is one of Plato's early dialogues. Its assertions do represent Plato's thinking at that time, but, given the great shifts that occur between the early, middle, and late periods of his work, one cannot point to *Ion* for a resolution of Plato's conflicted opinions about poetry and the poet.

Twentieth-century Freudian criticism would take a much different approach, one that, instead of reconciliation, would offer an psychological interpretation of Plato's attitudes. Harold Bloom's (1973) theories of poetic influence inevitably insert themselves here. To what extent, Bloom's adherents might ask, is Plato's struggle with Homer one in which he strives to break free from the influence of his precursor?

Rhetoricians take yet another tack: Plato mistrusted poets for their failure to strive toward the truth. As C. Jan Swearingen (1991) explains, a long tradition in our culture is that which associates rhetoric, irony, literature, and writing with lying. When poetry came to be thought of as a "made thing," it took its place with these others. All are *doxa*, "mere" opinion. For Plato, truth is the provenance of philosophy.

Sidney's dilemma persists. How can we reconcile Plato's rejection of poets with his continuing admiration for them? In the *Republic* (1916), he goes so far as to exclude poets from the ideal city-state—because they encourage disrespect for the gods. Yet in *Phaedo* (trans. 1981), which, like *Republic*, comes from the middle period of his work, Plato invokes Homer for evidence from authority. Plato's Socrates cites the *Odyssey* (Homer, trans. 1967) as evidence for the argument that the soul is not a harmony, and in that context, he refers to "the divine poet Homer" (Plato, trans. 1981, 95a). And although Socrates says, early in the dialogue, that poets make fables rather than arguments (61b), he also cautions Cebes against letting "some malign influence upset the argument we are about to make." Socrates's antidote is to "come to grips with it in the Homeric fashion" (95b). The Socrates of *Phaedo* does not specify what the "Homeric fashion" is. It may refer to a method of argument—a perverse connection, given Socrates's previous dissociation of poets and argument. Or it may refer to the storytelling that is soon to follow, when Socrates recounts his youthful enthusiasm for natural science (96–99). Either possibility is an interesting one—the former because it allows poets some role in argument, the latter because it suggests that storytelling can rescue an endangered argument. And both possibilities gain potential support in the conclusion to Socrates's argument in *Phaedo*:[2] that conclusion is itself a fable about what happens to the soul after death (108–114). Socrates acknowledges that the fable may not have a basis in fact but that it nevertheless makes a worthwhile contribution to belief-formation:

> No sensible man would insist that these things are as I have described them, but I think it is fitting for a man to risk the belief—for the risk is a noble one—that this, or something like this, is true about our souls and their dwelling places, since the soul is evidently immortal, and a man should repeat this to himself as if it were an incantation, which is why I have been prolonging my tale. (114d)

Plato is demonstrating what I have called the mimesis/originality binary and what Thomas McFarland (1985) calls the "originality paradox." In the *Republic* (1916), Plato rejects Homer—to whom he was intellectually indebted, as *Phaedo* (trans. 1981) illustrates. In order to understand his attack on Homer, we must understand that poetry in Homeric culture was far more significant than it is today; it constituted a "tribal encyclopedia"; it was a "social, not an individual manifestation," for it was orally memorized (McFarland, 1985, pp. 18–21).

Individual authorship, says Eric Havelock (1995), is "strictly a literate conception," whereas the two Homeric epic poems are the result of "collegiate activity on the part of generations of composers" (p. 692). I doubt that the categories are mutually exclusive. But I do agree with Havelock's premise: Cultural changes, such as changes in literacy and writing technology, affect dominant representations—and actions—of authorship. Plato's contempt for the poets is thus a rejection of a textual strategy, mimesis, that he believes to be in eclipse. Again, McFarland (1985):

> In this understanding, the attraction/rejection tension between Plato and Homer is the counterpart of the individual/tradition tension that constitutes the originality paradox, and is in fact the archetypal exemplification of the depth, unavoidability, and constancy of that paradox.... The essence of Plato's point, the raison d'être of his attack, is that in the poetic performance as practised hitherto in Greece there was no "original." (p. 21)

The key word in this passage from McFarland is "unavoidability." Plato's dilemma is not, despite Sir Philip Sidney's (1995) best efforts, ever resolved—in Plato or in the centuries of Western culture that have since elapsed. Mimesis and tradition may characterize oral culture, and originality and individuality may characterize the literate culture that displaced it. We may trace the rise and fall of influence among the "sides" of the authorship binaries. But the entire congeries of textual values encompassed by these binaries is always already participating in Western textual values at any given moment. And the "rise and fall" does not follow any sort of linear progression from ignorance to enlightenment, but rather resembles something more like the ocean's tides—or, more accurately, traffic in New York. The rise and fall of poles in the authorship binaries responds not to forces of nature, but to cultural demands, notably those created by technology and the economy.

QUINTILIAN: IMITATION IN THE ASCENDANT

Harold Ogden White (1935) describes the dominant theory of authorship in classical letters: "[I]mitation is essential; fabrication is dangerous; subject matter is common property" (pp. 6–7). The fragmentary texts of Dionysius of Halicarnassus from the 2nd century B.C. are the earliest exposition of *imitatio* in oratory (Kennedy, 1980). Imitation solved a problem for Dionysius: He believed that the era in which he lived was intellectually inferior to the classical age that had passed. By imitating the Attic orators and historians, though, he could participate in the excellence of their era. For Dionysius, imitation was not just a way of learning; it was a way of *being*. Imitating classical writers merged his identity with theirs and elevated the general tenor of his own times. Thomas Greene (1982) affirms this perspective on classical theory of authorship:

> The treatment of *imitatio* during the first century A.D. is colored progressively by the sense of decline that seems to have been virtually universal during that era. Thus imitation, when it is perceived as desirable, tends to emerge as a technique for mitigating the general lowering of standards. (p. 72)

What both White (1935) and Greene (1982) describe is the dominant theory of authorship in the ancient West. Close reading of any single rhetoric text of the time nevertheless reveals the continuing congeries of textual values. The competing values of autonomy and collaboration, originality and mimesis, are evident, for example, in the *Institutio Oratoria*. Quintilian (1987), great synthesist of rhetorical theories, offers a three-step sequence of activities for he who would maintain and develop the skills in eloquence that he has already acquired. As the orator's objective, speaking comes first; then imitation; then writing. When Quintilian refers to imitation, he means reading for the purpose of studying models, and he specifies that, especially at first, only the best models should be studied: "For a long time...none but the best authors" should be read, with "as much care as if we were transcribing them" (X.1.20). In studying a model, the orator should not simply seize upon only that which can readily be understood, for often these passages represent the dross, the least valuable parts of the source. In a passage in which Quintilian seems to be talking about patchwriting or its close kin, he says that the source model is only diminished when it is followed too closely. "The first consideration, therefore, for the student, is, that he should understand *what he proposes to imitate*, and have a thorough conception *why it is excellent*" (original emphasis, X.2.18). Clearly, Quintilian has reservations about imitation, and clearly he believes in the possibility of originary composition: "[I]n the originals, which we take for our models, there is nature and real power, while every imitation, on the contrary, is something counterfeit..." (X.2.11).

However, despite these reservations, Quintilian (1987) espouses the dominant theory of authorship in the ancient period: He recommends imitation as the primary means of honing and developing one's skills in oratory.

From these authors, and others worthy to be read, must be acquired a stock of words, a variety of figures, and the art of composition. Our minds must be directed to the imitation of all their excellences, for it cannot be doubted that a great portion of art consists in imitation—for even though to invent was first in order of time and holds the first place in merit, it is nevertheless advantageous to copy what has been invented with success. Indeed, the whole conduct of life is based on the desire of doing ourselves that which we approve in others. (X.2.1–2)

THE MEDIEVAL WEST: IMITATION AS DOMINANT MODEL

Medieval notions of literacy emphasized tradition and the accumulation of knowledge, while de-emphasizing the individual writer.[3] These constitute a shift in emphasis from antiquity: appreciation for or even attention to the individual author was at an all-time low. The notion of individual authorship was, in fact, more foreign to the Middle Ages than to either antiquity or the modern world. Hans Robert Jauss explains, "[I]n contrast to humanist and modern authors, the medieval writer wrote 'in order to praise and to extend his object, not to express himself or to enhance his personal reputation'" (qtd. in Lunsford & Ede, 1990, p. 78). In the Middle Ages, when St. Bonaventure theorized four methods of composition, completely original work was not among them.

The mimesis characteristic of the Middle Ages has a different motivation from that of the ancient West: Literacy, produced in and controlled by the Church, has the primary task of furthering God's purposes. The individual writer in this economy of authorship is beside the point, even a hindrance. Instead, the writer voices God's truth (even if the document he is writing is a forgery) and participates in the tradition of that truth-telling. Even in patron-sponsored writing for the purposes of entertainment, the writer's identity and originality are only tangentially at issue. In the Middle Ages, the ancient dynamic between the textual values of imitation and originality had shifted so much that Giles Constable (1983) says, "The term plagiarism should...probably be dropped in reference to the Middle Ages, since it expresses a concept of literary individualism and property that is distinctively modern" (p. 39). Constable is correct, of course, in identifying originality as the hallmark of modern notions of authorship, but it would be a mistake to think that this textual value was invented in the Modern period. It is apparent in ancient rhetoric, submerged in the Medieval period, and in the modern world emerges as the dominant textual value.

Instead of placing a premium upon autonomous composition and individual presentation, medieval textual practice privileged the sources from which the writer works. Writing contributed to the accumulation of knowledge, and the individual writer might apprehend that which had previously gone unrecognized. But that apprehension was due not to the writer's personal attributes, but to the high quality of the sources from which "he" worked.[4] In the Middle Ages, mimesis was the means of establishing one's authority, as well as being an expression of humility.[5] The notion of the individual author, autonomous, original, and proprietary, played only the smallest role in this economy of authorship. With those textual values so much in decline, plagiarism was hardly an issue. The concern for plagiarism is an ancient one, dating back to the Roman poet Martial, who applied the word to textual activities and not just to the kidnapping of slaves. But in the medieval West, plagiarism was a concern that seldom arose.

The mimesis-based medieval textual values are evident in the metaphor of standing on the shoulders of giants, an aphorism today commonly attributed to Isaac Newton, but in fact of much greater antiquity.[6] Robert Merton (1965) observes that although Robert Burton and *Bartlett's Familiar Quotations* attribute it to the ancient writer Lucan, the phrase "standing on the shoulders of giants" can first be authenticated only as early as the 12th-century Bernard of Chartres.[7] John of Salisbury reports Bernard's use of it, and 20th-century scholar Roger Sarton translates it from Salisbury's Latin into English: "In comparison with the ancients, we stand like dwarfs on the shoulders of giants." In Merton's view, Sarton's translation aptly captures the assertion that the writer is not as great as his source. Merton observes, though, that the aphorism in the Middle Ages, and specifically in Salisbury's Latin, also expresses "the singularly important idea that the successors need be no brighter than their predecessors—nor even *as* bright—and yet, the accumulation of knowledge being what it is, they can know far more and thus come to see farther" (p. 41). It is the process of the accumulation of knowledge that is the hero of medieval textual theory.

Bernard of Chartres uses the metaphor to explain the statuary and stained-glass representations in the medieval architectural showcase Chartres Cathedral,[8] but the theme echoes again and again, in a variety of contexts. Constable (1983) finds it in a late 12th-century letter by Peter of Blois. In this letter, it is clear that the imitation and collaboration to which the metaphor of standing on the shoulders of giants refers is a language-specific imitation and collaboration. Peter is not talking about imitating rhetorical structures; he is talking about reproducing, recontextualizing, and reviving the actual language of a source text:

> We are like dwarfs on the shoulders of giants...by whose kindness we see
> further than they do, when we adhere to the works of the ancients and

arouse into some newness of being their more elegant sentences, which age
and human neglect have let decay and become almost lifeless. (qtd. in Constable, 1983, p. 34)

Peter's metaphor might attribute superiority to the dwarves, who can
see further; or to the giants, who are larger and stronger. But, says Constable, "In the Middle Ages it meant...that modern people must be more
perspicacious than people of Antiquity precisely because they are further
from the fountain of truth" (p. 37).

Like the textual values to which it refers, the metaphor of standing on
the shoulders of giants is historically unstable. As the values it expresses
change, so does the meaning of the metaphor. As if to illustrate my point,
Merton (1965) finds another, almost contrary element emerging: the ele-
vation of the dwarf/pygmy. He who in the early uses of the metaphor was
a humble successor gradually becomes a superior creature. Merton is not
the first to recognize this shift; he says that Ludovicus Vivis, in 1531,
expresses exasperation with the combination of humility and egotism
found in the frequent use of the aphorism (pp. 63–64).[9] A century later,
Godfrey Goodman and Alexander Ross both use it as a means of lament-
ing the decay of civilization, but George Hakewill's 1627 use of the aphorism makes equals of the giants and pygmies, again emphasizing the
importance not of individuals, but of accumulated knowledge. Yet, true to
what I believe is a fundamental truth about theories of authorship, this
early modern tendency to elevate the pygmy was simply a shift in emphasis, not an innovation: Quintilian (1987) had spoken of the same phenomenon. In fact, he recommended that the imitator should always strive
to surpass his source: "Even those who do not aim at the highest excellence should rather try to excel, than merely follow, their predecessors..."
(X.2.9).

Surely today's patchwriting students—indeed, all patchwriters (which is
to say all writers), expert and novice—are on some level conscious of the
identity-fusion, the giant-pygmy collaboration, that takes place in patchwriting. A common contemporary response to patchwriting focuses on
appropriation—the patchwriter's appropriation of the source. From this
perspective, patchwriting is theft, a criminal act. But medieval textual theory reminds us that patchwriting's merger of self is bidirectional: The
patchwriter is acknowledging his writing persona as entailed rather than
autonomous, and he is acknowledging the authority of the source text.

If that merger of selves is criminalized, though—as it is in contemporary composition pedagogy—the patchwriter cannot, like Peter of Blois,
be standing on the shoulders of giants and seeing further than they, but is
instead lurking furtively in the shadow of those giants.

THE SHIFT TO THE MODERN:
ORIGINALITY IN THE ASCENDANT

After the passage of yet another century, the modern use of the aphorism is well established: "standing on the shoulders of giants" remains a declaration of modesty, but the usual emphasis is decidedly on the superior knowledge of the pygmies. In a 1670s quarrel with Robert Hooke, Isaac Newton uses it, and Merton (1965) concludes, "Newton was being humble at the very time he was denying, and rightly so, that any before him, and particularly not Hooke, had come upon the theory he had himself evolved" (p. 11).[10] In a transformation typical of modern textual values, the aphorism quickly gained a reputation as Newton's original saying (p. 34).[11]

Peter Gay's (1966) account suggests that the metaphor had a very specialized use in the 18th century. Not only was it a way of generally asserting the superior quality of contemporary thought, but it was also specifically a way for the philosophes to assert their superiority over their 17th-century predecessors. They acknowledged their debt to the 17th century, but asserted their pygmy superiority—partly on the basis of their own close attunement to the classical world, without the intervention of misguided 17th-century commentators:

> The philosophes were fond of saying that if they surpassed antiquity, they surpassed it because they were standing on the shoulders of ancient giants. As their distance from their ancient masters defined the amount of work they had done for themselves (or, they conceded, their seventeenth-century precursors had done for them), so their intimacy with them revealed how persistently and productively they were in touch with the best of Greek and Roman thought. (p. 121)

By the dawn of the Romantic era, it was no longer acceptable to stand on the shoulders of predecessors, nor even to use commonplace phrases like "standing on the shoulders of giants." Hence, when Edward Young (1759/1966) alludes to the tradition, he does not acknowledge that he is doing so, and he engages in a sufficiently sophisticated patchwriting that the "standing on the shoulders of giants" commonplace is not readily recognizable. In 1759, offering a Romantic revision of earlier textual values, Young says that if by sheer chance we write what the ancients have written, we "become a noble Collateral, not an humble Descendent from them" (p. 22). No longer must we stand on the shoulders of giants, recent or distant, in order to advance knowledge; and when we do work from sources, it is with grandeur, not humility.

PYGMIES NO MORE

In the modern textual economy, originality marks "true" authorship; derivative authorship must acknowledge its sources; and derivative authorship using unacknowledged sources is socially transgressive. From its emergence in the 17th century until the postmodern era of the late 20th century, this economy has steadily gained credence. The writer is no longer a pygmy obscured by giants. Even when they do work from sources, writers are at least the equal or colleague of (rather than pygmy to) those sources—as attested by Robert J. Connors's revision of the metaphor:

> We may not always be able to claim that we see far because we stand on the shoulders of giants; we do, however, stand on the shoulders of thousands of good-willed teachers and writers surprisingly like us, who faced in 1870 or 1930 problems amazingly similar to those we confront each time we enter the classroom. (1991, p. 49)

How did our basic notion of authorship accomplish such an about-face? One is tempted to begin searching for causal factors in the shift, but, as Foucault (1971/1977a) suggests, sociohistorical analysis is a dangerous business. The genealogy that Foucault prefers to history would seem equally difficult, though, in that it undertakes to identify and untangle the strands of discursive practices that seem natural and ahistorical. Genealogy, says Foucault, differs from history in that it "opposes itself to the search for 'origins'" (p. 140);[12] it does not undertake to assemble causal, linear, unified accounts. "Genealogy," continues Foucault, "is history in the form of a concerted carnival" (p. 161).[13]

In "What Is an Author?" (1977b), Foucault visits the concerted carnival of authorship, exploring the relationship of text and author—the way texts seem to point to "this figure who is outside and precedes it" (p. 115). Mark Rose (1993), in contrast, takes an historical rather than genealogical approach to authorship, and his explicit concern is not with the subjectivity of authorship but with its representation, through the notions of "property, originality, and personality" (p. 7). With Rose, I focus more on representations than on subjectivity. But with Foucault, I am wary of the search for origins of these representations. Rather, I would prefer to point to some of the notions with which they associate, notions which are customarily advanced as causes.

One of these associations is with individualism. Authorship in the West shifted from mimetic representations to autonomous representations at approximately the same time that individualism was "invented." Through his splitting of subject and object and his postulating knowledge within the subject, René Descartes (1637/1965) is one of the pivotal figures in this invention. He resolves to hold only those opinions that he can demonstrate as worthwhile—to reject all opinions, "in order to replace them afterwards, either with better ones, or else the same ones when I had raised them to the level of reason" (p. 13). In the Medieval period, knowledge resides in the community, but in the Modern period, it is within the individual. Both Descartes and John Locke (1960) are instrumental in articulating this modern epistemology. The two have very different approaches—Descartes credited with a Platonism that postulates innate, prediscursive ideas,[14] and Locke associated with the *tabula rasa* epistemology of observation and experience. Yet taken together, their theories assert that knowledge is within the subject rather than the community. Locke, moreover, invests enormous power in the subject when he says that the individual has the right of property to the labor of his body.

Certainly individualism is one of the discursive formations that accompanies the emergence of modern authorship, and Mark Rose (1993) asserts that the "complex layering of the literary-property struggle" included the ideological struggle for "possessive individualism" (p. 92). A corollary struggle played later in Germany. Martha Woodmansee (1994a) explains that Young's *Conjectures on Original Composition* (1759/1966) quickly achieved wide currency in Germany. Today, *Conjectures* is best known for being the first extended treatise on authorial originality, but it also supplied Johann Gottlieb Fichte with material from which he could assert that a book is the imprint of the individual who wrote it. Neoclassical theory had it that the pleasure of a book was in the reader's discovering himself in it (an idea based on the supposed universality of the human type), but in the hands of German philosophers Fichte, Herder, and Goethe, the pleasure of a book was in the discovery of the individuality of the writer.[15] "This radically new conception of the book as an imprint or record of the intellection of a unique individual—hence a 'tremendous betrayer' [Herder] of that individual—entails new reading strategies" (Woodmansee, 1994a, p. 55).

It would be tempting to posit from these observations that the rise of individualism is the cause of the modern value of authorial autonomy, but most theorists today would not endorse that causal sequence. Jacob Burckhardt's (1945) once-influential explication of the rise of Renaissance individualism would have contributed to such an interpretation, and individualism and authorial autonomy are certainly concomitant formations. Constable (1983) asserts, for example, that the anonymity of medieval art was on the decline by the 12th century.[16] A sense of "literary individuality," he says, is evidenced in the increasing numbers of accusations of literary theft in the 12th and 13th centuries (p. 32). But to identify individualism and authorial autonomy as concomitant formations does not necessarily establish one as the cause and the other the effect. In fact, Wendy Wall (1993) advises against conflating the Renaissance emergence of the individual with the emergence of the author. "The author that we see in early modern England," she says, "is not the same entity as the bourgeois subject...." (p. 346).

Contemporary theorists, when they reach for causes, are much more likely to credit the printing press,[17] which made the distribution of literature sufficiently large scale that it could be lucrative. Thus writers for the first time had the possibility of making an independent living at their writing, without the constraints of patrons.

We may associate manuscript culture with the system of literary patronage, and print culture with writers' making a living from the sale of their work. For a brief transitional period, Renaissance literate activity was characterized by a competition between handwritten codices and printed texts (much akin to the competition at the end of the 20th century between print and electronic distribution of texts). Manuscripts gained their "authority" by audience legitimation in high-status coteries—the court, the Inns of Court, the universities. Manuscripts were initially accorded higher social status than were printed texts. Whereas manuscript writing was a mark of gentility, print publication marked the "collapse of social difference" (Wall, 1993, p. 12), including the "difference" of both social class and gender: The audience of printed texts could not be as easily contained and limited as could the manuscript audience. It is hardly surprising, then, that in the early days of printing in England, the Queen forbade secret printing presses, confined legitimate presses to the city of London and the two universities, and attempted "to control the medium by censoring materials and regulating the daily operations of the printing business" (p. 343). The objective, of course, was to contain sedition; but the sense of danger, of the print medium's potential for rampaging, menacing difference, is underscored by the early efforts at official containment (not unlike contemporary legislation aimed at the Internet).

Despite Martin Luther's pronouncement that knowledge came from God and should be shared freely, England instituted its Ur-copyright law with the 1710 Statute of Anne.[18] That law not only separated right in copy once and for all from censorship, but also heralded the demise of the traditional patronage system in England. Copyright in England was first accorded to the publisher, later to the author. By the end of the 18th century, international copyright laws were being put into effect in France; other Western countries followed suit in the 19th century.

As Martha Woodmansee's (1984, 1994a, 1994b) various publications explain, yet another element was essential to the emergence of the modern author: the reader. The 18th century saw a dramatic increase in literacy in Western Europe, a commensurably greater demand for texts, and, as a result, enhanced possibilities for the emerging profession of writing.[19] In the Middle Ages, writers had depended upon their patrons and wrote to please them, but increased literacy rates created a more numerous and less homogeneous reading public. The printing press provided the means of reaching that larger audience, and copyright laws protected the writer's ability to make a living doing so.

The printing press, the assertion of text as abstract property, the notion of authorial creativity, the ideology of individualism, and an expanded readership are all essential components of the emergence of the modern author. "It was not the sudden proliferation of books or a sudden increase in literacy rates that created an impact...but the way in which writers began to represent and perceive print's cultural, literary, and political potential" (Wall, 1993, p. x).

What this attenuated portrait of different eras' approaches to writing demonstrates is the historical contingency of authorship. The representation of authorship at any given time in any given culture is tied to that culture's circumstances and needs. This can be a positive force within the culture, but when those circumstances and needs are not unitary, authorship can become a site of contest, with each "side" insisting on the naturalness and necessity of its representation. Such contests occur most readily when the circumstances of writing are in transition, as they were in the West in the shift from manuscript to print culture in the Renaissance—and as they are today in the shift from print to electronic literacy.

NOTES

[1] The feminine pronoun here is deliberate; many feminists have complained that it is by no coincidence that the death of the author came along at just the moment when women were gaining authorial status. In Gilbert and Gubar's (1979/1991) description, women writers today are in the heady milieu of creating a female literary tradition, of being the precursors whom Harold Bloom allows only to male poets. The death of the author threatens to close down the making of that tradition.

[2] The argument of *Phaedo* (trans. 1981) is an important contribution to the Theory of Forms developed in the middle period of Plato's work: the true philosopher will welcome rather than avoid death, because in death his soul will be freed from his body and thus will have the possibility of attaining (remembering) true knowledge.

[3] A number of fine treatments of medieval textual theory are available, including Giles Constable's "Forgery and Plagiarism in the Middle Ages" (1983), Hans Robert Jauss's "The Alterity and Modernity of Medieval Literature" (1979), and

Alastair J. Minnis's *Medieval Theory of Authorship: Scholastic Literary Attitudes in the Later Middle Ages* (1987).

[4] The masculine pronoun is well established as the only accurate one for discussions of authorship prior to the Modern period—and even to this century. Though medieval women did write, the male writer was plainly normative.

[5] Indeed, when George E. Rowe (1988) describes Ben Jonson's theory of authorship, he connects the Renaissance to the ancient world rather than to the intervening Middle Ages. In that context, he differentiates three types of mimesis:

> Classical and Renaissance discussions of imitation fall into three basic categories. The first, which is of little interest here, defines imitation as copying or following a model as accurately as possible. A second and much more influential approach describes it as an endeavor not to reproduce a model exactly but to transform that model in a manner suited to the imitator's personality and situation. Seneca is the major classical exponent of this viewpoint.... The third approach to imitation...defined imitation as an endeavor to compete with and surpass a model rather than merely alter it.... Its earliest known proponent is Hesiod.... Quintilian, however, was probably the most influential classical advocate of this viewpoint. (pp. 13–15)

Séan Burke (1995) categorizes ancient mimesis in a rather different way. He identifies a mimesis in which the rhetor is "copyist of reality" (p. 5), associating this approach with Plato. Burke cautions, though, that in this Platonic mimesis, what the rhetor copies is not Truth but only a distorted approach to it. Aristotle, too, represented mimesis in this way, except for him the imitation was of "significant reality." But a second type of ancient mimesis is described by Burke as the mimesis of literary tradition—in keeping with the metaphor of "standing on the shoulders of giants."

[6] Even when the aphorism is not attributed to Newton, it—or the assertion which it makes—is commonly considered of modern vintage. H. Floris Cohen (1994), for example, attributes to Condorcet (1743–1794) the first declaration that knowledge cumulates.

[7] Both Burton and *Bartlett's Familiar Quotations* refer to Lucan's evoking giants and pygmies in a work called "Didacus Stella," but Robert Merton (1965) notes that neither provides any information about this "Didacus Stella," in which the aphorism supposedly appears. Burton himself makes no mention of standing on the shoulders of giants in the first edition of the *Anatomy of Melancholy* (Merton, 1965, p. 7); he introduces the aphorism in the second edition by way of defending his heavy use of sources (p. 11). From these circumstances, it is easy to see why Merton believes that Burton's attribution of the aphorism to an ancient source is at least self-serving and even potentially fraudulent.

[8] The lancets below the South Rose Window, for example, depict Christian figures literally standing on the shoulders of Hebrew Testament patriarchs.

[9] Twentieth-century commentator Allan Bloom (1990) shares Vivis's exasperation. In the preface to his book, *Giants and Dwarfs*, Bloom wastes no time in announcing,

My title emphatically does not refer to the old saw "We are dwarfs, but we stand on the shoulders of giants." This expresses, in the guise of humility, too much self-satisfaction. Do giants let themselves be climbed so easily? Is it their function to carry dwarfs on their shoulders? Perhaps they were once so gracious but now have set us down on the earth and quietly stolen away, leaving us with an illusion of broader perspectives. The groundless assumption of intimacy with greatness soon gives way for a new generation which denies that there ever were giants and asserts that the whole story is a lie made up by their teachers to empower themselves. The giants are, I presume, looking down on this little comedy and laughing. (p. 9)

[10] Merton's adverb phrase "rightly so" reveals his own subscription to the modern valorization of pygmies who can and do create something new, themselves becoming giants.

[11] And to that reputation a certain stock of lore attaches. Raymond G. McInnis summarizes: "...in connection with Newton's use of the term, certain dark motives are involved. Allegedly, Newton used the metaphor as a put down of Robert Hooke, a contemporary scientist. Hooke was physically deformed, I believe what we call a 'hunchback.'"

[12] My reading of Foucault's (1971/1977a) essay on Nietzsche is not universally accepted. Ernst Behler (1991), for example, says that Foucault describes history as teleological, genealogy aetiological. Much more consonant with my interpretation is Judith Butler's (1990) account of genealogy: "A genealogical critique refuses to search for the origins of gender, the inner truth of female desire, a genuine or authentic sexual identity that repression has kept from view; rather, genealogy investigates the political stakes in designating as an *origin* and *cause* those identity categories that are in fact the *effects* of institutions, practices, discourses with multiple and diffuse points of origin" (original emphasis, pp. viii–ix).

[13] Susan Miller (1991) explains the meaning of the word *carnival* for critical theory. The carnival, as deployed by Bakhtin, Stallybrass and White, and Foucault, is a transient site where the dominant culture is suspended and inverted.

[14] The true philosopher, "as far as he can...turns away from the body towards the soul" (Plato, trans. 1981, 64e) because the soul can apprehend that which is constant, that which is real, whereas the body becomes confused by—and confuses the soul with—that which is apprehended through the senses, that which is constantly changing (79c).

[15] Patricia Phillips (1984) argues that the emergence of the notion of originality constitutes a resistance to the hegemony of Neoclassicism, with its strictures of erudition, form, and tradition. The literary value of originality enabled poets to shed these fetters and instead engage in experimentation.

[16] Many historians regard the 12th century as the end of the Middle Ages; the 13th and 14th centuries, in this interpretation, function as part of a pre-Modern or early-Modern period.

[17] Elizabeth Eisenstein's two-volume *The Printing Press as an Agent of Change* (1979) is widely considered the watershed statement of this point of view. More recently and more succinctly, Mark Rose (1993) explicates a similar thesis in *Authors and Owners: The Invention of Copyright*, as does Roger Chartier in "Figures

of the Author" (1994). Wendy Wall's *The Imprint of Gender: Authorship and Publication in the English Renaissance* (1993) demonstrates the gender representations occasioned by authorship in the early print medium.

[18]The law was passed in 1709 and enacted in 1710.

[19]In *The Author, Art, and the Market*, Woodmansee (1994a) notes that in Germany, the rise of mass literacy took place somewhat later. German writers compensated by energetically promoting the value of writing and reading "high" literature.

5

Modern Authors

[A] reformed vision of how specifically written discourse originates can rescue a concept of the "subject" or "author" of writing from its currently precarious theoretical and philosophical place. We can, that is, explain historically why it remains feasible to investigate the human "writer" without necessarily surrounding that person with the now easily deniable claptrap of inspired, unitary "authorship" that contemporary theorists in other fields have so thoroughly deconstructed.

Susan Miller (1989)

In the Middle Ages, textual theory depicted authorship in near-exclusive terms of mimesis and writer-text collaboration. Textual theory in the Modern period has shifted to the opposite pole: authorship is now depicted in exclusive terms of originality and autonomy.

In the preceding chapters, I have argued that the competing terms of the mimesis/originality and collaboration/autonomy binaries, together with a variety of lacunae and points of instability, have been a part of Western textual theory throughout its recorded history. We have not "invented" a new sort of author in the Modern period; rather, the balance in those binaries shifted toward the originality and autonomy poles.

In the Modern period, we do, nevertheless, have some innovations. For the first time, one pole of the binaries has been accorded outlaw status. With the outlaw status comes a new binary: plagiarist/author. What was, through the Ancient and Medieval periods, a legitimate set of textual practices is now labeled illegal and immoral. Writers who are mimetic and who collaborate with their texts are not authors. They are, at best, students. If they fail to acknowledge their mimesis or their collaboration with source texts, they are plagiarists. If they are both plagiarist and student, they are punished. This is new; a "relatively recent invention."[1]

According to most historians of authorship, economic and technological conditions caused the shift from the accretive textual values of the medieval West to the individualistic ones that emerged in the 18th century and continue today. Notions of authorship are culture-specific, arising not as a description of foundational facts about writing, but as cultural arbitraries that support larger social trends. From the early modern development of print publication and copyright come autonomy and proprietorship as attributes of authorship. To some extent, the attribute of originality can also be traced to that period. However, in the 19th century, originality gains the textual prominence that we know today, and with its emergence comes the notion of morality as an attribute of true authorship. In the Romantic imagination, the character of the writer is reflected in the felicity of his words.

With the economic and technological rationales, I would emphasize a third causal factor in the hegemony of the originary, autonomous, proprietary, moral modern author and in the commensurate criminalization of the mimetic, collaborative, larcenous, immoral modern plagiarist. The economic and technological changes may have been the proximate causes of the modern author. But they were also the proximate causes of the destabilization of the intellectual status quo. The need to shore up that status quo, to establish new justifications for it that could replace those threatened by economic and technological change, became the proximate cause of the rise of the modern plagiarist.

An incredulity toward the autonomous, originary author is now gaining ground in critical theory, bolstered by the new digitized information systems and by postmodern literary theory. Nevertheless, the figures of the autonomous, originary author and the unethical, larcenous plagiarist persist in textual studies and prevail in the academy. Therefore, composition studies, in its gatekeeper function, is faced with the task of upholding contradictory textual values. As it strives to maintain the author-plagiarist dichotomy and to include patchwriting in the category of plagiarism, the role of composition studies in maintaining and reproducing intellectual hierarchy becomes increasingly evident and increasingly disturbing.

PROPERTIES OF AUTHORSHIP

The textual values that composition instruction is expected to uphold can be articulated as "properties" of authorship. I identify four: autonomy, proprietorship, originality, and morality. These are not, by any means, a complete list of properties attributed to modern authorship; nor are they the only possible means of categorizing those attributes.[2] They are at best a terminological convenience, a way of genealogically discovering the *author*, towards the objective of describing that author's supposed opposite, the *plagiarist*. An understanding of each of the properties in isolation helps to demonstrate just how arbitrary are our received representations of the plagiarist.

Proprietorship

Though Charles Dickens worked hard for international copyright as a means of protecting his proprietary rights in his publications, Gerhard Joseph's (1994) reading of Dickens's works reveals that, even in an age when the principles of copyright were being energetically formulated and even though Dickens worked toward those ends, he experienced mixed feelings about the proprietary quality of authorship. Specifically, in *Martin Chuzzlewit*, Pecksniff's appropriation of young Martin's architectural drawings stands for Dickens's own concerns about appropriation of his writings. At that time in England, it was legal for Pecksniff to appropriate Martin's architectural drawings, but Dickens has questions. Those questions, says Joseph, destabilize "nineteenth-century assumptions about the ownership of intellectual property" (p. 265). Pecksniff's theft "serves [the] critical function [of] putting into question the egoism and pride of ownership out of which [Martin's] outrage arises" (p. 267).

> [T]he very fact that intellectual rather than monetary rights are in dispute for Martin would seem to argue, in the displacement I posit, that for Dickens the money seemed (or so he would have told himself) less important than the principle of a creator's "natural rights" to his words subject to whatever contractual arrangements he might wish to make. (p. 269)

In other words, in *Martin Chuzzlewit*, Dickens is playing with both sides of the paradox described by both Gerhard Joseph and Thomas McFarland (1985), in which "originality and imitation have never existed in isolation but have always been two terms of a ratio...." (Joseph, 1994, p. 267).

But despite this conceptual tension, both plagiarism and copyright were energetically articulated in the 19th century. Although plagiarism and copyright are not covariant, they do borrow metaphors from each other, and they both contribute to and draw from the economy of authorship whose properties include autonomy, proprietorship, originality, and morality. It is worthwhile, therefore, to trace the emergence of propri-

etorship in copyright theory, in order to understand the role that proprietorship plays in the discourse of plagiarism.

The early rights for printing were extended not to authors but to print-
ers, and the purpose of these "rights" was for the state to ascertain who
might be held legally responsible, should the text prove seditious. The
transition from royal patents to authorial copyright was a time-consuming
process to which considerable energy in 17th- and 18th-century England
was devoted. Indeed, copyright law continues to be revised in England,
the United States, and elsewhere, to the present day. From the first
English royal patent issued to a printer in 1518, it took two centuries
before the 1710 Statute of Anne made copyright possible not just for a
Stationers' Guild member, but also for the author.[3] In that transition,
printed texts became what Foucault (1977b) calls "objects of appropriation"—property protected by copyright laws (p. 124).[4]

Aside from the tangible issues of censorship and commerce that pro-
pelled the transition from patents to copyright, certain ideological rationales supported the change, and it is this ideological apparatus that proves
most relevant to the problems of plagiarism that vex textual studies
today. The initial ideological argument for copyright was an argument
advanced on a variety of fronts. I am labeling this argument *proprietorship*:
a man has a right to the labor of his body; writing is a labor of the body;
and a writer therefore has the right of property in what he writes.[5] This
syllogism has far-reaching consequences for composition pedagogy.
Lester Faigley (1992) complains about one: In claiming to give students
"ownership" of their texts, teachers "conflat[e] the capitalist notion of
property rights...with autobiographical writing" (p. 128).

At first it was the booksellers who gained most from the new copyright
laws, although as they argued for the legislation, they spoke of the bene-
fits that would accrue to the authors. Most authors of the period did not
want to dirty themselves with the taint of commerce that copyright carried; they sold their works outright to the booksellers. An exception was
Alexander Pope, who, despite representing himself as a gentleman who
wrote for the purpose of entertaining friends, brought charges against
Edmund Curll for the unauthorized publication of his letters. The case
was important for establishing that property rights in letters belonged to
the writer, not the receiver. Whereas medieval literary property had
reposed in the physical text itself, the case of *Pope* v. *Curll* moved literary
property another step into the abstract domain (Rose, 1993).

The booksellers differentiated literary property from other types of
property: Literary property is *created* by he who possesses it. In the second
half of the 18th century, William Blackstone (1765–1769/1979) endeav-
ored to define literary property as analogous to real property.[6]

But prior to Blackstone, Thomas Hobbes's (1988) and John Locke's (1960) theories were integral to the emergence of the authorial characteristic of proprietorship. Locke believes that by natural right a man owns his body and the products of his labor:

> Though the earth and all inferior creatures be common to all men, yet every man has a property in his own person; this nobody has any right to but himself. The labor of his body and the work of his hands, we may say, are properly his. Whatsoever then he removes out of the state that nature has provided and left it in, he has mixed his labor with, and joined to it something that is his own, and thereby makes it his property. It being by him removed from the common state nature has placed it in, it has by this labor something annexed to it that excludes the common right of other men. For this labor being the unquestionable property of the laborer, no man but he can have a right to what that is once joined to, at least where there is enough and as good left in common for others. (p. 17)

Natural right, then, is a right of *person*. It is a common-law right that, elsewhere in the *Second Treatise*, Locke contrasts with absolute (statutory) rights. Whereas absolute rights depend upon the legislations of the political unit, natural rights transcend time and context. Absolute rights may change; natural rights cannot.

Rose (1993) explains how readily Locke's (1960) principles attach to authorship: "Extended into the realm of literary production, the liberal theory of property produced the notion...of a property founded on the author's labor, one the author could sell to the bookseller" (p. 6). Françoise Meltzer (1994) agrees that for Locke, property entails ownership and that it invades authorship when it makes writing a sort of labor. But she also asserts, without explaining why, that in Locke's account, property and original genius are mutually entailed. She seems to see connections and significances in Locke that she cannot explain. And Rose says outright that he cannot fully ascertain Locke's attitude toward authorship.

I cannot either; but I *can* supply a missing premise in Meltzer's (1994) assertion that for Locke, property and original genius are mutually entailed. Evidence for that interpretation, I believe, lies in Hobbes's (1988) notion of the person as a site of attribution, his distinction between the natural and the feigned person. In Chapter 16 of *Leviathan*, Hobbes says that when one engages in words and actions that *others attribute* to oneself, one is a "natural person." If, however, one engages in words and actions that *others attribute* to someone else, one is a "feigned person." Although we must acknowledge Locke's *Second Treatise* (1960) as a sustained argument with Hobbes, it also builds upon *Leviathan*. Specifically, Locke's notion of literary property's deriving from authorial labor assumes that labor to be authentic, not feigned. An author cannot claim ownership to writing that someone else labored to produce. If labor is a function of the body, then, the author who is entitled to claim literary property cannot but be original, a site of authentic attribution.

Locke's (1960) notions of proprietary authorship readily assume the status of foundational facts rather than cultural arbitraries arising from economic and technological conditions. Economist Jane Humphries (1987) says, "Capitalism, as a mode of material production, is obsessed like no other with the notion of property" (p. 20). I would observe that capitalism as a mode of *literary* production is even more obsessed with the notion of property. Friedrich Engels demonstrates my assertion: In his book, *The Origin of the Family, Private Property and the State* (1884/1986), he denounces material property as the oppressor of the body, the cause of both slavery and the subordination of women. Yet in the introduction to the volume, Engels affirms literary property when he complains of those who would plagiarize the work of Marx. He assures his readers that he is not among those plagiarists.

Engels (1884/1986) recognizes one form of property—literary property—even while he rejects all other forms. Perhaps this is because the Lockean legacy makes literary property a part of natural rights and other forms of property a part of statutory rights. From Locke's (1960) distinction between natural and statutory rights, Engels is apparently willing to leave one precept of natural rights intact: the natural right of literary property.

Autonomy

If it is Hobbes (1988) and Locke (1960) who articulate principles integral to the assertion of authorial proprietorship, then it is René Descartes (1637/1965) who offers an epistemology whereby the property of autonomy is readily attached to the author. *Discourse on Method, Optics, Geometry, and Meteorology* describes thinking as the essence of man, a function of the soul. Our senses sometimes deceive us, but some of our thoughts—placed in us by God—we know to be true. Descartes therefore resolves to study the book of nature, free of the opinions of others and true to the "certain laws which God has so established in nature, and the notion of which he has so fixed in our minds" (p. 31). The thinker and therefore the writer, from the Cartesian point of view, can act autonomously to apprehend and express ideas that are unmediated by social discourse. With his emphasis upon the autonomous thinker—from which the autonomous writer can so readily be extrapolated—it is not surprising that Descartes was concerned with the possibility of plagiarism. He accused Hobbes of wanting to plagiarize from him, and, interestingly, Descartes was himself accused of plagiarizing from Leibnitz (see Merton, 1965).

Just as Locke's *Second Treatise* (1960) critiques Hobbes's *Leviathan* (1988), so his *Essay Concerning Human Understanding* (1979) argues with Descartes (1637/1965). The social aspect of language and knowledge that Descartes rejects is the very thing that Locke acknowledges. Both Locke and Descartes "locate...the production of knowledge within individual minds" (Crowley, 1990, p. 5). However, whereas Descartes believes that this knowledge can be validated through an authentic, unmediated relationship with the natural world, Locke (1979) believes that only simple ideas, such as names for colors, can be validated in their reference to the things of the world.[7] Our abstract ideas, he says, are the result of bundling simple ideas together and then ranking and categorizing them. We believe that they, too, refer to and can be validated in the world external to the thinker; but in fact all we are doing is validating our abstract ideas by finding that they accord with others' abstractions; and this "validation" does not in fact tell us whether our abstract ideas are true. To that extent, therefore, no abstract idea can be verified as true or false (Locke, 1979, II.32.1–9).

It is Descartes's (1637/1965) epistemology, however, that resonates with Romantic thought; it also makes possible the autonomous author who can apprehend Truth without recourse to social discourse. Locke, in contrast, was regarded in 19th-century England as the "evil genius of the eighteenth century" (Aarsleff, 1982, p. 121).

Originality

In addition to proprietorship and autonomy, originality is a third essential property of modern authorship. For all that commentators may strive to make it appear so, it is hardly a straightforward concept. In *The Lady of the Aroostook* (1879), William Dean Howells's character Staniford, who fancies himself a cosmopolitan, tries very hard to adopt a superior stance toward his new acquaintance from the provinces, Lydia (whom he calls "Lurella" Blood). He fails, of course, and eventually marries her. But while he is vainly attempting to resist her charms, he remarks to his friend Dunham, "If she were literary, she would be like those vulgar little persons of genius in the magazine stories" (p. 91). To illuminate the tensions in Staniford's feelings for Lydia, Howells here draws upon the intelligentsia's disdain for mass culture, encapsulated in the "magazine stories." The "vulgar little persons of genius" in those stories are, obviously, the masses' mistaken representations of that which they do not understand. When Staniford declares that Lydia is "merely and stupidly pretty," Dunham avers,

She is not merely and stupidly pretty!... I don't mean that she's like the women we know. She doesn't say witty things, and she hasn't their responsive quickness; but her ideas are her own, no matter how old they are; and what she says she seems to be saying for the first time, and as if it had never been thought out before. (p. 92)

In the character of Dunham, Howells not only demonstrates the dichotomizing of high and low literacy that has been commonplace since the rise of mass literacy, but he also represents the complex of attributes of authorship. He asserts originality, yet acknowledges that it may not actually be original.

As originality gained the ascendancy (signaled by Edward Young's 1759 book, *Conjectures on Original Composition),* the long-standing valorization of imitation declined. The importance of originality increased as a result of "the industrial revolution, the deluge of books, and the increase of population" (McFarland, 1985, p. 6). Marilyn Randall (1991) adds that "the artistic value of originality" arose as "a consequence—or an index— of the social, economic, and political evolution of the notion of the individual and of the conventions and rules governing public and private property" (p. 528). All of the "causes" (or corollaries) of modern authorship—individualism, the printing press, an expanded readership—contribute in turn to the emergence of originary composition as a cultural value. Originary composition is, moreover, entwined with the proprietorship and autonomy that are attributed to the author in the Modern era. Rose (1993) observes that James Thomson's poem *The Seasons* is the subject of "two landmark literary-property cases"—the *Donaldson* v. *Becket* case in 1774 and the *Millar* v. *Taylor* case in 1769. In Thomson's poem, we see literary property defined not just in the Lockean sense, as the product of a writer's labor, but also in the modern sense, as the work of an individual. "The basis of literary property, in other words, was not just labor but 'personality,' and this revealed itself in 'originality'" (Rose, 1993, p. 114).

Somewhat later, in Romantic rhetoric, the word *genius* comes to be associated with authorship, expressing the notion that a writer can not only compose autonomously, but can also be the source, the origin, of ideas and their expression. It is in William Wordsworth's *Essay, Supplementary to the Preface* (1798/1974), that most historians of authorship locate the canonization of this representational figure:[8]

Of genius the only proof is, the act of doing well what is worthy to be done, and what was never done before: Of genius in the fine arts, the only infallible sign is widening the sphere of human sensibility, for the delight, honor, and benefit of human nature. Genius is the introduction of a new element into the intellectual universe: or, if that be not allowed, it is the application of powers to objects on which they had not before been exercised, or the employment of them in such a manner as to produce effects hitherto unknown. (p. 82)

The historical sequence of the emergence of proprietorship and originality as attributes of authorship gives rise to the speculation that the valorization of originality was, from its inception, economically motivated. Money was to be made in print publication; attributing originality to authors justified their proprietary rights.

Wordsworth was working in a tradition that emerged in the 18th century. Joseph Addison was one of the first to argue for originality instead of mimesis; Henry Fielding and Samuel Richardson continued in the same vein (see Rose, 1993). Eighteenth-century European theorists deemphasized the craftsman component of the Renaissance writer, and they "internalized" the source of inspiration. "'Inspiration' came to be explicated in terms of *original genius*, with the consequence that the inspired work was made peculiarly and distinctively the product—and the property—of the writer" (Woodmansee, 1994a, p. 37). Alexander Pope illustrates the tactic. His 1709 book, *Essay on Criticism*, still proposes a craftsman view, but also proposes that the poet who breaks the rules of his craft can accomplish something new. Gradually, the originary writer, inspired from within, displaced the craftsman, and the writer became an author.

In 1759, Edward Young devoted his treatise *Conjectures on Original Composition* to differentiating the genius from the imitator. Genius, which he calls a "fertile and pleasant field," partakes of the Divine and equates with Virtue. Young invokes the now-familiar organic metaphor to scorn those who would imitate other authors:

An *Original* may be said to be of a *vegetable* nature; it rises spontaneously from the vital root of Genius; it *grows*, it is not *made*: *Imitations* are often a sort of *Manufacture* wrought up by those *Mechanics, Art*, and *Labour*, out of pre-existent materials not their own. (original emphasis, pp. 11–12)

Miriam Brody (1993), details how firmly these notions became entrenched in composition studies.[9] Organic writing in composition textbooks "connected the separate dimensions of thought and language" (p. 163). Foerster and Steadman's 1931 composition text advised,

The words required for the expression of the thought or feeling are the words inherent in the thought or feeling itself. They are not cunningly devised by the writer, invented and arranged by him with a view to impressing the reader. He does nothing but find them in the place where they spring to life, i.e., in the mind. (qtd. in Brody, 1993, p. 164)

"Composition," says Sharon Crowley (1984), "becomes an afterthought on the Romantic model, something attended to when inspiration, the real stuff of poetry, declines." And the audience of poetry must be attuned to the poetry "[i]n such a way as to obviate the need for clarity" (p. 22).

Nevertheless, even as the genius who produces original writing became canonical in composition theory, so did what Harold Bloom (1973) has called the "anxiety of influence." If the only true author is "he" who produces original text,[10] then the task of the author is to avoid influence. Edward Young (1759/1966), as he makes his clarion call for originality and refuses to be influenced by the giants of the past, warns:

> But why are *Originals* so few? not because the Writer's harvest is over, the great Reapers of Antiquity having left nothing to be gleaned after them; nor because the human mind's teeming time is past, or because it is incapable of putting forth unprecedented births; but because illustrious Examples *engross, prejudice,* and *intimidate.* They *engross* our attention, and so prevent a due inspection of ourselves; they *prejudice* our Judgment in favour of their abilities, and so lessen the sense of our own; and they *intimidate* us with the splendor of their Renown, and thus under Diffidence bury our strength. (original emphasis, p. 17)

The task is not as simple as that of avoiding influence, for even as the author tries to work in solitude, he or she is dogged by the fear that the task is impossible—that all writing is dependent on others. Françoise Meltzer (1994) explains Descartes's and Freud's anxieties about originality: Writers who want recognition must assert priority; to assert priority is to assert originality; and to assert originality engenders a fear of being robbed. Behind that fear of being robbed is "the larger fear that there is no such thing as originality" (pp. 40–41).

That fear is articulated in William Dean Howells's (1902/1968) speculation that all writers are plagiarists. Similar speculations emerge at least as early as Hellenistic rhetoric, which expresses the fear that all the good ideas had been exhausted in the Classical period. Such fears arise in Quintilian's and Dionysius of Halicarnassus's treatments of imitation, and they lurk in the heart of every undergraduate who is today faced with the task of writing a library research paper. Such fears can be allayed by the suggestion that creativity is independent of originality. M. J. Stevens, an undergraduate student in a course on print culture studies, offers her own definition of what she calls "originality," but what might more aptly be termed "creativity":

> Developing the intellect for personal definition, as well as for employment purposes, requires that a student learn how to be original—originality being here defined as synthesizing or adding on to the body of knowledge in order to produce an improved or advanced product. (1994, n.p.)

Writers in the modern tradition of originary authorship are always in danger of working not on the shoulders but in the shadow of their precursors, and this shadow falls over both style and substance. Walter Pater declared, "Good style is the 'absolute accordance of expression to idea,'" (qtd. in Crowley, 1984, p. 25), which can most easily be accomplished in poetry but which can be approached in other modes of writing as well. Having quoted Pater, Crowley describes the Romantic program:

> Poetry reflects valuable human truth through its being given to especially sensitive writers to transfer their insights to capable readers. Further, the linguistic surface of the poetic work is neatly fitted to the message it carries. The concept of the perfect fit between inspiration and expression fosters a disdain for composition as an art which served only those readers who are unable to share the poetic insight without its assistance. Romantic theory leaves the more mundane work of appealing to audiences, dealing with facts, and addressing the niceties of composition to nonpoetic modes of discourse. (p. 26)

Plagiarism, the derivative rather than original use of language, the surreptitious borrowing of others' words and ideas and representing them as one's own, inevitably accompanies the notion of the originary author, in Ralph Waldo Emerson (1836/1950) as in Young:

> The corruption of man is followed by the corruption of language. When simplicity of character and the sovereignty of ideas is broken up by the prevalence of secondary desires—the desire of riches, of pleasure, of power, and of praise—and duplicity and falsehood take place of simplicity and truth, the power over nature as an interpreter of the will is in a degree lost; now imagery ceases to be created, and old words are perverted to stand for things which are not.... In due time the fraud is manifest, and words lose all power to stimulate the understanding or the affections. (p. 17)

Emerson demonstrates, though, how unstable are representations of originality. Thomas McFarland (1985) points out that although Emerson is recognized as "an unequivocal spokesman for originality and individuality," he also (in his 1841 essay "Self-Reliance") acknowledges "the full claims of tradition," not only in poetry, but also in science and philosophy (pp. 14–15).

Morality

Absent from Emerson's (1836/1950) account—as from most testimonials to modern authorship—is acknowledgment of the role of the reader. That acknowledgment is, however, integral to postmodern treatments of authorship. An author's name, Foucault (1977b) explains, differs from other proper names in that it functions as a means whereby readers classify and establish relationships among texts. The author-function is most of all a rational entity constructed through a complex process that includes our projecting dimensions of our "way of handling texts" upon an individual author-function, as we assign qualities like "profound" or "creative" to it (p. 127).

As these qualities came to be assigned to individual authors, the work of writers such as Ben Jonson and Alexander Pope came to be devalued because they were deemed imitative. William Shakespeare, in contrast, was touted as original, even though he, too, "participated in a mode of cultural production that was essentially collaborative...." (Rose, 1993, p. 122). Shakespeare's transition to author-function was fueled by how little was known about Shakespeare the man. The name even came to be dissociated from the person of William Shakespeare, when, for example, it was suggested that Francis Bacon had actually written what had previously been attributed to Shakespeare. Once an author's name has been attached to works rather than to the author, the meaning of that name changes not when new data about the author becomes available, but when readers' perspectives on the author's works change. Yet the high or low value of the works amounts to a commensurate valuation of the author. By the middle of the 18th century, Shakespeare had come to represent "a human being so extraordinary that all the value radiating from that galactic center was in turn the sign of his personal worth" (Rose, 1993, p. 123). The personal worth that accrues from the attribution of value to one's written texts is expressed in terms of the author's originality, which in turn is typically taken to be a sign of high character. Young (1759/ 1966) makes the equation explicit:

[F]or what, for the most part, mean we by Genius, but the Power of accomplishing great things without the means generally reputed necessary to that end? A *Genius* differs from a *good Understanding*, as a Magician from a good Architect; *That* raises his structure by means invisible; *This* by the skillful use of common tools. Hence Genius has ever been supposed to partake of something Divine. (original emphasis, pp. 26–27)

Immediately after this passage, Young correlates Genius with virtue.

This equation of genius and virtue—the equation of originality and morality—had begun to assume an important place in Western letters by the mid-19th century.[11] The "morality" to which I refer is a specific sort of textual morality that alludes not to the author's philanthropic or egalitarian impulses nor to his refraining from pornography or sedition, but to the morality of creativity, the high character demonstrated in one's ability to be original.

It is in Romantic literary theory that the element of personal virtue moves into the foreground of the emergent formation of authorship. Thoreau (1950) goes to Walden Pond to join the "benefactors of the race" who are "bearers of divine gifts to man" (p. 32). Emerson (1836/1950) explains the means whereby divine gifts are borne; it is through personal virtue derived from an attunement with Nature:

> Nature stretches out her arms to embrace man, only let his thoughts be of equal greatness.... A virtuous man is in unison with her works, and makes the central figure of the visible sphere. (p. 12)

And from personal virtue, Emerson says, comes a facility with language:

> A man's power to connect his thought with its proper symbol, and so to utter it, depends on the simplicity of his character, that is, upon his love of truth and his desire to communicate it without loss. (p. 17)

Words, the right words, arise from the writer's harmonious participation in nature. From those words a reader might make judgments of character about the writer:

> [P]icturesque language is at once a commanding certificate that he who employs it is a man in alliance with truth and God. (p. 17)

It is in these Romantic terms of personal virtue that 20th-century society describes plagiarism. Associating personal virtue with true authorship makes it possible to assert an absence of virtue for authorship's opposite, plagiarism. The ethically based opposition of authorship and plagiarism then supports an intellectual hierarchy that needed new definition in the 19th century. The naturalizing of the properties of authorship has meant the naturalizing of the authorship-plagiarism dichotomy and with it, the intellectual hierarchy it supports.

INTELLECTUAL HIERARCHY

Copyright laws began to be enacted in Ben Jonson's time, but it is only in the 19th century that the idea of originality— fueled by Romanticism— becomes important; and thus it is only in the 19th century that plagiarism begins to be a social concern. The theoretical articulation and subsequent codification of plagiarism as an ethical transgression deals an apparent death blow to the cultural value of mimesis. By the end of the 19th century, people like William Dean Howells are exhorting against the immorality of plagiarism,[12] and in the early 20th century, composition texts are enjoining students against the feminine activity of plagiarism and instead urging them to manly originality.

From 19th-century notions of authorship arise the concern for student plagiarism that has today escalated to what Andrea A. Lunsford and Lisa Ede (1994) call an "obsession" (pp. 436–437). At its inception, this obsession is part of the gendering of composition instruction. As Brody (1993) has established, the Romantic model that dominated early 20th-century composition textbooks imagines true authors as "strong," masculine writers, whereas derivative authors are weak and feminine.[13] Social class, apparent in the intellectual categories of high and low culture, is also involved in the strand of modern authorship that constructs student plagiarism.

Indeed, both the gendering of plagiarism and its intellectual class associations must unavoidably be associated with the reaction of 19th-century intellectuals to the perceived evils of mass education.[14] From 1800 to 1914, the population of Europe increased by 250 percent, and at the same time literacy was on the rise. These concurrent developments caused considerable alarm among the traditionally educated and privileged group. Many intellectuals, including Friedrich Nietzsche, associated the population increase with an increase in lower-class culture. John Carey (1992) points out that in *The Will to Power*, Nietzsche (trans. 1967b) describes the "majority of men" as "a misfortune to higher men" (Carey, 1992, p. 12). "Nietzsche's message in *The Will to Power* is that a 'declaration of war on the masses by higher men is needed'" (p. 4). Many intellectuals depicted the masses as lacking souls and not really being alive.

Not only Nietzsche, but also T. S. Eliot and D. H. Lawrence opposed universal education. Woodmansee (1994a) says that by the 1790s there was a "veritable war on reading" in Germany (p. 89), born of fear that reading might lead the downtrodden to have misplaced ambitions, which might in turn lead to something like the French Revolution, the later stages of which most Germans watched in horror. In England, too, where mass literacy was somewhat earlier in arriving, the intelligentsia were on the one hand grateful for the potential of a larger readership for their publications, but were on the other hand worried about how their writing might be affected by lowbrow tastes. If the reader affected the writing—if in no other way than the writer's shaping the text for the anticipated reader—and if the reader were a lowbrow, then the principles of art and culture dear to the intelligentsia were at risk. Nor did a larger literate public necessarily translate into a larger readership for the texts of the intelligentsia. Instead, it translated into a new breed of texts, written for the functionally, instrumentally literate. These texts took the form of magazines, cheap novels, and newspapers. In the United States, writers like Emerson, Hawthorne, Thoreau, and Melville found themselves with a relatively small readership, whereas the "scribbling women" of the 1850s, whom Hawthorne deplored, were enjoying brisk sales of the novels they were writing for mass consumption (see Gilbert & Gubar, 1986; Gilmore, 1985; Smith, 1974; Ticknor, 1913).

Two cultural phenomena of deceptively disparate appearance bracket and gloss the mid-century indignation expressed by the American Romantics. The insurgent 19th-century cultural importance of the notion of plagiarism, moreover, must be understood in the context of these phenomena. The first of the two phenomena is the 1830s emergence in England of the expression "the Great Unwashed." In the Stallybrass and White (1986) etymology, the phrase expresses the fear of contamination that ran rife in English society. "'Contagion' and 'contamination' became the tropes through which city life was apprehended" (p. 135). The second cultural phenomenon is the development of the concept of the literary canon, in place by the end of the 19th century (Miller, 1991). The two may seem unrelated unless we consider Stallybrass and White's contention that the fear of contamination extended beyond hygiene to a fear of the "spiritually inferior" (p. 136). It is not any coincidence that by 1926, Robinson Shipherd would compare plagiarism "to a sexually transmitted disease, calling it the 'moral problem of our subject,' our 'bete noir of sex hygielle'" (qtd. in Brody, 1993, p. 174). The originary literary canon hypostatized the spiritually pure; plagiarism identified the spiritually contaminated.

A binary literacy arose—one literacy for the masses (among whom women were numbered), the other for the intellectuals. The intellectuals were threatened by a primary medium for mass literacy—newspapers—because the newspapers escaped the intelligentsia's control. Pictorial journalism came in for particularly virulent criticism because, it was alleged, it toadied to feminine tastes. "Women habitually think in pictures, [Holbrook Jackson] explains, whereas men naturally aspire to abstract concepts. 'When men think pictorially they unsex themselves'" (Carey, 1992, p. 8). English culture in the 19th century divided along a fault line, with the penny-newspaper-reading masses on one side, and the intellectuals whose standards, opinions, and writing were increasingly devalued on the other.

The tendencies that Carey (1992) describes in English culture are mirrored in the United States. As preface to his diatribe against the mind-deadening "Little Reading" offered in his Circulating Library, Thoreau (1950) declares,

> The works of the great poets have never yet been read by mankind, for only great poets can read them.... Most men have learned to read to serve a paltry convenience, as they have learned to cipher in order to keep accounts and not be cheated in trade; but of reading as a noble intellectual exercise they know little or nothing; yet this only is reading, in a high sense, not that which lulls us as a luxury and suffers the nobler faculties to sleep the while, but what we have to stand on tip-toe to read and devote our most alert and wakeful hours to. (p. 94)

Even in the 20th century, Theodor W. Adorno and his colleagues at the Frankfurt Institute for Social Research "shared the view that mass culture and the mass media, as developed under capitalism, had degraded civilization in the twentieth century. They blamed radio, cinema, newspapers and cheap books for 'the disappearance of the inner life'...." (Carey, 1992, p. 43).

The denigration of "low" literature has become a rhetorical commonplace in "high" literature today: it is a commonly-held belief that needs no arguing and upon which enthymematic arguments can be based.

The 19th-century intellectuals' solution to the problems of widespread literacy was to demonstrate that, despite the shared experience of literacy, we are not all equal—a task that participated in the liberal-culture rhetoric described by David R. Russell (1988) and James A. Berlin (1996). The intelligentsia's making their writing inaccessible to the masses was one means of accomplishing this demonstration. Samuel Taylor Coleridge, for example, begins *On the Principles of Genial Criticism* by saying that he is going to explain to the burghers how to understand the aesthetic experience; but his argument quickly becomes far too convoluted and dependent upon the readers' previous knowledge of esoteric philosophy. Finally, then, he refuses to engage the people whom he declares are the audience of the treatise (see Woodmansee, 1994a).

Carey (1992) turns to Herbert Marcuse for another demonstration of the tendency. Marcuse, he says, "preaches the confessedly 'élitist' doctrine that genuine art must be inaccessible to the masses. Only the individual can appreciate 'high' culture—and mass civilization threatens to obliterate the individual" (p. 43). This "solution" is apparent not only in Marcuse but everywhere. The common representation was of a binary contest between fact and art. The masses, it was believed, were so consumed with getting correct facts that they could not appreciate art. Photography was one of the arenas in which this binary was enacted. In the early days of photography, the camera was regarded as an extension of the masses' need for facts, and it was therefore reviled by Baudelaire and Lady Eastlake (Carey, 1992, p. 31).

American evidence for Carey's argument abounds. Alfred Stieglitz (1899), for example, was one of the first persuasive voices in defense of photography; but he defends it not by challenging the binary of fact versus art but by drawing upon it. Stieglitz divides photographers into what he calls three classes: "the ignorant, the purely technical, and the artistic" (p. 528). He derides the first two classes, "the brand of mechanism, the crude stiffness and vulgarity of chromos, and other like productions." He exalts the third class, which can include both the professional and the amateur, as long as they use their materials "as tools for the elaboration of their ideas, and not as tyrants to enslave and dwarf them...." (p. 529). Stieglitz's artistic photographer stands in no one's shadow. The intelligentsia—the artistic—are giants, whereas the masses, with their craving for fact and their ignorant or merely mechanical photography, are pygmies dwelling in the shadows, incapable even of climbing upon the giants' shoulders.

In terms of writing, the intellectuals' negative opposite is the plagiarist, the writer who is dependent and derivative rather than autonomous and original. The dichotomy has only gained strength in the 20th century. According to Lester Faigley (1992), a 1931 report issued by a CEEB commission declared, "true originality will be the result of discriminating and vigorous perception and thought." Clearly, says Faigley, this group was dedicated to the "preservation of an asymmetry of literary taste" (pp. 118–119). Equally obvious, the commission's preservation of that asymmetry depended upon the valorization of originality.

In that asymmetry, students become the representatives of the masses, their teachers the representatives of the intelligentsia. Plagiarism fits too neatly into the liberal-culture program of differentiating high and low literacy. Students are imagined as having lowbrow reading tastes that must be elevated: They must be weaned from purely instrumentalist reading, from trashy novels, and most importantly, from visual media. They must be educated to an appreciation—or at least an awe—of the classics. They must be guided from *Beavis and Butthead* to *War and Peace*.

As writers they are imagined as error-makers ("They can't even write a decent sentence!") and as low characters who would cheerfully "steal" the work of others—whether from Cliffs Notes, purchased term papers, or their roommates—unless the wily professor can prevent them. They are taught, in the contrast between their composition class and their literature class, that they are the inadequate—the Great Unwashed—whereas Milton and Woolf are perfected and are thus included in the literary canon. By such means are students placed not on the shoulders but in the shadow of giants.

NOTES

[1]The phrase is Martha Woodmansee's, and in several of her texts (1984, 1994a, 1994b) she uses it in reference to the emergence of the originary, autonomous modern author.

[2]Mark Rose (1993), for example, traces the representation of authorship through three, rather than four, properties: He names originality, proprietorship, and a third category that he calls "personality" (p. 7). While agreeing with him that originality and proprietorship are two of the key properties that our culture attributes to "true" authorship, I would divide his third category, personality, into two separate categories, which I am calling autonomy and morality.

[3]Rose's book, *Authors and Owners* (1993), a fresh, concise overview of the development of literary property, is my primary source for the history of copyright, and my account is substantially indebted to his.

[4]In his book, *The Order of Things* (1973), Foucault describes this transition as a "deep cultural rupture." In the Classical Age, grammar, natural history, and wealth were "double representations—representations whose role is to designate representations, to analyse them, to compose and decompose them in order to bring into being within them, together with the system of their identities and differences, the general principle of an order." After the rupture, "words, classes, and wealth will acquire a mode of being no longer compatible with that of representation" (p. 221).

[5]The syllogism is John Locke's (1960).

[6]The analogy, says Rose (1993), doesn't work because of the "radical instability of the concept of the autonomous author" (p. 8).

[7]Mine is not a universally accepted interpretation. Crowley (1990), for example, cites Locke's *Essay Concerning Human Understanding* (1979) to assert that for Locke, thought refers directly to "things of the world" (Crowley, 1990, p. 9). In Book II, though, Locke specifically states that ideas are labeled with words so that they can be stored in memory; thus words link ideas to things of the world. We are mistaken, Locke says, when we think that ideas relate directly to things; they are mediated by words.

[8]Among these historians of authorship, Martha Woodmansee has made a particularly lucid case for the role of organic theory in the formation of modern authorship. See not only "On the Author Effect: Recovering Collectivity" (1994b), but also Chapter 2 of her 1994 book, *The Author, Art, and the Market*.

[9]The received date for the "beginning" of composition studies as a discipline is 1963, but Sharon Crowley (1990) persuasively argues that composition studies began with composition teaching. Until the second half of the 20th century, most of it proceeded on the basis of composition textbooks—so that composition teachers knew no more than that which they were teaching to their students. Given Crowley's case for the centrality of textbooks not only to pedagogy but to composition studies, Brody's (1993) observations about organic theory in composition textbooks amount to assertions about organic theory in composition theory.

[10]Again, it makes greatest sense to use the masculine form, not as a generic pronoun but as a gender-specific one: discussions of influence—most especially Bloom's 1973 discussion—postulate only a male writer.

[11] It was not a 19th-century innovation. Sidney and his contemporaries, for instance, asserted a presence in texts, a presence that was the writer's power, "which retrieves the ancient spoken presence of individual prophecy, divination, and powerfully composed oratory" (Faigley, 1992, p. 95).

[12] Novelist, essayist, critic, and editor first of the *Atlantic Monthly* and then *Harper's Monthly*, Howells was perhaps the most influential voice in *fin-de-siècle* American letters.

[13] Sharon Crowley's 1990 account of composition and rhetoric separates Romanticism from current-traditionalism, which she credits with the theories of invention that came to dominate composition instruction in the early 20th century. The two cannot, however, be fully separated; and in terms of the representations of authorship that have informed composition instruction throughout the 20th century, Romantic rhetoric provides substantial theoretical premises.

[14] Martha Woodmansee and John Carey offer provocative accounts of the results of mass literacy. In *The Author, Art, and the Market* (1994a), Woodmansee explains how mass literacy changed writing and the construction of authorship, and in his book, *The Intellectuals and the Masses* (1992), Carey argues that the notion of high culture was born of the intelligentsia's reaction to mass literacy. Peter Stallybrass and Allon White identify Pope's *Dunciad* as well as other 18th-century texts with defending authorship from being contaminated by an association with low culture. Their book, *The Politics and Poetics of Transgression* (1986), persuasively argues for the 18th-century emergence of the high/low culture dichotomy, whereas Carey's is a powerful interpretation of the tendencies of 19th-century intellectual culture.

6

Modern Plagiarists

I think that we are all influenced, in more than one instance here and there, by the thoughts, words, and creations of others. If we sat around and continually attempted to be original, we might go mental. As we do anything in life, we are influenced and guided by previous knowledge, etc. I do not believe that this is necessarily "plagiarism" by my definition.

Paul Verbitsky (1994)

The widespread literacy and distribution of texts that heralded the Modern era effected a revolution in Western letters. One outcome of that revolution is a new binary of authorship, inherently hierarchical. At the privileged pole of this hierarchy is the true author, who can be recognized by his or her autonomy and originality. Composing alone, independent of influence, this author produces original ideas or expressions that have not previously been thought of or used. The properties of autonomy and originality earn great respect for the author, who is thereby accorded proprietorship of the words and ideas he or she has produced and who is also taken to be of high moral character.

At the other pole of this new binary is the plagiarist.

Curiously, the poles of this binary are not coeval. One pole, that of the autonomous, originary author, has identifiable origins in ancient commentators' respect for originality and for the individual author. Indeed, as the rhetoric of Quintilian demonstrates, this originary author was the privileged member of a binary. In the ancient world, however, it was not the plagiarist but the mimetic writer who occupied the opposite pole. Nor was this mimetic pole a negative opposite, as the plagiarist is today; the activity of mimesis was considered not only legitimate, but necessary. Originary and mimetic writers were both respected.

The new, hierarchical plagiarist/author binary is a radical revision of the relatively neutral mimesis/originality binary whose traces mark the entire history of Western letters. The great majority of us subscribe to this new binary as an unexamined precept, on the assumption that it expresses a fundamental truth about the nature of writing. In contemporary Western culture, the plagiarist/author binary is regarded as an ahistorical fact, not as a military occupation and simplification of a complex, interactive textual culture that informed a long, rich history of Western letters.

The figure of the modern author, together with the copyright laws reifying that figure, assumed importance three centuries ago and have been energetically developed ever since. The figure of the plagiarist and the institutional and pedagogical policies outlawing his or her activities are innovations of the 19th and 20th centuries.

The 20th-century plagiarist potentially engages in any one of a disparate set of textual activities. He or she may (1) purchase, download, or copy a term paper; (2) copy text without supplying quotation marks; copy text without identifying the source; use ideas from a source without acknowledging the indebtedness; or (3) talk about a source while using language clearly derived from it. Nor is the collection of these varied activities under the unitary label *plagiarism* an accident. Including #2 (failure to cite) and especially #3 (patchwriting) in the same company with #1 (ghostwriting) substantially serves liberal cultural ideals.[1] It accomplishes the cultural work of separating the geniuses—those for whom stylish, seemingly originary writing is an untaught gift—from the plodders, the mere copyists whose textual appropriations are so painfully obvious that the attribution of originality is impossible.

The truth, though, is that we are all plodders, in the sense that we all collaborate with source texts, not just conceptually, but also linguistically. Hiding the traces of linguistic writer/text collaboration is an esoteric skill that only those immersed in textual studies are likely to develop.

When the inability or failure to hide those traces is conflated with the willingness to fraudulently represent someone else's text as one's own, a lack of advanced textual skills becomes a crime. By such means are now-traditional sociointellectual hierarchies preserved. At one time, being literate was a mark of membership in the intellectual elite. Now the great majority of the populace is literate. How, then, do intellectuals mark their superiority? By making nonmembership (signaled by the absence of a difficult textual skill) a crime, and by persuading everyone—members and nonmembers alike—that the definition of this crime is not arbitrary, but that it proceeds from natural, necessary textual values expressed in the binaries of collaboration/autonomy, mimesis/originality, and, especially, plagiarism/authorship.

THE MODERN DEVELOPMENT OF PLAGIARISM

Until the mid-19th century, writers and critics participated in the formulation of copyright law. But from the time of William Wordsworth, literary theory began instead to elaborate a separate ethical discourse of authorship, one that focused on plagiarism as the criminalized opposite of originality (and thus of authorship).

Although legal and textual studies parted company in their deliberations on authorship more than a century ago, each has continued to appropriate metaphors from the other. This mutual appropriation obscures the differences between the two. While copyright legislation and regulations against student plagiarism are both functions of the modern textual economy, they are not parallel discourses. Copyright legislation strives to protect the rights of the individual author, whereas regulations against student plagiarism strive to protect the community of letters. Copyright is governed by the state, plagiarism by society. Copyright, in other words, is a legal formation, whereas plagiarism is a matter of local norms, notwithstanding those norms' codification in universities' and professional organizations' regulations against plagiarism, a codification that gives them the appearance of law.[2]

Peter Jaszi and Martha Woodmansee (1994) warn against conflating copyright and plagiarism:

> The stakes are high in disciplinary actions against students accused of intramural offenses against authorship. Indeed, our institutions underline the seriousness of these proceedings by giving them the form, as well as some of the content, of legal actions for violations of copyright law. (p. 9)

Notions of authorship, they observe, are changing radically in literary theory, whereas the law is always slow to change.

This is especially problematic in the case of students, who are still punished for violating codified norms that no longer reflect prevailing textual theories in the academy. If we mistakenly equate plagiarism with copyright, we will mistakenly assume that plagiarism regulations cannot be changed unless copyright changes first. One way, in fact, that injunctions against plagiarism gain their power is by an apparent identity with copyright. But even though they are born of the same parent, plagiarism and copyright have for the past century functioned as separate discourses. The discourse of plagiarism operates primarily within academic discourse, supporting the principles of the academy. As those principles change, so can the discourse of plagiarism—provided that we recognize it as a cultural arbitrary that is subject to change, and provided that we don't confuse it with copyright.

Prior to his/her installation as the binary opposite of the originary author, the plagiarist was a familiar, derided figure in Western letters. The plagiarist receives the vitriol of the ancient Roman writer Martial:

> Plagiarism, as an epithet for the theft of another writer's language or ideas, was invented by the Roman poet Martial. Excoriating Fidentinus for "recit[ing] my works to the crowd, just as if they were your own," Martial compared him to the worst thing he could think of—a slave stealer, a *plagiario*. (McCormick, 1989, p. 133)

From time to time, complaints about plagiarism pop up in the works of other ancient and medieval writers. But when the individual, proprietary author gains importance in the 17th and 18th centuries, the textual equation begins to shift. The valorization of mimesis and the emphasis on the accumulation of knowledge retreat to the background, and the autonomous author takes center stage. His nemesis, the plagiarist, begins to take shape. Constable (1983) observes, "It is no accident that the term plagiarism first appeared in English in the seventeenth century, since it depends upon the distinctively modern concept of creativity and originality as the personal property of individuals" (p. 26).

It is Ben Jonson, in fact, who first used the word *plagiary* in English. George E. Rowe (1988) quotes Jonson's description of imitation—which obviously glosses the "standing on the shoulders" aphorism: "It is true they [the ancients] open'd the gates, and made the way, that went before us; but as Guides, not Commanders." Rowe says that Jonson had ambivalent feelings about imitation, rejecting the imitation of contemporaries (pp. 16–17); yet Susan Miller (1989) asserts that Jonson and his contemporaries "stole from each other with great goodwill" (p. 87). Jonson derides the likes of Montaigne for the abuse of slavishly copying the latest thing one has read, and he clearly subscribes to the notion of originality. However, following Quintilian, he also believes in imitation. "The grown man is *confirmed*, made more himself, by the tincture of otherness," says Jonson (qtd. in Greene, 1995, p. 275). The tension between imitation and origination constitutes what Thomas Greene calls a "dialectic of selfhood through his work." But in that dialectic, imitation takes the negative role: "Imitation raises a man above himself, leads him to self-forgetfulness and prevents his return to his basic selfhood, discolors his native purity by an osmosis of otherness" (pp. 276–277).

In the work of Ben Jonson, mimesis begins to be conflated with plagiarism. Jonson still ascribes positive value to imitation, but his attitude is ambivalent. To establish the author as independent and as the equal of the ruler who may yet be his patron requires a fresh way of looking at the business of writing. That fresh way, evident at its inception in the career of Jonson and fully articulated in the following century by Edward Young (1759/1966), is the authorial property of originality. That value can most readily be expressed in contrast to some sort of opposite. Initially, the binary opposite of originality was imitation. However, establishing a negative value for imitation required negating a long, honorable tradition. Thus plagiarism, a negative though minor construct long established in the discourse of Western letters, replaced mimesis in the binary.

Meanwhile, originality gained importance by becoming a defining characteristic of authorship. Replacing the old, neutral binary of mimesis/originality, the new plagiarism/authorship binary functioned in hierarchical terms that readily supported the economy of print culture and self-supporting authors. It was only a matter of time before the negative intersection of imitation/plagiarism would be simplified to a unitary construct and rejected altogether.

The fact that the figure of the plagiarist gained importance in the West at the same time that literacy was passing from manuscript to print culture and at the same time that copyright laws were being formulated does not mean that it was regarded in the same way that it is today. Heterogeneity characterizes early modern textual theory, and the ideas of a single commentator—for example, Ben Jonson—are characterized as much by dissonance as unity. In the early Modern period, imitation was still a means of establishing one's authority, as it had been in the Middle Ages. *Bartlett's* attributes the familiar epigram, "Imitation is the sincerest flattery," to Charles Caleb Colton's *Lacon* (1820–1822). In that epigram, we can detect an enduring valorization of imitation, even into the 19th century, but it is a transformed valorization, one that evokes one individual writer flattering another—not a communitarian tradition of giants and pygmies. The flattery of this imitation does not involve an accumulating cultural tradition, but only a lateral copying. Just as manuscript and print culture competed for a brief period in the Renaissance, so plagiarism and mimesis competed for the status of the true, natural, obvious interpretation of the circumstance in which a writer collaborates with a printed source. That competition lasted considerably longer than the one between manuscript and print culture, and it has never been resolved as conclusively. It did, however, reach apparent closure in Romantic rhetoric, a closure that is now ruptured by the technological and ideological circumstances of postmodern culture.

PROPERTIES OF PLAGIARISM

As a result of that closure, plagiarism now occupies the bottom of the authorial hierarchy. The plagiarist is the thief who is not original, but derivative; who works not in solitude, but in the company of others' texts; and who pirates from these texts and represents the piracy as his or her own. For the representation of plagiarism, the most important property of authorship is that of morality. The property of morality is itself dependent upon the belief that originality, proprietorship, and autonomy are "natural truths" about "real" authorship, rather than cultural arbitraries. Therefore, the discourse of plagiarism often invokes these assumptions.

The image of the autonomous author is very powerful in composition studies. Lester Faigley (1992), though warning against imagining "dichotomous categories" of modernism and postmodernism in composition studies, ventures to say,

> Where composition studies has proven least receptive to postmodern theory is in surrendering its belief in the writer as an autonomous self, even at a time when extensive group collaboration is practiced in many writing classrooms. Since the beginning of composition teaching in the late nineteenth century, college writing teachers have been heavily invested in the stability of the self and the attendant beliefs that writing can be a means of self-discovery and intellectual self-realization. (p. 15)

For students, the most powerful property of modern authorship may be the property of originality. The aphorism built upon the key phrase "standing on the shoulders of giants" articulates the belief, dominant in the medieval and early modern West, that the source (the giant) is greater than the writer (the pygmy) who uses it, even though the pygmy writer may add to the knowledge transmitted by the giant source. Overwhelmed by data that washes over them in ever-increasing waves—now reaching them through the burgeoning Internet—today's students hold quite a different view of authorship. Many will readily endorse the idea that originality is the hallmark of a "true" writer *and* that the original ideas are all used up. They therefore believe that nothing is left to them but imitation—a belief only bolstered by writers like Ezra Pound (1935), with his list of the authors "who actually invented something" (pp. 27–28). Today's students' imitation is not the glorious affirmation of the medieval and early modern writers, but the sorry repetition of the disempowered modern writer. They stand not on the shoulders of giants, but in the shadow of them. Many of these student writers are haunted by college regulations against plagiarism that they suspect they regularly break, since they "know" that nothing they write is or can be original and that they do not acknowledge every single source.

THE HEROIC PLAGIARIST

Paradoxically, the authorial hierarchy is not ordered solely according to the originality of writers, for some writers at the very top of the textual hierarchy appropriate text yet seem immune to the charge of plagiarism. Kathleen Hall Jamieson (1988) documents case after case of political ghostwriting. She offers very good reasons for ghostwriting's having become the norm in late-20th-century American politics: Jimmy Carter, for example, was called upon to deliver approximately one speech per day as President. He could hardly have time to write all those speeches himself (pp. 212–213). While Jamieson herself expresses grave reservations about the liabilities of ghostwriting for American politics,[3] she also describes ghostwriting—in the political arena, an acceptable practice—as the norm in American politics today.

In the literary arena, Marilyn Randall (1991) describes situations in which plagiarists are forgiven: a renowned author who plagiarizes is less likely to be accused than is an unknown. Moreover, a chosen few are regarded as having established such a high level of character or as being of such great value to society that even if they are found to have plagiarized, their reputations can carry them through. Dennis Baron (1994) names three: "I do not propose that we need to rethink the greatness of King or Jefferson or even Coleridge—theirs is a Teflon greatness that mere plagiarism cannot tarnish" (p. 87).

Not only can this chosen few, the Teflon plagiarists, avert or survive public exposure, but the plagiarism of others is actually appreciated. These are the "great wits," the "good poets." Baron adduces a quotation from an 1863 issue of *Blackwood's Magazine*: "Little wits that plagiarise are but pickpockets; great wits that plagiarise are conquerors" (p. 87). T. S. Eliot (1932) established his place in this same critical tradition when he declared, "Immature poets imitate; mature poets steal; bad poets deface what they take, and good poets make it into something better, or at least something different" (p. 153). Given the extent to which plagiarism is generally regarded as a threat to high culture, it might seem ironic that Eliot celebrates the heroic plagiarist even as he believes that he, as an intellectual, is responsible for transmitting timeless values. Great-wit plagiarism, then, is presumably one of those values.

In addition to political necessity, Teflon greatness, and great wits as apologias, postmodern critics appreciate plagiarism that constructively challenges the supposed naturalness of the authorial properties of autonomy, proprietorship, originality, and morality. Nowhere is the case made more explicitly than by Ellen McCracken (1991), who suggests that the complex webs of signification constructed and celebrated in postmodern discourse challenge and offer alternatives to literary capitalism, in which words are the property of authors. She details an illustrative case: Ricardo Piglia writes a short story, "Luba," which is plagiarized from a short story written by Leonid Andreev. Piglia prefaces "Luba" with "a parodic scholarly essay," which he entitles "Homenaje a Roberto Arlt." In the essay, he declares Roberto Arlt to be the original author of the short story. Nowhere in the story or the essay does he mention Leonid Andreev, but he does leave textual clues that would lead what McCracken alternately calls the "vanguard reader" or the "postmodernist reader" to discover Andreev as the real source of Piglia's appropriation. Piglia is not the first to invite detective work from the vanguard reader.

Randall (1991) notes that Georges Maurevert's 1922 book, *Le Livre des Plagiats*, attempting to rehabilitate plagiarism as a literary practice, describes delighted readers' successive uncoverings of Anatole France's plagiarism. "Maurevert's study reveals that the shift from open imitation to original composition entails a redefinition of the critic's role from recognition to revelation" (p. 529).

In constructing their intricate webs of intertextuality, Piglia and Maurevert join Michel Foucault (1977b) in declaring the primacy of discourse over concerns about proprietary authorship. Piglia's case is made even more subtle and complex by his choice of Roberto Arlt as the supposed original author of the plagiarized short story. Since Arlt himself questions the ownership of words and ideas, by claiming to plagiarize from him Piglia offers his own double-layered challenge to print capitalism and offers ironic tribute to Arlt's beliefs.

That Piglia has plagiarized is not the point. *How* and *why* Piglia has plagiarized—the purposes to which he puts plagiarism—is. McCracken (1991) speaks for many other literary theorists in suggesting that formal textual features are insufficient for determining questions of authorship. Plagiarism lies not in the text, but in the author's intentions—and the readers' reception. The only readers who can appreciate the purposes to which Piglia has plagiarized are postmodern readers who must "on one important level engage in a patient, close decoding" of the text and who must then "extrapolate from [the text] to come to grips with the larger philosophical currents that underlie Piglia's use of parody and metaplagiarism" (pp. 1073, 1080).

Marilyn Randall (1991) observes that for both author and reader, post-modern plagiarism can also serve in the cause of decolonization, "in which the struggle for a national identity against a dominant and oppressive force is often expressed in cultural production" (p. 525). Plagiarism, she says, can have political motivations:

> The theoretical construction of the colonized subject may be seen to justify "plagiarism" as an appropriate revolutionary move in the process of the creation of a new identity, while censure or recuperation can be seen as strategies of self-protection exerted to assure the hegemony of the institution. (p. 532)

Plagiarism accomplishes this revolutionary move by prompting an attention to difference that the ideal of originality would erase. Randall cites two examples of a "poetics of plagiarism." One is Hubert Aquin's 1968 book, *Trou de Mémoire*, published in English as *Blackout*, which made plagiarism an overt subject by having characters discuss it and by having a whole apparatus of fictive attribution. It also made plagiarism a covert subject by its unattributed indebtedness to other sources. Randall's second example is Yambo Ouologuem's book, *Le Devoir de Violence*, published in Paris in 1968 and hailed as an authentic African novel. It was later revealed to be plagiarized from multiple sources—many of them not even African. Ironically, in the novel Ouologuem recommends that African writers stick to mystery novels, which can be formulaically assembled, since that is the highest literary form to which they will be allowed to aspire; meanwhile, Ouologuem writes his literary novel by those very means.

A number of other critics and artists would endorse the efforts of McCracken and Randall to move plagiarism outside the confines of orig-inary authorship. Stanley Corngold and Irene Giersing (1991) wrote a novel in whose protagonist the polarities of originality and plagiarism collapse; Linda Hutcheon (1986) asserts that intertextuality rescues the postmodern reader from the Romantic author-centered tyranny transmitted through modernism, as evidenced in D. M. Thomas's *The White Hotel*; and Alasdair Gray's 1981 novel, *Lanark*, pokes fun at plagiarism, particularly the structuralist taxonomies of plagiarism.

Like the great-wit and Teflon-greatness theories, postmodern theory establishes circumstances in which plagiarism is not condemned. However, postmodern criticism differs from the great-wit and Teflon-greatness theories in that it does not endorse the economy of authorship while noting exceptions. Rather, it seeks to dismantle that economy.[4] Postmodern plagiarism is an act of resistance.

In four scenarios, then, plagiarism is considered acceptable: political, Teflon, great-wit, or postmodern plagiarism. In political plagiarism, society acknowledges the impossibility of candidates' composing their own texts. In Teflon plagiarism, society tolerates plagiarism when the author's corpus is highly valued. In great-wit plagiarism, criticism celebrates the "transgression" when the author makes something new and better of the appropriated materials, thereby demonstrating a type of originary genius. In postmodern plagiarism, criticism celebrates the nontransgression, the "appropriation,"[5] when the author *intended* to plagiarize in order to critique the notion of originary genius. The first scenario assumes that plagiarism is regrettable but necessary in the complex, demanding world of contemporary American politics. The second assumes that plagiarism is always a bad thing, but that in certain situations it can be forgiven. The third assumes that plagiarism is usually a bad thing, but that there are exceptional cases in which it may be a good thing. The fourth, because it assumes that the whole idea of plagiarism derives from a misunderstanding of the nature of authorship, attaches no value judgment to plagiarism, except when it reveals the arbitrariness of modern notions of authorship—in which case it is a good thing.

None of these four scenarios, however, addresses students' plagiarism; in all four, the author in question is a professional writer, not a student. According to contemporary commentators, students can be forgiven for plagiarizing under certain circumstances, but not for the positive reasons of their political,[6] Teflon, great-wit, or postmodern plagiarism. Their plagiarism can be forgiven—or their punishment lessened—for a separate, fifth reason: their ignorance of academic citation conventions. This fifth scenario, which attributes a negative characteristic—ignorance—to the plagiarist, is usually applied successfully only to student writers.

In composition studies, most published discussions of student plagiarism proceed from the assumption that plagiarism occurs as a result of an absence of ethics or an ignorance of citation conventions. Some students don't appreciate academic textual values and therefore deliberately submit work that is not their own; others don't understand academic citation conventions and therefore plagiarize inadvertently. Both of these are negative interpretations, postulating an absence—of either ethics or knowledge—in the plagiarist. Christopher S. Hawley (1984) states it succinctly:

> Plagiarism is not carried on exclusively by evil students whose sole intent is to defraud the unsuspecting professor. Much unacceptable documentation, in fact, may come more from simple ignorance than deceit. (p. 38)

Similarly, Edith Skom (1986) gives a fine example of patchwriting and attributes it to the writer's lack of knowledge about "the mechanics of quoting and footnoting" (p. 4). Then she describes another patchwriting student who clearly did intend to plagiarize, who concealed and even denied the source from which she patchwrote huge portions of her paper. These are the only interpretations allowed in traditional representations of students' patchwriting.

Only in very recent commentary emerging from composition studies does a positive apologia that might apply to student plagiarists appear. Students sometimes engage in patchwriting, a textual practice classified as plagiarism, as a means of learning unfamiliar discourse and engaging difficult texts. Recognition of this sixth apologia, which we might call entry-strategy plagiarism, remains very much a minority discourse in composition studies. What prevails is the notion that students plagiarize either because they are of low character or because they are ignorant of citation conventions. The citation conventions thereby serve not merely as a textual convenience, but as the repository of textual ethics. To teach citation is to teach ethics.

Attributing either immorality or ignorance to a student plagiarist postulates plagiarism as a moral offense. Laws regarding plagiarism and copyright are believed to legislate not just property, but also morality; those who violate the "laws" of print capitalism allegedly reveal weak character and indifference to the future of a civilization threatened by a decay in values.

PLAGIARISM AS CHOICE BEHAVIOR

Buttressing this interpretation is a still-influential Romantic axiology in which writing is an expression of immanent experience with truth; in which the writer has to isolate himself from others and keep his ideas differentiated from theirs; and in which his original, felicitous expression *reveals* the high character that enabled his originary vision. To speak of ethics in the context of plagiarism—even if one asserts ethical relativism or students' capacity for ethical behavior—is to reproduce the Romantic axiology that obscures plagiarism as a cultural arbitrary and that makes it difficult to imagine students' plagiarism as anything but an absence of ethics or an ignorance of them. The situation is only compounded by the authority of quantitative inquiry into plagiarism, which investigates not only the incidence of plagiarism (e.g., Allen, 1994; Dant, 1986; Fass, 1986; Hawley, 1984; Schab, 1980) but also students' attitudes toward it (e.g., Fass, 1986; Kroll, 1988). Most of these studies agree that students are concerned about plagiarism, but still feel compelled to do it. Statistics are thus marshaled, however unintentionally, for the juridical episteme that asserts plagiarism as an ethical issue and that reveals students' unethical choices.

Not everyone, of course, adheres to an ethical paradigm for interpreting plagiarism. In a letter to the *Council Chronicle*, Robert G. Wood (1994) asserts that it is not ethics but the ownership of words and ideas that is at issue in plagiarism; hence he advocates our speaking of plagiarism not in terms of ethics but in terms of commerce. Nor does everyone who applies an ethical paradigm to student plagiarism posit a binary framework for the discussion. Both Gerry H. Brooks (1989) and Keith Miller (1993) believe that ethics is the fundamental issue in plagiarism, yet Miller argues in favor of ethical relativism. Brooks declares the problem of student plagiarism more complicated than is usually recognized. The problem, he says, is that student plagiarists operate on an inappropriate set of moral principles. Students' difficulties in learning to acknowledge sources, Brooks says, may stem from values learned in their home communities (which, he notes, include college fraternities). Papers submitted from fraternity files operate on the moral principle of the good of the fraternity: by keeping up one's grade point average, one advances the stature of the fraternity. Brooks concludes that when students plagiarize by submitting their friends' papers, their conduct "is ethical, bound by sets of rules that they can elaborate and test, which implies that they are perfectly capable of learning the practices of attribution in a scholarly community" (p. 35).

Most discussions of student plagiarism—even with caveats such as those of Miller and Brooks—do postulate an ethical basis to plagiarism. The supposed immorality of the plagiarist serves as an important unifying factor in the representation of plagiarism as a stable category. In this community episteme, plagiarism is believed to derive from what anthropologist G. N. Appell (1988) would call "choice behavior": "Choice is constrained but not fully determined by the system of morality in which the choice is made..." (p. 34).

In such a framework, plagiarism, in all its types, is an ethical—or, more accurately, an unethical choice that a writer consciously makes. Appell (1988) describes the signifying practices that support notions of choice behavior: "[T]he greater the freedom to choose, the greater the scope for good or bad choices and the greater the need for ethics, rules, and laws for defining prohibited alternatives...." (p. 34).

Such moral criteria for plagiarism seem natural and necessary, drawing as they do upon widely held assumptions. The lexicon of choice behavior invokes not only ethics and morality but also property and the law. This juridical lexicon is widely available and very familiar. James Atlas (1991), former editor of the *New York Times Magazine*, writing about novelist John

Gardner and politician Joseph R. Biden, Jr., wields the language of property ("stealing," "shoplifting," "pilfering") and attributes flagging "moral character" to those who succumb to the temptation to plagiarize (p. 2). Chris Raymond's (1990, 1991) reports on Martin Luther King, Jr., in the *Chronicle of Higher Education* also associate flawed character with plagiarism. Raymond says that one of King's biographers believes a writer's very identity is revealed by plagiarism. Now that he knows about King's transgressions, historian David Levering Lewis has quite a different picture than he did when he wrote the biography: "Who he was [had] simply escaped me" (qtd. in Raymond, 1991, p. 11).

These are descriptions of professional writers charged with plagiarism, but the same language fuels representations of student plagiarism, even when published by composition scholars in composition journals. Although it might seem appropriate to discussions of "intentional" but not "unintentional" plagiarism, the juridical lexicon is sufficiently powerful that it engulfs the entire field of plagiarism, becoming the language for all commentary. That it is inappropriate to discussion of unintentional plagiarism goes unnoticed. It seems neither oppressive nor hegemonic, but "natural," since it accords with the modern properties of authorship.

The seemingly natural judiciomoral vocabulary for discussing plagiarism abounds in composition studies. Frank J. McCormick (1989), in the *Journal of Teaching Writing*, talks about crime and honor; Augustus Kolich (1983), in *College English*, about moral standards and citizenship; Elaine E. Whitaker (1993), in *College Composition and Communication*, about academic integrity; and Edith Skom (1986), in the *AAHE Bulletin*, about crime, theft, and the plagiarist as "less of a person" (p. 3). George L. Dillon (1988) remarks that we "all know" that "verbatim use of another's words without setting them off in double quotes is an act of fraud—misrepresenting another's property as one's own...." (p. 63). Barry M. Kroll (1988) depicts plagiarism as an issue of "moral reasoning" (p. 220). The "Official Guidelines" for the 1988 Glatt Plagiarism Screening Program (a computer software program advertised in the April 1992 issue of *College English*) speaks of plagiarism as a "temptation" from which students must be deterred. Hawley (1984) describes the difference between acceptable and unacceptable textual practices as an "ethical threshold" (p. 35), and Dennis Baron (1994) speculates on the possibility of a "low moral threshold" in plagiarists (p. 90). Lorna Peterson (1986) would solve the problem by implementing Kohlberg's theory of moral development. David L. Ison (1994) observes the paradox of the moral student who would steal: "The problem English faculty deal with repeatedly is that students in our composition and general literature courses have no handle on 'what means theft,' though these students are generally moral" (p. 10). When the *Council Chronicle* asks readers to submit their definitions of plagiarism

("We Want to Know: How Do You Define Plagiarism?," 1993), the sub-heading describes the endeavor as an "ethics case study."

The juridical stance of such commentary constitutes an essential component of the economy of authorship. It supplies an ethical discourse that discourages would-be transgressors, and it supports a legal apparatus for punishing any transgression that does occur. Plagiarists must be punished—for their own good and for ours. In crimes of writing, the conversion of the subject is the outcome of its adjudication. "The subject after conversion appears as the integrated and authentic offspring of a writing that the law has produced by command" (Stewart, 1991, p. 23).

Operating with an ethical paradigm and a juridical lexicon, published discussions of plagiarism in contemporary composition studies depict plagiarism as a unified field of transgression against common morals—even as these same publications may be striving for humane responses to student plagiarists. Those who would argue with the ethical paradigm are represented as enemies of traditional values, as victims of postmodern delusion, or as the uninformed.

The discourse of modern authorship elides all alternative interpretations, notwithstanding that alternative interpretations abound: Lester Faigley (1992), Andrea Lunsford and Lisa Ede (1990), Susan Miller (1991), and Susan Stewart (1991) are among the many textual scholars who reject the possibility of autonomous authorship. That rejection, if widely accepted, would dismantle the entire plagiarism/authorship binary. Autonomy is not a sufficient cause of the modern author, but it is a necessary one.

Much of the complexity of authorship is bracketed from consideration by defining plagiarism according to textual features alone. Universities' policies describe plagiarism in terms of the morality of the writer when they classify it as a form of "academic dishonesty." At the same time, though, these policies define plagiarism in formalist terms, as features of texts. Plagiarism policies may even specifically exclude the writer, stipulating that plagiarism is plagiarism even if the writer is ignorant of its prohibitions. The morality of the writer is thereby extrapolated exclusively from mediating textual features rather than from any direct consideration of the writer himself or herself.

The distinction between "intentional" and "unintentional" plagiarism might seem to offer a counterdiscourse, one that provides for facilitative response to the unintentional plagiarists. Certainly the words *intentional* and *unintentional* seem to reach beyond the text to speak of writers, and thereby to provide space for facilitative pedagogy. The distinction is commonplace in composition studies; Alice Drum (1986) and Susan H. McLeod (1992) are two of the many scholars who make it. In one of the best available overviews of the issues involved in adjudicating student plagiarism, Dorothy Wells (1993) endorses McLeod's and Drum's distinction between intentional and unintentional types. She goes on to suggest that unintentional plagiarism, wherein students "just did not bother to document bits and pieces of material from secondary sources," deserves greater attention than it has previously received (p. 60).

Indeed, the distinction between "intentional" and "unintentional" plagiarism often alludes not to an actual assessment of the writer's intentions, but to salient features of the text. If it is a purchased term paper, it is "intentional" plagiarism; if it is patchwriting, it is "unintentional." The writer's intentions are present only insofar as they might be inferred from the genre of plagiarism, with the terms "intentional" and "unintentional" functioning as convenient labels for texts rather than as descriptions of writers. Thus the representations of both intentional and unintentional plagiarism participate in the liberal culture gatekeeping function of plagiarism discourse.

As a result, the recommended teachers' responses to patchwriting (which is classified as "unintentional" plagiarism) often have little bearing on the actual needs of the student writers. The label "unintentional plagiarism," moreover, relieves teachers of the burden of observing the real intentions of their patchwriting students and obscures from them the cues available from the contexts in which the patchwriting occurs. As they are currently applied to students' plagiarism, the labels "intentional" and "unintentional" ironically serve to safeguard teachers from involvement in writers' actual, indeterminate, elusive intentions. A powerful appeal of text-based definitions of plagiarism—obvious in software that purports to detect plagiarism but also evident in text-based extrapolations of writers' intentions—is that it keeps the person who is making the judgment away from the messy business of dealing with real people, people presumed to be of questionable morals or insufficient knowledge.

The label "unintentional plagiarism" offers teachers two possible responses. One is the juridical response, which says that students must take responsibility for their textual practices because ignorance is no excuse for breaking the rules. Beverly Palmer (1994) declares, "In my writing class, I emphasize that copying another's language or opinions even without the intent to deceive is still plagiarism" (p. 11). William L. Gray (1994), writing to the *Council Chronicle*, also rejects lack of intent as an "excuse" for plagiarism. And Hildegarde Bender (1994) tells her high school students,

> If you give me plagiarism, I will give you an "F." I am not concerned with the idea of "intent to deceive" since my experience tells me two things: the world doesn't care about intent; and since I give very thorough instruction

regarding plagiarism prior to expository writing, if it occurs, there *is* intent to deceive.

The other possibility is the pedagogical response of teaching citation conventions. McLeod (1992), for example, argues for prosecuting only intentional plagiarism. To prosecute unintentional plagiarism, she says, is both legally and morally shaky. The unintentional plagiarist should instead be taught citation conventions.

This latter option seems far more "humane"—especially if the plagiarism is indeed not intentional. However, teachers who elect it can too easily satisfy themselves that they have taken the high road when they teach citation conventions in response to students' patchwriting.

For plagiarism to function as a choice behavior, the culture must have a system of ethics, rules, and laws. These come in the form of originality as the mark of high character (cf. Emerson, 1950); plagiarism as the mark of low character (cf. Lewis, 1991; qtd. in Raymond, 1991); universities' plagiarism policies as the means whereby writers of low character are punished and those of high character protected from the contaminating influence of the miscreants; and style sheets (e.g., MLA, APA) as the mechanisms whereby writers demonstrate their ethical adherence to the prevailing textual values—and also declare their application for membership in the academic discourse community. Within this system of ethics, rules, and laws, the student plagiarist is either an unethical person of low character (one who chooses to violate community values) or a pre-ethical person, a nonmember of the discourse community (one who is ignorant of citation conventions). Commentators who portray plagiarism as a moral choice behavior often acknowledge this latter possibility, calling it "unintentional," "inadvertent," "unconscious," or "accidental" plagiarism. In these descriptions, unintentional plagiarism is the product of writers who do not know how to cite or whether to cite.

Thus, embedded in the juridical lexicon of modern authorship is the assertion that plagiarism is a choice behavior. When juridical language is used, the accusation of immoral choice attaches even to the plagiarism that the commentator declares "unintentional." The conversion of the student subject to the ethics of textual purity remains the desired outcome of teachers' responses to both intentional and unintentional plagiarism.

But the entire issue of choice is irrelevant to most instances of patchwriting. Though seldom acknowledged in composition pedagogy, patchwriting is a means of learning the language and ideas of the source, and for some, it may be the only means available. Patchwriting is, at least in some cases, the mark of writers who do not understand what they are reading and who therefore must work with it monologically, merging their voice with that of the source as a way of collaborating with its language and ideas. Patchwriting, in this interpretation, constitutes a positive learning strategy.

NOTES

[1] In "Romantics on Writing," David R. Russell (1988) explains that the rhetoric of liberal culture, derived from Romantic theory, maintains that writing cannot be taught directly. Instead, it should be taught indirectly, through students' exposure to great works of literature. Elitist adherents of liberal culture see the "democratic reforms" of which composition is a part as "a threat to the standards of taste that liberal culture defended" (pp. 133–134).

[2] These codifications become unintentionally polysemous when one university copies its plagiarism policy from another institution. See Mallon (1989) for a chronicle of this phenomenon.

[3] Jamieson (1988) leaves no doubts about her own perspective:

> When the ghosted text contains words the speaker can say truthfully and comfortably, speechwriting's divorce of speaking from thinking simply obscures our view of the thought processes and mind of the speaker, denies the speaker the advantages that come from writing one's thoughts, and deprives the public and the political process of public rhetorical exchange of ideas that can refine proposals and educate the audience. When the ghosted text sunders the speech act from the speaking self additional problems emerge.... Those who live by scripts alone may find that their own ability to think, speak, and write have gone the way of our sixth toe. (p. 220)

[4] Even by opposing proprietary authorship, postmodern criticism participates in it, thus contributing to its reproduction. That which has opponents has a life. Judith Butler (1990) outlines an approach to the apparently "natural" category of gender that is equally applicable to the apparently "natural" category of plagiarism:

> Obviously, the political task is not to refuse representational politics—as if we could. The juridical structures of language and politics constitute the contemporary field of power; hence, there is no position outside this field, but only a critical genealogy of its own legitimating practices. As such, the critical point of departure is *the historical present*, as Marx put it. And the task is to formulate within this constituted frame a critique of the categories of identity that contemporary juridical structures engender, naturalize, and immobilize. (p. 5)

Plagiarism, then, counts among the "categories of identity that contemporary juridical structures engender, naturalize, and immobilize."

[5] Marilyn Randall (1994) says that pre-modern plagiarism was the bad application of good rules, whereas postmodern plagiarism privileges the transgression of aesthetic norms. "Plagiarism" is covert, whereas "appropriation" is overt.

[6] The pedagogical—and hierarchical—implications of this phenomenon are not lost on Jamieson (1988):

> [O]ne of the major changes in communication in the twentieth century is the extent to which not only the public political words spoken but the ideas they express originated in someone else's mind. The resulting double standard is stark. When students fail to acknowledge the sources from which their essays are drawn or, worse, when they expropriate the language of another, we righteously cry plagiarism and penalize them; once the student attains the status of senator, congressperson, or president, the rules change. Feigning authorship of another's thoughts and words is then not only expected but publicly funded. (p. 230)

III

Collaborators: How Can We Get Out of this Mess?

7

Contemporary Alternatives

[T]he challenge of responding to contemporary critiques of the author and of the subject comprises one of the most important tasks faced by those in composition in the coming years.
Andrea Lunsford and Lisa Ede (1990)

P ower, dominance, and the status quo—even when backed by juridi-cal force—are never unitary and never completely successful in silencing opposition. They are always destabilized by difference within and by alternative discourses. Even though the 20th century's criminalization of plagiarism strives to legislate, at last, one model of authorship, successful alternative discourses continue.

COLLABORATION IN NINETEENTH-CENTURY WOMEN'S STUDY GROUPS

One of these alternative models of authorship is only now beginning to be excavated: the collaborative reading and writing practices of 19th-century women's literary clubs. With the textual difference and resistance of these clubs only now being recognized, it is too early to gauge the extent of the clubs' influence on 20th-century theories of authorship or to determine the extent to which the textual practices of these groups can or should be revived. Certainly, though, they demonstrate that, even while one model of authorship was being legalized as the sole model, others thrived.

At a time when modern authorship was being codified in individualistic terms, many women belonged to literary study groups whose model of authorship and literacy was based on collective principles. These groups persist, somewhat changed, in today's society, but Anne Ruggles Gere (1994) describes the distinctive features of their 19th-century form:

> [E]ven as the interrelated concepts of intellectual property and authorship were solidifying their positions in the dominant culture, alternatives to these concepts were being developed by the women's clubs that began to emerge during the last three decades of the nineteenth century. (p. 384)

These clubs appeared innocuous: they were based on self-improvement; they accepted women's domestic roles; they afforded women an alternative to the social penalties visited upon feminist radical reform groups; and they sought sanction from patriarchal religious leaders. Yet the study clubs "foster[ed] literary activities that resisted the concepts of intellectual property and authorship as defined by the dominant culture," a practice which "offered an alternative way of thinking about writers and texts" (Gere, 1994, p. 387).

These "alternative ways" affected all aspects of the literary experience. Reading was "communal and corporeal," by virtue of the practice of reading aloud to the group, a practice that "offered an alternative erotics of learning" (Gere, 1994, p. 390). The formal study of literature in higher education, in contrast, was dominated by historical and "scientific" philological approaches. The women's clubs also produced communally owned, collaboratively produced texts.

Pleasure was an important part of the literary experience in these clubs. "The view of intellectual property that commodified texts gave little quarter to the pleasure to be derived from texts. In contrast, pleasure took a central place in the way women's clubs saw and dealt with their texts" (Gere, 1994, p. 394). One sort of pleasure, humor, had an honored place in the clubs. And one important form of humor in the study clubs was parodying mainstream texts.

It is worth pausing to consider Judith Butler's (1990) perspective on parody: "The parodic repetition of 'the original'...reveals the original to be nothing other than a parody of the *idea* of the natural and the original" (original emphasis, p. 31). Such parody has, in recent court cases, become a criminalized form of authorship. Martha Woodmansee and Peter Jaszi (1995) describe the rap group 2 Live Crew's successful defense of its parody of Roy Orbison's song "Pretty Woman" in the lower courts: Their "parody of the original song...expose[d] the blandness and banality of the original song" (p. 773). But the state eventually responded with a defense of proprietary authorship that is more stringent, less flexible, than ever before. The U.S. Court of Appeals, reviewing *Acuff-Rose Music, Incorporated v. Campbell*, reversed the lower court's decision, concluding that the 2 Live Crew parody was an infringement of copyright.

> As this decision shows, the penumbral reach of the "work" protected by copyright has expanded to include not only translations but a seemingly infinite series of imaginable variations thereon—including variations as opposite as parody. Indeed, *Acuff-Rose* seemed to render all critical commentary suspect insofar as it must make use of quotation and is carried on in the expectation of some kind of profit. (Woodmansee & Jaszi, 1995, p. 773)

Although parody is now adjudicated as a potentially transgressive authorship, in 19th-century women's study groups it was a form of pleasure. These groups were formed for the purpose of *study*—learning, education—just as are our composition classrooms. Key differences, though, are the women's groups' inclusion of pleasure, parody (a creative form of mimesis), the physical erotics of reading, and a collaboration that blurs boundaries between "individuals."

Even in the presentation of her autobiography, Victorian writer Margaret Oliphant described authorship in collaborative terms. She rejected the heroic individualism implicit in what she saw as Harriet Martineau's self-aggrandizing autobiography. Oliphant described her own autobiography as a family production, and she applauded other women writers who strove to make authorship part of and subordinate to the domestic realm (see Peterson, 1997). For many women in the late 19th century, collaboration was a desirable model for both reading and writing.

MIMESIS IN NON-WESTERN CULTURES

In many non-Western cultures today, collaboration—the writer/text collaboration of mimesis—is the normative model of authorship. That model becomes a source of conflict when students from these cultures attend college in the United States. A familiar problem in teaching writing to international students is that many non-native speakers of English have difficulty in adhering to Western conventions for interacting with source material. These students may go so far as to copy whole passages of text without citation; or they may engage in patchwriting, blending their words and phrases with those of the source—with or without acknowledgment.

The cause of this phenomenon is not universally agreed upon. Working from a cognitivist interpretive framework, Cherry Campbell (1987) compares the textual strategies of native and non-native speakers of English and concludes, "[T]he non-native speakers relied on the background text significantly more than the native speakers for getting started in their writing" (p. 23). By "relying on" background sources, Campbell means, among other things, what I call patchwriting, which she calls "near copies":

> a borderline between word-for-word copying and paraphrasing.... [N]ear copies behave more like *paraphrases* than *exact copies*. They might be considered faulty *paraphrases* in that they exhibit...inappropriately few syntactic or semantic changes from the original reading text. (original emphasis, p. 25)

The salient question for Campbell is whether the student is working in optimal circumstances—doing the writing out of class or in—and the issue is one of ability: "These students may have the *ability* to incorporate information from a background reading text without copying, but that ability may not emerge under the constraints of the classroom" (emphasis added, p. 26). Non-native speakers, she believes, face problems in cognitive processing when they write about texts in English, and those cognitive problems impair their *ability* to write without overreliance on sources.

I always find the invocation of writers' "ability" disturbing. Pierre Bourdieu (1983/1986) helps articulate the implications of *ability,* a word which commonly functions as a synonym for *aptitude.* Bourdieu's interpretation of *ability/aptitude* derives from his taxonomy of *capital.* Cultural capital, which is acquired through laborious education, sometimes masquerades as symbolic capital, which means that it is seen not as capital, the product of work, but as "legitimate competence"—the product of ability. Bourdieu explains that when it translates into academic success, the commonsense view regards it as a "natural aptitude." In terms of human capital, on the other hand, ability or talent is seen as "the product of an investment of time and cultural capital" (p. 244). Aptitude, says Bourdieu, should be examined in terms of its unequal distribution among classes. Ability or aptitude, in other words, are tropes whereby a society holds individuals responsible for—and incapable of changing—their sociointellectual positions.

That this trope might be invoked with regard to international students' acquisition of Western rhetorical forms seems peculiar indeed. Still, Campbell (1987) does postulate the possibility of crosscultural concerns in students' use of sources: "Cultural differences regarding use of text information," she says, "warrant investigation...." (p. 33).

Not all cultures today endorse the autonomous, originary author, and not because they lack the "ability" to do so. Susan H. McLeod (1992) calls the autonomous author a "profoundly Western" notion; many non-Western cultures value a writer's ability to incorporate the words and ideas of canonical sources. In some Asian countries, for example, textual values approximating those of the ancient and medieval West prevail, insofar as a writer's work is valued for its use of authoritative sources. To cite those sources would be a crass insult to the readers' erudition. Carolyn Matalene (1985) explains that the Chinese audience is expected to "infer meanings"; rhetoric proceeds by indirection (pp. 801–802). "The most acute disagreement and misunderstanding that occurred between me and my wonderfully quick and highly motivated Chinese students was over [the] issue [of plagiarism]," Matalene says. Imitation is considered essential in China, "especially [in the words of a Matalene student] for a beginner" (p. 803).

The *Council Chronicle* acknowledges the struggles of international students to learn the textual values that prevail in the United States. Testimony from the University of Illinois illustrates the point: "Numa Markee, director of the university's ESL Service Courses, says that in Chinese rhetoric in particular, good writing honors the ideas of grand masters, with original thought having much less, if any, value" ("University of Illinois International Students Learn about Plagiarism in Class," 1994, p. 6). The article quoting Markee and describing crosscultural issues of textuality applauds instruction at the University of Illinois

> which combines a focus on writing skills with content about plagiarism. Upon completing the unit, international students should be able to define plagiarism, to recognize plagiarized passages, and to write effectively while avoiding plagiarism in their own work. (p. 6)

The outcome of crosscultural textuality, in this model, is the conversion of the international Other to the textual values of Us. Matalene, on the other hand, describes Chinese rhetoric in terms of her own failure to teach her students appropriately during her stint in a Chinese university. Having since learned more about contrastive rhetoric, she feels that she might now do a better job.

But what if we were to contemplate, for a moment, what the Chinese model might offer Western textual values? What about a Western composition curriculum that encouraged students to adopt the voices of authoritative texts, thus enlarging their stylistic and conceptual repertoires? This is not to speak of Asian students' adaptation to Western rhetoric, nor Western teachers' adaptation to the Asian context, but of crosscultural rhetorical "fertilization": If authorship in the West is once again changing, again beginning to value mimesis and collaboration (as evidenced in postmodern celebrations of deliberate plagiarism and in composition studies' increasing adherence to collaborative learning and writing), what can the Western academy learn from cultures that do not adhere to individualistic notions of writing? One possibility is the pleasure of the text, an erotics derived from physical interaction with the text. Chinese students, in Matalene's (1985) description, read aloud for the purpose of memorizing the text (p. 791). And, in Fan Shen's (1989) description, their critical response is to call forth a creative, personal response to the text (p. 464). What connections can imitation and personal response have? In the West we consider the two to be opposing forces. If in the East they are not opposing tendencies, then in fact we may have a model on the basis of which we might maintain our cultural value of "authentic," "creative" rhetoric in the presence of the newly re-emergent value of imitation as a (or the) means of learning.

VOICE-MERGING IN AFRICAN AMERICAN FOLK PREACHING

Here in the United States, too, we needn't look far for mimetic models. Dennis Baron (1994) uses preachers' textual strategies in composing their sermons as an example of free-wheeling mimesis in contemporary American culture: "[P]lagiarism, the ultimate academic sin, is simply a way of life for the clergy, who have found a loophole in the commandment prohibiting theft. And it is the ministry, not the professors, who are, after all, the guardians of our public morality" (p. 86). Tongue in cheek, Baron highlights the contrast between the actual practice of a respected sector of the culture and the textual values espoused by that culture—values predicated on authorial morality. Should we take this as an indication of the collapse of our civilization when the guardians of it—literally, its priests— engage in textual practices that our culture widely deems immoral?

The question is not a facetious one, but my own answer is, of course, that our civilization will not only survive but will be undamaged by ministers' textual collaborations. Keith D. Miller (1992) identifies mimetic ministerial textual values with the discourse community of African-American folk preachers. Verbal skills, say social psychologists Hecht, Collier, and Ribeau (1993), are important to that community, as evidenced in the preaching style. Mimesis would presumably be one of the verbal skills that is valued.

Miller acknowledges that White preachers, too, engage in wholesale unattributed borrowings from each other: Harry Emerson Fosdick, for example, was once introduced to a group of ministers as "someone 'whose sermons you have heard and preached'" (Miller, 1992, p. 126). However, Miller says that the practice is most characteristic of African American folk preaching. The Black folk tradition was oral, since slaves were denied written literacy. That oral tradition therefore depended upon repetition and borrowing.

African American folk preachers today merge their voices with those of biblical sources, telescoping biblical time and the present into what Miller (1992) calls "sacred time." They merge their voices with those of their fellow preachers, emphasizing the commonality of religious experience. And they merge their voices with those of theologians, emphasizing the continuity of theology and religious experience. To cite any of these sources would be to distract the faithful from the purpose at hand: participation in the shared religious experience.

In this sermonic tradition, sermons are "shared blessings, not personal belongings" (Miller, 1992, p. 135). Borrowing gives preachers a number of advantages: it recognizes the culture's valorization of authority and appropriateness over originality; it provides a different mode of establishing sacred time; and it subordinates the speaker to the word of Jesus. Miller's interpretation would assert that we are not discovering that our priests violate public morals, but rather that their traditions endorse an alternative set of textual morals.

Miller's book, *Voice of Deliverance* (1992), by offering an extended treatment of the textual strategies of Martin Luther King, Jr., provides a case study in a contemporary American textual culture that is based on mimesis, not originality. In his various articles and in *Voice of Deliverance*, Miller argues that Martin Luther King, Jr., was engaged in "voice merging"— the African American folk preaching tradition of patching together unattributed words, phrases, and even extended passages from theological sources, the Bible, and other preachers' sermons. He attributes King's "plagiarism" (a word that Miller himself seldom applies to King's textual practices) to the oral traditions of King's primary community. King's composing practices originate in the oral traditions of the African American church, where discourse is "communal wealth." "By enlarging the pool of discourse and the size of audiences, print altered King's rhetorical universe without disturbing its premise that words are shared assets, not personal belongings" (Miller, 1990, p. 79). To academic and political discourse, Martin Luther King, Jr., brought textual values from the discourse of African American folk preaching. Regardless of what he may have known about the textual values of the academy, in his dissertation and speeches he engaged in voice merging. David J. Garrow (1991), among others, argues energetically that King was well aware of and therefore should have adhered to academic injunctions against plagiarism. But one must ask whether this is a realistic demand. Considerable linguistic scholarship in code-switching asserts that the extent to which a speaker engages in accent convergence depends upon the extent to which that speaker identifies with the listener. Code-switching may take the form of converging toward the power dialect or diverging from it, depending upon the situation and the strength of the speaker's identity with a minus-power group. Dialect code-switching is not just initiated by performance errors and variable rules, but also by communicative strategies triggered by the ethnic identity of the listener. Would not rhetorical code-switching follow similar rules? Can it be either a great surprise or a source of justifiable outrage that Dr. King did not identify with the European-molded academy to the extent that he would abandon all the rhetorical strategies of his home culture?

This is not to say that all multicultural rhetors experience cultural conflict. On the contrary, Shen (1989) describes ready shifts between Chinese and Western rhetoric, depending on the occasion, and depicts rhetorical code-switching as a matter of "creating and defining a new identity and balancing it with the old identity" (p. 466). Hecht, Collier, and Ribeau (1993), however, consider code-switching to be an activity at the heart of personal identity formation. Their focus is on linguistic code-switching, but because rhetoric is part of language, I believe that the principles of dialect code-switching are plausibly applicable to rhetorical code-switching as well. "The self can be thought of as an organized system of meanings created through social interaction" (p. 47). It is "both a psychological and a communication process" (p. 36). Identity is part of the self, an orientation of self "toward a particular ethnocultural framework" (p. 34). It is a conscious choice. What does this have to do with Dr. King? "Identity can...be seen as motivating behavior" (p. 48).

Following Keith Miller's lead, I would like to assert the possibility that the voice-merging of Martin Luther King, Jr., that persisted even in his academic and public writing was a part of his maintenance of ethnic identity: "Language clearly does play a role in African American ethnic identity" (Hecht, Collier, & Ribeau, 1993, p. 67). According to the formulations of social psychology, King's ethnic identity may, I believe, have motivated his textual behavior. Individual strategies for coping with "pressures on language identity" include code-switching (Hecht, et al., 1993, p. 54). Martin Luther King's strong identification with the ethnic group of African Americans can hardly be contested; his life's work centered on asserting the value of that ethnicity for American public life. Hecht, Collier, and Ribeau point out that many European Americans have a negative attitude toward the use of African American Vernacular English in intellectual discussions. African Americans, too, may regard their language with disdain, calling it "slang." "This makes it difficult for them to form and maintain a positive identity. This ambivalence may play itself out in many forms, prominent among which is code or style switching" (p. 67).

King was hardly ambivalent, but he was also faced with the rulebound procedures for obtaining academic degrees. Those procedures include the prominent expectation that essays and dissertations will be written in the power dialect, Standard Written English. King adhered to that expectation; the dialect code in his writing displays accent convergence. But one way—whether conscious or unconscious—of maintaining his ethnic identity while gaining European-American credentials would be to engage in divergent rather than convergent rhetorical code-switching: to apply the textual ethics of African-American folk preaching to all of his writing. "While effective communicators adapt their style to fit the situation regardless of their ethnicity, the power dynamics of U.S. society and the history of African American oppression imbue [convergent] switching with a political meaning" (Hecht, Collier, & Ribeau, 1993, p. 90). Martin Luther King, Jr., may on some level have been aware of that meaning as he engaged in accent convergence, and his divergent rhetorical code-switching may have been imbued with positive political meaning for his African American ethnic identity.

Does King's voice merging offer a model that might inform composition pedagogy? Does it connect with the practices and problems of international students writing in American college settings? Joseph Harris's (1989) recommendation seems germane: "Rather than framing our work in terms of helping students move from one community of discourse into another...it might prove more useful (and accurate) to view our task as adding to or complicating their uses of language" (p. 17). Martin Luther King, Jr., and the international students described in the *Council Chronicle* are writers working simultaneously in multiple communities, bringing the traditions of one into another. It would be naive to expect that education would teach them to maintain their memberships as sequential and mutually exclusive rather than as simultaneous and mutually entailed experiences.

I am suggesting that we consider these cases not as problems to be solved, but as opportunities to be seized. Dorothy Wells (1993) brings together the cases of international students and African Americans when she reviews Susan McLeod's 1992 article on adjudicating plagiarism: "McLeod gives examples from Mike Rose and Fan Shen suggesting that the problem [of plagiarism] is especially pervasive among minority students and those from non-Western cultures, but her treatment of this aspect is cursory" (pp. 60–61). Having brought the two together, however, Wells does not ponder their similarity. Although she herself has long experience in teaching at a historically Black college, she does not connect Shen's observations to her own student population. While bringing paratactic commonality to the textuality of African American and international students, she does not explore any positive options that the two together might offer. They each function, in other words, as problems to be dealt with, rather than as opportunities offered to an American economy of authorship that is swamped by the complex interactions of textuality, property, and pedagogy.

These alternative textual values might be acknowledged and then set aside as the values of the Other, except that Asian and African American students attend college in the United States, where the model of the autonomous, originary author prevails. Even then we might simply demand that these students learn and participate in the values of the academy. But when one of those students is an African American preacher who, regardless of whether he learned the values of the academy, does not participate in them but instead brings the textual strategies of African American folk preaching to his academic writing, the situation becomes more difficult. When that preacher's academic texts are, according to the modern academic economy of authorship, plagiarized, yet when they precipitate and fuel a civil rights movement so successful that its author has a national holiday designated in his honor, the situation becomes desperate. The editors of the preachers' papers must consider when and how to announce the discovered plagiarism; the institution that granted the doctoral degree must consider whether to rescind that degree; a biographer must consider whether to retract the approbation previously extended; the *Journal of American History* (Thelen, 1991) must devote an entire issue to ethical debate of his plagiarism; the American public must come to terms with having heroically canonized a plagiarist; and composition scholars must consider the possibility that textual values are part of a person's cultural repertoire—that, like dialect, they cannot always be readily turned on or off.[1] And composition teachers, if they are alert to the possibility, can consider what this circumstance might teach us not just about how writers operate in their social communities, but also about how the changing textual values of the academic community might be embraced in our classrooms.

PLAGIARISM IN CRITICAL THEORY

Contemporary critical theory offers yet another site at which we might discover models for revised pedagogy. A crucial difference, however, is that critical theory represents a different kind of community from those I have just described. In differentiating these communities, we might make use of Marilyn M. Cooper's (1989) definition: "Some—but not all—scholars...discriminate discourse communities from speech communities on the basis that discourse communities are defined by the use of written language" (p. 204). Walter R. Fisher (1992) offers a different sort of distinction, but one that equally illuminates the difference I am asserting between the communities of 19th-century women's study groups, Chinese students, and African-American folk preachers on the one hand and critical theorists on the other:

> It seems to me that there are two essential sites of community: interpersonal relationships, such as families, friendships, social groupings, and some professional associations.... The other site is what MacIntyre calls practices, including medicine and law, sport and scholarship. (p. 212)

Critical theory would, in Fisher's formulation, be a "practice" rather than a spatially located group.

Critical theorists are challenging every premise of the modern author. Séan Burke (1995) warns that the property of autonomy is hard to elude: In the modernist equation, the author is possessed of "autonomous agency" (p. xxviii). From the postmodern perspective, the author is the conduit of language, and "language is sacralized." The difference between the two lies "only in the designation of the alterity by which the recipient is overtaken" (p. xvii). Marilyn Randall (1991) postulates "the artistic value of originality as a consequence—or an index—of the social, economic, and political evolution of the notion of the individual and of the conventions and rules governing public and private property" (p. 528). Assailing the authorial property of proprietorship,[2] Susan Stewart (1991) rejects the Lockean assertion of dominion over one's ideas that is echoed by the U.S. Supreme Court yet contradicted by "the intangibility of literary property." "If ideas and words were not inherited," says Stewart, "every idiolect would be incomprehensible" (p. 25). Thomas Pfau (1994) speaks to the property of morality: "Traditional" approaches to authorship, he says, subscribe to a "genetic paradigm" that construes authorship as "inward subjectivity," whereas Pfau approaches it teleologically to ask about the relation between morality (an "inward category") and discourse; about how inward morality becomes collective; about the causal relationship between "moral authority and authorial competence"; and about what features of a text prompt readers to construe an author (p. 134).

Some literary critics focus on the role of the vanguard reader in constructing plagiarism. The reader, in some sense, becomes the plagiarist, along with the writer; it is the reader, according to Linda Hutcheon (1986), who activates the relationships that are plagiarism. "The neo-Romantic among us understandably feel more comfortable detecting sources, influences, even plagiarism. The formalists still want to consider only the text. But those other players—the readers—demand to be taken into account too..." (p. 237). Nor is it just the reader's role in plagiarism that critical theory can offer a revised composition pedagogy; it is also the notion that plagiarism is constructed not in the text and not just by the reader's interpretations, but also by the writer's intentions. Randall (1991) specifies that the determination of plagiarism depends upon both authorial intention and the reception of the text. Parodic metafiction like *The White Hotel* (Thomas, 1981/1993), says Hutcheon, is meaningful only in the context of authorial intent; yet in recognizing the necessary operation of the reader, it is also intertextual.

> ...in this debate on *The White Hotel* I believe we are viewing only an overt version of a contemporary critical muddle regarding the *status* and, more significantly, the *locus* of textual appropriation. On the one hand, we are dealing with *authorial* intent and with the historical issue of sources and influences; on the other, it is a question of *reader* interpretation whereby visible sources become signs of plagiarism, and influences yield to "intertextual" echoes. (original emphasis, p. 230)

From one perspective, critical theory challenges the originary, autonomous, proprietary, moral author; but from another, it offers positive value for pedagogy.[3] Critical theorists' "take" on authorship constitutes a site from which pedagogy might model useful alternatives to the dominant academic economy of authorship. Of most obvious use is their challenge to the possibility of a plagiarism that excludes authors' intentions and readers' participation. They even assert that what we call "plagiarism" actually describes how everyone writes. These critical assertions are made about the "high" texts of literature, but it takes only one small step to apply them to the writing of students as well—as does George Dillon (1988):

> Finding one's language, one's voice...is not finding something which is out there, or in here, but is forged dialogically in response to the already written and in anticipation of the hearer's responsive word—it is forged on the borderline.... Finding one's voice is...not just an emptying and purifying oneself of other's words...but also an admitting, an adopting, an embracing of filiations, communities, and discourses." (pp. 70–71)

If we are to regard critical theory as a legitimate site for considering a revised composition pedagogy, then we must include writers' intentions and readers' interpretations in the construction and interpretation of student authorship.

THE REVOLUTION IN ELECTRONIC COMPOSITION

Another site that offers powerful alternatives to the autonomous modern author is electronic composition. Our situation bears some resemblance to that of Ben Jonson. George E. Rowe (1988) describes Jonson as working in and contributing to a period in which critical theory was undergoing a fundamental change, away from an allegorical interpretation that referenced texts in external, unchanging truths and toward a critical theory that allowed authorial intention and historical context as arbiters of meaning. Moreover, authors, for the first time, were being described as the natural proprietors of texts they wrote. The legislative cohort to these shifts in critical theory was the passage of the first British copyright law.

Like Jonson, we live in an age in which important shifts in textual relations are apparent. In his world, authorship was being profoundly changed by the technology of the printing press. In our world, authorship is being profoundly changed by the technology of the computer. That a greater span of years separates the introduction of the printing press from Jonson's day than separates the introduction of the computer from ours only demonstrates what Henry Adams (1918/1973) warned of nearly a century ago, a phenomenon with which we are all now familiar: The pace of technological change constantly increases, allowing us less and less time to respond and adjust.

Today, the technological innovation of the computer is precipitating and accompanying shifts in textual values that fast approach proportions comparable to the early-modern emergence of the normative autonomous, individual author. In this new textual economy, Woodmansee (1994b) says that the computer is "dissolving the boundaries essential to the survival of our modern fiction of the author as the sole creator of unique, original works" (p. 25). Just as 19th-century intellectuals felt their work to be a respite from and a rising above the threats of industrialization, so once again intellectual culture today finds itself at odds with the machine. Jay David Bolter (1990) sums up the threat: The personal computer is changing our relationship to literacy, offering us "a new kind of book and new ways to write and read" that will change "the idea and the ideal of the book" (p. 2).

Part of the "ideal of the book," for our culture, is the mutually entailed notions of its autonomy, originality, and integrity, providing premises for copyright laws' protection of intellectual property. But as Richard Lanham (1994) explains, "Electronic information seems to resist ownership.... [W]e will have to create a new marketplace based on a new conception of intellectual property and copyright protection...." (pp. 19–20). Not only the electronic revolution, but also postmodern culture in general threatens those concepts of autonomy and originality of books and authors.

A fundamental problem of property in the digitized environment is that electronic text is not fixed, whereas our notions of literary property are. Transformed into law, the government's preliminary "White Paper" would shut down the free exchange of texts and information on the Internet. Only after years of wrangling did the Executive Branch acknowledge, in 1998, the impossibility of complete government control of the Internet. Copyright, though, is another matter: New legislation extends copyright protection by another 20 years—*in addition to* the copyright protection for the author's lifetime plus 50 years that had already been provided by the American copyright legislation of 1978. The balance between proprietor and user is shifting ever more heavily in favor of the proprietor. What is it that precipitates the State's tightening of laws regarding intellectual property, at the very time that electronic composition insistently undermines the model of authorship that supports laws on intellectual property? The question, it seems, answers itself. It may well be *because of* the threats to the common assumption underlying the State's regulation of authorship. In her undergraduate textbook on ancient rhetoric, Sharon Crowley (1994) asserts that the conclusion of an enthymeme may be more effective when it is based on law than when it is based on moral principles. Now that moral principles can no longer be relied upon as a common belief on which arguments regarding proprietary authorship can be based, the law must escalate its role in fulfilling that function.

Mark Rose (1993) tries to explain why our culture clings so determinedly to copyright as a foundational principle. Copyright, he says,

> is an institution whose technological foundation has recently turned…into an enemy. Copyright developed as a consequence of printing technology's ability to produce large numbers of copies of a text quickly and cheaply. But present-day technology makes it virtually impossible to prevent people from making copies of almost any text—printed, musical, cinematic, computerized—rapidly and at a negligible cost. (p. 142)

Yet, Rose adds, we don't follow Foucault's call to forget the author and circulate texts anonymously; we don't abandon copyright, because it is "deeply rooted in our economic system" and in our "conception of ourselves as individuals with at least a modest grade of singularity, some degree of personality" (p. 142). Behind proprietary authorship, in other words, lurks always-vigilant American individualism.

Illustration of Rose's assertions comes in the form of a report, *Intellectual Property and the National Information Infrastructure: A Preliminary Draft of the Report of the Working Group on Intellectual Property Rights*, issued in

July 1994 by the United States Department of Commerce. Composition teachers deliberating issues of intellectual property were not impressed:

> [The National Information Infrastructure] Copyright Protection Act of 1995 as currently framed does not serve the public interest. We fail to see how the public interest will be served if students are not allowed to browse digital materials, or if universities are required to do more snooping and to allot additional resources to support network use, or if this legislation has the effect of transforming the Internet into another version of the Home Shopping Channel and of discouraging students' writing. (Caucus on Intellectual Property of the Conference on College Composition and Communication, 1996)

The preceding quotation is excerpted from a statement issued by the 1996 Caucus on Intellectual Property of the Conference on College Composition and Communication, a group interested in expanding rather than shrinking the scope of texts in the public domain. It is a group alarmed by what proposed restrictions on electronic transmissions will mean for composition pedagogy—so alarmed that it sent a petition to the Senate Judiciary Committee in response to the intellectual property legislation proposed by the "White Paper" (see United States Department of Commerce, 1994). That petition characterizes the proposed legislation as "an attempt to restrict to the point of near elimination any sense of educational Fair Use as it might apply to computer-generated materials."

In 1995, Woodmansee and Jaszi published an article in *College English* arguing that the decision in the 1991 court case *Basic Books v. Kinko's* adheres to an excessively limited view of creativity. Teachers putting together course packets, they say, engage in a cutting, pasting, arranging, and contextualizing of published materials that itself amounts to creativity. The issue for them is one of "fair use." The constitutional provision for copyright suggests a balance between authors' rights in copy and the public's fair use of published materials. In Woodmansee and Jaszi's estimation, course packets are a form of fair use rather than copyright infringement.

Woodmansee and Jaszi, as well as the CCCC Caucus on Intellectual Property, are moving into terrain that only a few years ago was *verboten* in the discipline of composition studies. In much less than a decade, a monumental shift on issues of textual boundaries has taken place within the discipline. That the entire discipline has engaged in this shift is anything but true. Equally undeniably, though, this shift is led not by the lunatic fringe, but by well-respected members of the discipline.

In sharp contrast is another logic, wherein some of our present indeterminacy might be resolved by mechanization. The April 1993 issue of the

Chronicle of Higher Education reports a "computerized method of detecting plagiarism" developed by Walter W. Stewart and Ned Feder (see Magner, 1993). These two scientists, in the employ of the National Institutes of Health (NIH), studied the work and sources of Stephen B. Oates, a historian who had previously been accused of plagiarism. In its deliberations, the American Historical Association had not declared Oates guilty of plagiarism.[4] The January 1994 *Chronicle of Higher Education* story carries a picture of Oates sitting at his computer (see Magner, 1994).

Enter Stewart and Feder, whose computer program turned up fresh evidence that they forwarded to the AHA in the form of a 1,400-page document (Gray, 1993). Even their program, though, didn't answer the underlying question. As a writer for the *New York Times* put it, the question remained: How many duplicated words constitute plagiarism—or perhaps it is a question of which ones? Must the copying be deliberate, or is the fact of duplication enough? (Hilts, 1993). Not only did Stewart and Feder's work not bring closure to the question of Oates's textual practices or the definition of plagiarism, but it also earned them a reassignment in the NIH. *USA Today* reports that, because they examined the work of a historian rather than a scientist, they had "moved outside the mission" of their organization and would thus not be allowed to continue computer-assisted, NIH-sponsored investigation of plagiarism (see Levy, 1994, p. 5D). The story carries a picture of Stewart sitting at his computer.

Despite the NIH's response to the focus of Stewart and Feder's efforts, it remains a fact that the NIH originally funded their research, predicated on the notion that plagiarism is a function of texts and thus can be detected by machines—a notion that, in its positivistic assumptions, has great appeal.[5] In the April 1992 *College English*, Glatt Plagiarism Services, Incorporated, advertised software that will detect plagiarism and teach students how to avoid it. Frank McCormick (1994) explains this software and offers his own system for plagiarism detection that, like Barbara Glatt's product, uses cloze structure techniques but does not require expensive computer software.

The irony of mechanical means for detecting plagiarism, especially as such means are enacted by computers, should not be overlooked. Plagiarism-checking software would mechanize the monitoring of textual purity, excluding all but textual criteria. Plagiarism-checking software excludes both authorial intention and reader interpretation in the construction of authorship. By automating textual purity, plagiarism-checking software naturalizes the increasingly embattled modern economy of authorship, even as the human factors that it elides would reveal that economy as a cultural arbitrary. In the face of a revolution in authorship that rivals the introduction of the printing press, plagiarism-checking software would deploy digitized information technology to protect that which is threatened. Instead of transforming the ways in which we think of reading and writing, this technology would freeze and reassert the notion of authorship in which writing is unitary, originary, proprietary, and linear, and in which the text is the locus and sole arbiter of meaning. Reassuring us that these machines can be marshaled in the service of the familiar textual regime, such text-only, mechanized criteria for discovering plagiarism assuage an epistemological longing from which *fin-de-millénnium* culture suffers.

Monitoring plagiarism via machines contributes to the juridical formation of plagiarism. It is similar to Foucault's (1979) description of 18th-century technological advances in that it offers hierarchized surveillance that is anonymous in its operation because it depends upon mechanized (or in this case, digitized) systems. The power of the hierarchy derives not from a person at the head of the pyramid, but from the unrelenting surveillance of the mechanism, simultaneously invasive and impersonal, indiscreet and discreet. By removing people from the functioning of the hierarchy, the mechanization of the hierarchy makes it seem natural— and inevitable.

Lester Faigley (1992) points out that in many cases, electronic technology in composition classrooms has been employed in the service of modern notions of writing. Myron Tuman (1992) identifies this impulse with what he calls the "first generation of writing teachers to use computers": their concern is to identify "the impact of word processing on the students' ability to write college essays and other traditional assignments" (p. 8). By means of questions like "Does the use of computers prompt more revising?," Faigley says we confine the effects of revolutionary technology: we use it to sustain the status quo that preceded it.

In a variety of ways computers are put to such purposes. John Schilb (1992) recalls, "David Harvey in *The Condition of Postmodernity* and Jean-François Lyotard in *The Postmodern Condition* point out how electronic modes of transmitting and storing information enable multinational firms to consolidate their power even more" (p. 114). Similarly, plagiarism-catching software hides the operation of power. The machine's indiscriminate operation makes us believe that what historian Jaime Sokolow did (see Mallon, 1989), what Martin Luther King, Jr., did, and what patchwriting students do is the same. The plagiarism-detecting machine takes us where Henry Adams (1918/1973) feared, where no one is any longer in control, exercising critical judgment. Only technology is in motion. Once a cultural arbitrary becomes mechanized, it becomes extremely difficult to recognize as a cultural arbitrary; it exerts its own naturalizing force.

Despite all this repressive and regressive activity, though, electronic composition is changing authorship by providing new models of and venues for collaboration and mimesis. Textual boundaries collapse in electronic composition. The exact causal sequence is hard to determine: Is authorship changing because of the electronic environment—or is the electronic environment a product of changed notions of authorship? Faigley (1992) ponders the question:

> Instead of a scenario of technological determinism where computers are changing radically how we think and how we teach writing, perhaps radical changes in our thinking are embodied in the software for hypertext and electronic written discussions and in the ways writing might be taught using hypertext and electronic written discussions. (p. 166)

Writing in 1986, Hutcheon would date the shift from modern/Romantic authorship to postmodern authorship at about 1970—well before hypertext or even the personal computer became commonplace:

> [T]he dominant *new* critical ideology, in the last fifteen years, both on the continent and in North America, has been, I think, basically an anti-Romantic one: perhaps only in a Romantic (and capitalist?) context where individuality and originality define art can the "borrowing" from other texts be considered plagiarism—or "stealing." (p. 234)

Like Hutcheon, Marilyn Randall (1991) would seem to attribute change not to technology, but to critical and cultural theory. She says that the emergence of postmodernism in the 20th century has given rise to the notion of "the subject as being divided against itself" rather than that of the centered, unified subject. "The loss of the authority of the subject has, in turn, produced a crisis of the notion of authorship and consequently of authenticity and originality in aesthetics" (p. 525).

Regardless of the causal sequence, though—and regardless of the State's attempts to preserve the established economy of authorship—it is clear that there is no going back now that the Internet revolution is upon us. It is not—and I cannot overemphasize this point—that one model of authorship is destroying the other. But it is the case that one is dislodging the other; the formerly subordinate is claiming the ascendant. The linear, print-exclusive literacy headed by an autonomous, originary author that has dominated the Modern period is being displaced by multidirectional, multimedia composition headed, in some case, by no single individual who can be identified.

> As the collaborative nature of contemporary research and problem-solving fosters multiple authorship in more and more spheres, electronic technology is hastening the demise of the illusion that writing is solitary and originary. Even in the still relatively primitive applications that are widely

available—the communication networks and information services like Internet, Bitnet, and Compuserve—not to mention the more sophisticated hypertext applications that are just beginning to be developed, the computer is dissolving the boundaries essential to the survival of our modern fiction of the author as the sole creator of unique, original works. (Woodmansee, 1994b, p. 25)

Hypertext is the electronic site at which the changes are most obvious. In hypertext, readers make additions and changes without necessarily leaving any trace of who contributed what, and a text is never "finished." "Hypertext," Peter Holland (1993) says, "enables us to reconsider the whole notion of the intellectual status authorship confers, not least since it creates two types of authors/editors, refusing to distinguish between the two: those who write sentences and those who restructure materials" (p. 21).

Like the textual values of international students and African American folk preachers, hypertext provides a possible model for revised textual values in the composition classroom. Hypertext makes visible what literary critics have theorized: the cumulative, interactive nature of writing that makes impossible the representation of a stable category of authorship and hence a stable category of its cohort, plagiarism. It provides composition pedagogy with models for interactive, indeterminate composition that flaunts traditional linearity. Multimedia composition has long been the objective of writers such as William Blake; hypertext makes these possibilities realizable in ways that were not technologically available to Blake. And it suggests that for composition pedagogy—regardless of whether that pedagogy is enacted on computer networks—print-exclusive, linear composition (of which citation and documentation is a constituent) is not and should not be the sole model of authorship in a composition curriculum.

All of these potential sites—19th-century women's writing groups, Chinese textual values, the voice merging of African American folk preaching, the formulations of contemporary theory, and the realities of electronic composition—offer important principles for building a composition pedagogy that (re)habilitates mimesis as a means of learning. At these sites we find the principles of the physical pleasure of mimesis, as well as its intellectual subtleties; its ability to shape personal identity and define community allegiance; its involvement of reader, writer, text, and context; and its welcoming of authorial instability.

The simultaneous presence of and tension between mimetic and originary models of authorship explains many of the contradictions apparent in contemporary culture's putatively unified approach to plagiarism. After describing the contradictions and ambiguities produced by this tension, Thomas Mallon's book, *Stolen Words* (1989), chooses sides, excoriating those who do not energetically denounce and punish plagiarism. By means of juridical force he seeks to rout, once and for all, the mimetic competitor to originary authorship. The modern culture that valorizes originary authorship has already branded its competitor an immoral lawbreaker; now Mallon would, by enforcing the laws of autonomous authorship, undertake to end the competition once and for all.

Mallon (1989) assumes that our ambivalence about plagiarism derives from a wavering moral fiber. I would propose that the ambivalence comes, instead, from the recognition that the modern academic economy of authorship is not a unified field and that it cannot by itself account for the way in which we compose. The evidence is everywhere among us: in Freud's fear of reading Nietzsche and thus being unduly influenced by him, and in the famous plagiarisms of Leibnitz, Samuel Johnson, Ben Jonson, and Samuel Taylor Coleridge—the very people who worked so hard to establish the autonomous, originary author. Though Wordsworth's 1798 preface to the *Lyrical Ballads* is considered an event of "uncontested originality" marking "the advent of the Romantic movement," a 1954 article by Robert Mayo points out that most of the components of the Preface existed in previous literature (see McFarland, 1985, p. 14). Can it mean that these canonized writers' work is a sham—that they are not, after all, "true" authors? Or might it mean that authorship "means" something other than—or at least something more complicated than—"autonomous" and "originary"?

NOTES

[1] Unsettling, too, is the realization that, although Martin Luther King, Jr., was a great orator whose textual practices certainly created something new and important—a successful and socially transformative civil rights movement—he frequently does not receive the accolades of T. S. Eliot's (1932) heroic plagiarist, who has shaped the source material "into something better, or at least something different" (p. 153), but is instead condemned as if he were a student who had submitted a purchased term paper. Once again, it becomes clear how steadfastly the construct of plagiarism operates to validate and protect the traditionally powerful group and to keep outsiders such as students and African Americans firmly excluded.

[2] Some commentators are challenging those literary theorists. E. Christian Kopff (1993) declares, "A tidal wave of intellectual, and sometimes financial, fraud is hanging above the happy tropical village of American academia, threatening to crash down on it and sweep it away into the off-shore reefs" (p. 19). Deconstructionists, he says, are frauds, as demonstrated by the fact that some of De Man's translations are inaccurate. Kopff deems it scandalous that we have a national hol-

iday for a "plagiarist." The ruling elites of universities are corrupted and corrupting, advancing the notion that plagiarism is acceptable and truth relative. But truth, he assures his readers, still exists—in the work of scientists.

[3]To refer to an "it" here is not, of course, to suggest homogeneity in contemporary criticism. I do, however, group together a variety of critics' perspectives insofar as together they collectively constitute a "new" approach to authorship.

[4]It is worth noting here that the AHA has historically been reluctant to censure plagiarism—a tendency that has earned the organization the wrath of many, including Thomas Mallon (1989). Though the AHA found that there is "no evidence that Stephen Oates committed plagiarism as it is conventionally understood" (qtd. in Magner, 1994, p. A17), Oates was dissatisfied with the vagueness of this finding and declared his intention to sue the organization.

[5]The particular feature of positivism that applies in this circumstance is what ethnographers Hammersley and Atkinson (1983) call its grounding in universal laws: Events are interpreted according to universal laws external to the data-collecting situation, and the value of research is measured by the generalizability of findings (which themselves become universal laws for subsequent research). In *Rhetoric and Reality* (1987), James A. Berlin outlines the history of positivism in composition theory. That an organization of scientists like the NIH would, in its representations of authorship, draw upon positivism, which has or at least has had its own adherents among composition scholars, seems altogether natural. In composition scholarship, positivism has become a form of invective (see Berlin, 1987), and even in science it now has its detractors (see, for example, Chalmers, 1990). Yet it remains a powerful interpretive force, even in matters of textuality deliberated by textual scholars.

8

Pedagogy for (Re)Formative Composition

Invention builds on a foundation of knowledge accumulated from previous generations, knowledge that constitutes a social legacy of ideas, forms, and ways of thinking.

Karen Burke LeFevre (1987)

Clifford Geertz (1983) argues that the academic disciplines are so discontinuous as to render crossdisciplinary communication difficult or even impossible, and that key terms are the locus of that discontinuity. If we faculty have difficulty comprehending and manipulating the languages of the various academic cultures, how much more difficult a task do undergraduate students face as they are presented with a bewildering array of discourse, none of which resonates with the languages of their homes and secondary schools? How much more difficult is the task when students facing this cacophony are denied one of the basic tools—patchwriting—for sorting through and joining the conversations? If we can begin recognizing our students' work ("even" when it obviously includes patchwriting) as the work of authors, we will be helping them to become more successful authors.

The work of Mikhail Bakhtin provides an important source for the composition scholars who are developing classroom practices in which students are accorded author status. Given that the received academic model of authorship is fundamentally hierarchical (with the student writer located at the bottom of the hierarchy), postulating author status for composition students necessarily participates in the project of establishing composition pedagogy as a site of resistance to the modern author.

In scholarship on the revision of the author—some of that scholarship only incidentally self-identified with revision of the author—the theories and authoritative weight of Bakhtin are regularly invoked. Hence Anne J. Herrington (1992) endorses the familiar pedagogy of peer review to further a goal that she extracts from Bakhtin—the goal of producing "internally persuasive discourse":

> In "Discourse in the Novel," Mikhail Bakhtin introduces two terms that help conceptualize [a] personal challenge: "authoritative discourse" and "internally persuasive discourse." "Authoritative discourse" is that language we take on from other authorities and never really make our own. It remains distanced from us. "Internally persuasive discourse" is that language we internalize and interweave with our own language to use for our own purposes. (p. 111)

Bakhtin's theory of dialogism denies the possibility of anyone's owning language and acknowledges how much influence context has over the reception of a text. Obviously, the text is especially authoritative in the context of school. The conclusion that many scholars reach from a consideration of Bakhtin's theories is that it is natural for writers to collaborate with source texts.

For the specific task of authorizing patchwriting, I would also offer the theories of Friedrich Nietzsche. This might seem a peculiar move, since Nietzsche is so much a proponent of intellectual hierarchy.[1] Yet while Nietzsche does consider himself a member of a superior group, he also provides a compelling analysis of the means whereby the "priests" install their own qualities as "good" and label the qualities of the "herd" as "bad." That analysis has been a significant source for the development of postmodern thought, and its influence is evident throughout this book.

However, the use of Nietzsche that I wish to make in this chapter has to do with a specific textual theory that he calls "rumination." He introduces the idea in the preface to his 1887 book, *On the Genealogy of Morals*. Speaking very highly of his previous publications—both for their complexity and for their rewards—he advocates rumination as a strategy of reading. Some readers of his earlier work, he says, complained about its aphoristic style. They missed the point; they needed to *ruminate on* the commentary that followed each aphorism.

To be sure, one thing is necessary above all if one is to practice reading as an *art* in this way, something that has been unlearned most thoroughly nowadays—and therefore it will be some time before my writings are "readable"—something for which one has almost to be a cow and in any case *not* a "modern man": *rumination.* (original emphasis, p. 23)

Let me begin *my* commentary on this quotation/aphorism on the most shallow level: we might conclude that Nietzsche offers very good advice for students. They should not just seize the most readily available information from a source, but should engage its difficulties and complexities. As this chapter will explain in some detail, I believe summary-writing to be a first-rate vehicle for engaging readers in the complex, difficult meanings of a text.

Let me continue, though, by engaging some of the more complex meaning of this passage from the *Genealogy* (1887/1976a). I would like to take Nietzsche's metaphor seriously. He chooses the figure of the cow, she of the multiple stomachs, to allude to thorough contemplation of a text. The connection is inescapable. *To ruminate* means "to meditate," but it also means "to chew cud." That cud is inside the chewer, and instead of passing from the first stomach on through the digestive system, it is regurgitated and chewed again. Nietzsche is advocating a reading method in which ideas are not turned loose easily and in which they become part of the reader. Formal summary cannot accomplish goals such as these. Formal summary is, indeed, a method of writer-text collaboration. But because it keeps source text and summarizer neatly separate, it does not promote rumination.

Nietzsche (1887/1967a) calls it "rumination"; I call it "(re)formation." In this book, I have deliberately introduced a variety of terministic screens to describe a single concept. None of them is synonymous with the others; their accumulative riches bring depth to that single concept. Explaining a complex textual activity (such as the one under discussion in this book) with a single term and a unitary description is helpful but ultimately false. I find the word *patchwriting* useful for differentiating among types of textual activities customarily labeled "plagiarism." Within the category of plagiarism are the failure to cite, the purchase of term papers, and the mixing of one's language with that of a source text. By labeling this third textual activity "patchwriting," I can more readily assert that mixing one's language with that of a source text may not be a form of academic dishonesty, and thus should not be categorized as plagiarism. I have also used the words *imitation* and *mimesis* to talk about this same textual practice. The Greek *mimesis* and its Latin counterpart, *imitation,* are useful for pointing out the long, honorable history that mixing one's language with that of a source text has had. I have used the term "writer-text collaboration" to assert that mixing one's language with that of a source text bears some relation to an already-sanctioned textual practice, collaborative writing. I am intrigued by "rumination" because it suggests making a text one's own, through contemplation, internalization, and change.

Now I offer the term "(re)formation," whose inception I owe to the collaborative work of the (In)Citers, a scholarly group of which I am a member. The term is a development of one that Jerome McGann (1998) has used to describe his work on the Rossetti archive. McGann characterizes that work as "deformative criticism." Comparing copyright to the hand of the dead, he favors the complete abolition of intellectual property. In his work with the Rossetti archive, McGann challenges the originary, proprietary, and autonomous properties of authorship when he uses computer-imaging programs to change the face of Rossetti's artwork. Such changes McGann calls "deformative criticism," and he ranks their results with Rossetti's originals.[2] They are derivative of Rossetti's work. Rossetti's visual texts, in this project, are neither fixed nor sacrosanct. Recalling Emily Dickinson's advice that a reader should peruse a poem backwards, McGann recommends similar tactics for texts as well as images; the critic should be no respecter of fixed words.

As rhetoricians, the (In)Citers are more concerned with composition than with criticism; but as critics of the proprietary author, they have made their own ruminations on McGann's (1998) argument. Engaging in the very sort of deformative criticism that he advocates, they have come up with the term "(re)formative composition" to describe polyphonic writing. The present focus of the (In)Citers's (1998) ongoing work is on citation practices, which are beyond the purview of *Standing in the Shadow of Giants*. Here, I merely borrow the term to point to one possibility of the related activity of patchwriting. (Re)formative composition opens up the possibility of acknowledging the polyphony of all writing; of teaching students that polyphony is not a sin; and of teaching students how to manage their patchwriting in ways that are stylistically sophisticated and academically acceptable and that contribute to the writer's understanding of the source text.

When Sandra Jamieson and I wrote *The Bedford Guide to Teaching Writing in the Disciplines* (1995), we described patchwriting and recommended pedagogical rather than juridical responses to it. We did not, however, go so far as to describe patchwriting as an occasion for pedagogical celebration. The same is true of my 1993 article, "A Plagiarism *Pentimento*." Our book and my article both represent a sort of transitional stage in my own thinking, from where I was in 1986 to where I am as I write this book. In that transitional stage, I recognized noncriminal motivations for patchwriting, yet described summary-writing as a fine corrective; today, I perceive positive pedagogical value in patchwriting. I believe that it is the basis of all writing from sources. There is no corrective, no more advanced stage; there is only more sophisticated, more polylogic patchwriting.

COGNITIVIST PEDAGOGY

Some of my pedagogical recommendations regarding patchwriting are learner-internal, focused on the student's understanding of a source text. This is my "safer" material; it does no violence to established textual beliefs. Modestly, it proposes that patchwriting signals not a student's absence of ethics, but his or her struggle to understand a text.

My saying that a learner-internal approach does not upset the textual status quo does not constitute an oblique criticism of summary-writing. As a teacher, with each year I am increasingly concerned about my students' reading skills. Summary-writing is the most effective way I have found of helping them with those skills.

Regardless of whether I am teaching composition, literature, rhetoric, or linguistics, I often preside over in-class collaborative summary, with source texts closed. At the beginning of class, I call upon students to recount whatever they can remember of the assigned reading. I act as secretary, writing their recollections on the board. Other class members make their own contributions, and we piece together a summary of the assignment, with the entire class offering revisions. The silences in this collaborative text, the things the students have collectively forgotten, usually turn out to be the difficult passages of the assignment, the parts where, if I have assigned written summary, they have patchwritten; and we turn to these passages and enter them together in a spirit of questioning, supplementing, and wondering.

The following sequence of assignments (see Figure 8.1 to Figure 8.6) comes from a sociolinguistics course that I taught in 1995. The objective of the sequence is to bring students to a deep understanding of the assigned text. One important means whereby I measure that understanding is in the extent of visible, monologic patchwriting in their position statements. The sequence begins with summary and moves to argument. (With each assignment in Figures 8.1 to 8.6, I include my own teaching notes for the day.)

I was satisfied with the outcome of this sequence: By the end of the semester, only 2 of the 30 undergraduates (most of whom were in their first linguistics class) did any obvious patchwriting in the annotated bibliographies that they wrote for the course. My objective was to provide them with strategies that would increase their reading comprehension and thus move them beyond patchwriting. My concern was with patch-

First assignment

1. Read the first paragraph of the selection; then the first sentence of each succeeding paragraph; and then all of the final paragraph. Now set the book aside and write down everything you remember reading. Label this "First Reading."

2. Read the selection again, as fast as you can. Try to make your eyes take in two or more words at a time. Don't reread; don't underline or highlight; don't take notes; and don't worry about what you don't understand. Just keep reading, as fast as you can. Once you are done, set the book aside, turn to your "First Reading" notes, and revise them, adding whatever new information you can remember. Label this revision "Second Reading."

3. Now read the selection for real. Circle the words you don't understand. Highlight key phrases, but not whole sentences. Use the highlighter sparingly. Write in the margins any questions or observations that come to mind. When you are finished with this reading, set the book aside, turn to your "Second Reading" notes, and revise them, adding whatever new information you can remember. Label this revision "Third Reading."

> *Teaching notes: Ask one student to read "Third Reading" aloud. Then ask another student to read whatever he or she may have written that was omitted in the first student's writing. Proceed with two or three more students. Then turn to the selection and examine passages that the students omitted entirely; these are usually the passages that they didn't understand. Spend the remainder of the period discussing and explaining these passages.*

FIGURE 8.1.

writing as a sign of uneven reading comprehension. Hence I was pleased with the effects of the pedagogy.

This assignment sequence does not convey one essential component of my pedagogy of summary-writing; one or more of the assigned texts should be over the students' heads. It is in the struggle with difficult texts that the issues of patchwriting and reading comprehension emerge. In my first-year composition in the Fall of 1997, I assigned the Critical Art Ensemble's 1996 article, "Utopian Plagiarism, Hypertextuality, and Electronic Cultural Production." The students found it terrifying, both in its difficulty and in its radical textual proposals. And in the Spring of 1998, I assigned Kenneth Burke's "The Rhetoric of Hitler's 'Battle'" (1941) to

Second assignment

1. Go back through the selection and look up in the dictionary all the unfamiliar words you circled. Then pick out five of them that seem most important to understanding the meaning of the selection.

2. Draw a line down the middle of a sheet of notebook or typing paper.

3. List your five words in the lefthand column, and with each word, copy down the dictionary definition. (Don't transcribe portions of the definitions that seem irrelevant to this use of the word.)

4. Now go back to the selection. In the righthand column, make notes about how the context of the word might expand or specify the dictionary definition.

5. Go to the library and look up the words in a discipline-specific dictionary or encyclopedia. In the righthand column of your sheet, add whatever information seems pertinent to the context in which the word was used.

> *Teaching notes: Ask one student to select one word and discuss its meaning; ask other students who selected the same word to add to or revise the first student's statements. Engage the class in a discussion of whether the word in question is simply an esoteric word they had not previously encountered, or a key word specific to the development of the selection's ideas in its disciplinary context.*
>
> *Then ask another student to discuss another word. Repeat the process several times; then bring the students' attention to important words that they seem to be overlooking or taking for granted.*

FIGURE 8.2.

Third assignment

Select one of the issues raised in the selection and draft your own position statement on that issue. A position statement should state a belief—your belief about the issue in question—and your reasons for holding that belief. Write your position statement as if it were to be published in the same forum as was the selection; strive to achieve a similar tone.

> *Teaching notes: Peer response workshops.*

FIGURE 8.3.

Fourth assignment

In class, with no notes, books, or drafts, rewrite your paper.

Teaching notes: The in-class draft of the paper challenges the student, who is now familiar with the language of the selection and with his or her own position on it, to write authoritatively in his or her own voice, without extensive visible patchwriting.

FIGURE 8.4.

Fifth assignment

Read the handbook passages on source attribution.

Teaching notes: Peer group work, determining which passages of the in-class draft should be cited. This familiarizes students with the notion that they should cite sources of ideas as well as paraphrase, even in a one-source paper; and it also gets them accustomed to applying the specifics of the chosen style sheet (MLA, APA, etc.).

FIGURE 8.5.

Sixth assignment

Compose a final draft of your position statement.

FIGURE 8.6.

my sophomore composition class. They were fascinated by its analyses— once they had seized the argument. In both cases, the students were able to use summary-writing as a way of understanding the difficult text; and conversely, as a result of the exercise, they were possessed of a better means of text comprehension.

In evaluating students' work in response to such assignments, two criteria come to the fore: comprehensiveness and style. If the summary is being assigned as a means of teaching reading comprehension, the criteria for evaluation should focus on the evidence of comprehension that the summary provides. One of these is comprehensiveness: Does the summary cover the major assertions in the source? "Major," of course, is a matter of readers' interpretations. The teacher who encounters apparent omissions in the summary should pay attention to the summary's overall structure. What thesis has the student derived from the source? Even if it does not match the teacher's, is it nevertheless plausible? Does the summary include the major assertions from the source that contribute to that thesis?

A second source of evidence of the summary-writer's reading comprehension is prose style. The issue is not whether the student is mimicking the style of the source. Many teachers, among them Frank D'Angelo (1979), consider this a valuable pedagogy of imitation. But for issues of reading comprehension, the chief stylistic issue involves visible patchwriting. Does the summary include the key terms from the source? Does the summary go beyond key terms to an obvious dependence on the language of the source, one that would suggest that the writer might not fully understand the material? Equally important, does the summary resort to quotation? Quotation and visible patchwriting both indicate that the summary-writer can identify important passages, but neither testifies that he or she understands those passages.

SOCIAL CONSTRUCTIONIST AND POSTMODERN PEDAGOGY

Making patchwriting an issue not of plagiarism but of reading comprehension takes a significant—and essential—step toward a pedagogy that is responsive to the theory of authorship that now prevails in English studies. Even closer to home, it removes an artifact of liberal culture rhetoric and thereby opens the way for a less hierarchical, more democratic pedagogy. However, I am unable to stop there; I am unwilling simply to associate patchwriting with reading comprehension. As associations go, it is a vast improvement over the association with academic dishonesty, but the association with reading comprehension would make of patchwriting a learner-internal issue. In a contribution to the debates of the 1980s between cognitivist and social constructionist approaches to composition studies, Patricia Bizzell (1982) differentiates membership strategies from cognitive deficiency. When students have difficulty writing, she says, they should not be labeled cognitively deficient; rather, their struggles "should be understood as difficulties with joining an unfamiliar discourse community" (p. 227). This approach provides some relief, taking the onus off the student. No longer is patchwriting a matter of the student's "skill" (a word that too often functions as code for *ability*); now it is a community affair. Students' patchwriting, in this account, amounts to an application for membership in a target community.

Patchwriting surely qualifies as an instance of "authoritative discourse," the unassimilated discourse that Anne J. Herrington (1992), working with Bakhtin's theories, describes. From Herrington's perspective, the "personal challenge" is for the learner to achieve internally persuasive discourse (that which is not obviously patchwritten) by "inserting" herself into the discourse of the community, the discipline. That insertion, says Herrington, is facilitated by peer response to writing, by revising, and by teachers' responding to, rather than appropriating, students' drafts. Herrington also endorses Mina Shaughnessy's call for repeated practice.

Herrington (1992) in no way aligns herself with the recovery of *imitatio* or with the rehabilitation of patchwriting. However, by naturalizing the imitation of authoritative discourse, depicting it as a stage in the writer's movement toward the internally persuasive discourse that is more desirable because it facilitates community membership, Herrington potentially contributes to both those projects. Call it what you will—authoritative discourse, imitation, patchwriting—it is natural and necessary, not criminal.

Keith D. Miller's (1992) argument that Martin Luther King, Jr., was engaged in "voice merging" illuminates these issues. Miller's account attributes King's "plagiarism" to the oral traditions of King's primary community. Similarly, my account attributes students' patchwriting to issues of community membership—but in this case it is the target community, not the community of which the students are already members, that precipitates the textual strategy. Kathryn T. Flannery (1991), recapitulating Susan Miller, explains, "Students are always caught 'intertextually'— they are never inventing a new language out of nothing, but patch together fragments of the multiple texts, the multiple voices (as Bakhtin would put it) that are already available to them" (p. 707).

If students are working in discourse so foreign that the only voice available is the one that they are reading, the eclectic "patching" that is such a natural, normal resource for composing becomes limited to the text at hand. The students have no choice but to patch monologically from that text. In such cases, their patchwriting is a positive rather than negative trait. It is not "immature summary," much less "academic dishonesty"; it is the outsider's membership application, a way of acquiring the language of the target community.

The target community, the academy, will neither accept this application nor find it sufficient; valued members of the community of letters do not engage in obvious monological patchwriting. In the prevailing textual economy, patchwriting is plagiarism, a "crime"—specifically, a "theft" of another individual's "property." But as part of the writing process, patchwriting allows the writer to gain admission to a community by learning and employing its language.

This social constructionist account of patchwriting also makes a valuable contribution to the project of decriminalizing patchwriting, but, like the cognitivist account, it does not finish the job. Even with a social constructionist interpretation, one can still maintain a faith in established authorial hierarchies. The students' "membership strategies" come, after all, from outsiders, from the Great Unwashed.[3] Social constructionism does not necessarily counteract the liberal culture operation of hierarchy in composition pedagogy's criminalization of patchwriting. To declare the decriminalization of patchwriting and to alternatively describe it as a matter of reading comprehension or community membership does not address an important motivation for the criminalization of patchwriting: maintaining an authorial hierarchy in which professional writers (and professors) are those born with the gift—originary, autonomous, proprietary, moral—and students are (to use Nietzsche's objectionable word) the herd—derivative, dependent, textually impecunious, and unethical. In short, cheaters.

A 1989 article in the composition journal *Written Communication* opens a new door of opportunity. Glynda Hull and Mike Rose studied and report the textual strategies of a basic writing student whom they call "Tanya." Her strategies include patchwriting. Hull and Rose offer a refreshing perspective that is seldom acknowledged in composition scholarship on students' writing: They remind teachers that, although we have mastered the academic discourse rules of attribution, we, too, patchwrite.

> [W]e depend upon membership in a community for our language, our voices, our very arguments. We forget that we, like Tanya, continually appropriate each other's language to establish group membership, to grow, and to define ourselves in new ways, and that such appropriation is a fundamental part of language use, even as the appearance of our texts belies it. (p. 152)

Hull and Rose (1989) go far beyond the "refreshing perspective" of acknowledging that we all patchwrite. In a breathtaking step, they declare,

> A powerful pedagogic next move with Tanya...would be temporarily to suspend concern about error and pursue, full tilt, her impulse to don the written language of another. What she seems to need at this point in her reentry into the classroom is a free-wheeling pedagogy of imitation, one that encourages her to try on the language of essays...that...tie in with Tanya's hopes for herself. Then, gradually, the teacher could begin calling attention to certain sentence patterns through a more focused imitation, could help Tanya mark and develop discourse patterns—like the chronological one she's trying to follow in the summary we presented—could show her some

simple ways to effect coherent transitions from one bit of language to another, could teach her a few conventions that would enable her to use the texts of others in ways that show she is not copying. The teacher could, in short, help Tanya shape her writing in the way ... authors are shaping theirs. (p. 151)

The importance of this passage cannot be overstated. Hull and Rose are not just willing to forgive patchwriting, to decriminalize it; they are *embracing* patchwriting as a strategy that they would *encourage* their student to use, however temporarily. Their article was published in 1989; I first read it in 1991. But only after several years of rumination did I quit trying to fit it into received patterns of beneficent pedagogical "forgiveness" and instead comprehended that what Hull and Rose are saying has the potential for profoundly changing pedagogical representations of student authorship.

It is in reference to their work that Mary Minock (1995) introduces her postmodern pedagogy of imitation. Observing that Hull and Rose do not specify what their "free-wheeling pedagogy of imitation" would be, Minock supplies such a description. Hers is a pedagogy of repetitive experimental readings, often of texts that Minock herself has not read. Students' treating texts with reverence or regarding texts as banks from which they are to make withdrawals "interfere[s] with their ability to engage in dialogue" (p. 491). Much more fruitful is reading that takes place in Mary Louise Pratt's (1991) "'contact zone,' a place of potential conflict and 'misunderstanding'" (see also Minock, 1995, p. 491). Minock's concern is with liberating students from authoritative discourse.

Minock's (1995) pedagogy involves students' reading and responding at least a half dozen times over the course of a week, each time writing at least a one-page, single-spaced response; subverting her own authority (by not previously reading the texts herself); and discouraging students from abstracting the text or searching for its main idea. At times, Minock's role is that of "rhapsodist, performing spontaneous random readings of paragraphs of the text...." (p. 506). As a result, students engage in an imitation of the "syntax and...rhetorical structure" of the text, free of "reverence for or valorization of the text" (p. 492).

Minock (1995) is making some daring moves against hierarchical models of authorship, and she is making them in a place that counts, the classroom. She demonstrates that there *is* pedagogy outside the academic economy of authorship; it is not a matter of modernist pedagogy versus the abyss. Her article demonstrates, moreover, that postmodern pedagogy arises not *ex nihilo*, but from identifiable Western traditions. Among her acknowledged sources is Quintilian, whose "psychological insights...about memory and repetition support additional strategies for the *conscious* imitation procedures that he advocated in his influential *Institutio oratoria*." If one frees oneself from the notion of classical texts as "uncorrupted Antiquity" (the neoclassical point of view), one can "see imitation pedagogy as a workable tradition of intertextual learning adaptable to values and practices within particular cultures" (p. 493). Mary Minock's pedagogy challenges the very notion of textual boundaries.

This is (re)formative composition at its most vivid. The postmodern perspective of Minock (1995) that is enabled by the research of Hull and Rose (1989) amounts to a celebration of patchwriting, a genuine welcoming of its possibilities, an invitation to students to collaborate, unfettered, with their texts. This approach might not by itself accomplish the needed revisions in pedagogy's representations of the author. It could, however, work in tandem with a pedagogy of summary-writing, regardless of whether that pedagogy is presented in cognitivist or social constructionist terms.

CONTEXTUALIST STYLISTICS PEDAGOGY

As a theorist of authorship, I appreciate and even rejoice in this sort of pedagogy. The work begun by Glynda Hull and Mike Rose and continued by Mary Minock provides essential support for the new model of authorship endorsed in English departments and resisted by the legislators and corporations who are energetically moving to extend the scope and range of copyright. I fully endorse the cultural work undertaken by Minock, and I hope that many like-minded scholars join the exciting enterprise of designing pedagogies of unfettered authorship. My pedagogical plans certainly include some of these tactics.

However, I am still not satisfied, and my qualms come from my work as a writing program administrator. Every other discipline in the academy, it seems, gets to do its own work according to its own criteria. Compositionists, however, have to answer to the entire world: to state legislators, to standardized tests, to colleagues in other departments. Everybody believes he or she knows how composition should be taught, and everybody measures not just the success of composition instruction, but the very justification for its existence by his or her *own* criteria, not the discipline's. If the writing program's goals and criteria differ, the assumption is never that the writing program knows best, but that it is shirking its duty.

This portrait is painted in the hyperbole of the long-suffering writing program administrator, but it speaks to a familiar truth about composition curricula. The composition discipline has struggled to change lay perceptions of what constitutes good pedagogy,[4] and, thanks in large measure to the writing-across-the-curriculum movement, some changes have taken place in some localities. One thing that has not changed, though, is the laity's belief that they know how composition pedagogy should do its work.

One sticking-point has been the issue of correctness; hence landmark documents like *Students' Right to Their Own Language* (Butler, 1974). Another potential sticking-point is the issue of authorship. What happens if composition pedagogy *does* bring practice into line with theory? Is it enough to say that the author in composition pedagogy should accord with the author in English studies? If that takes composition pedagogy out of line with lay expectations, we have opened up another arena of strife. Then we will be not only the people who are shirking the job of teaching grammar, but also the people who are allowing plagiarism.

Effecting change in public perceptions is glacial work. The persistence of grammatical correctness as a lay goal for composition instruction demonstrates the point. I know of no reason to believe that the discipline of composition studies would have more success with promoting a new model of authorship.

It is a question of audience. We teach our students to be responsive to audience. They resist; they insist on speaking their "own minds," without being "influenced" by audience expectations. Or they resist by striving to capitulate utterly to the audience's demands. (This latter tendency is most evident in students' impulse to say "what the professor wants to hear" so that the paper will get an "A.") But after all that resistance, one hopes that the students come to see their writing as a conversation, a negotiation, even a collaboration with their audience.

A similar principle could profitably govern composition curricula. Designing pedagogy with only our own theories in mind, we would alienate an audience that, inside and outside the university, makes decisions that determine our fate. Conversely, utter capitulation to that audience (which is what a criminalized patchwriting amounts to) makes functionaries rather than professionals of composition teachers. But seeing our curricula and our pedagogies as conversation, negotiation, and collaboration with the rest of the academy and with the general public provides the genuinely exciting opportunity to make composition studies a relay point between theory, academic culture, and workplace demands.

Acting on this principle, one might consider a pedagogy of contextualist stylistics. Although instruction in style has lain fallow in composition studies for two decades, a victim of the rejection of textualist stylistics, literary theory is developing theories of contextualist stylistics that are potentially valuable for composition pedagogy. Richard Bradford (1997) explains: The "unifying characteristic" of the "disparate collection" of contextualist methods "is its concentration on the relation between text and context" (pp. 13–14). Then Bradford offers greater detail: The various factions of contextualist stylistics

> ...are united in their emphasis on the ways in which literary style is formed and influenced by its contexts. These involve (1) the competence and disposition of the reader; (2) the prevailing sociocultural forces that dominate all linguistic discourses, including literature; and (3) the systems of signification through which we process and interpret all phenomena, linguistic and non-linguistic, literary and non-literary. (p. 73)[5]

In patchwriting, the fundamental issues are power and style. A well-rounded pedagogy, one that takes its own theories and those of its audience into account, will teach students that obvious patchwriting is not appreciated in academic writing and is in fact punished in some quarters. It will teach students how to summarize in such a way that the traces of their patchwriting are erased. It will also allow them the *jouissance* of unfettered authorship, of exercises in which they play freely with language, without regard for ownership.

A pedagogy of disclosure can, in addition, acquaint students with the history of and current theoretical work in authorship, so that they come to realize that the autonomous, originary, proprietary, moral author is not a foundational fact, but a cultural arbitrary, one that still governs the expectations for their own writing but that is nevertheless ceaselessly undergoing change. Whether this disclosure is a matter of a few minutes' classroom talk or of assigned readings depends upon the context.[6]

Contextualist stylistics will add a rich understanding of the ways in which prose style constructs perceptions of the author. An exercise that compares and contrasts the use of sources by a star scholar, a beginning scholar, and the model essay in a writer's handbook would give students a greater understanding of what is expected of them as well as how those expectations will change with their professional status.

ONLINE PEDAGOGY

Conspicuously absent from this discussion is online authorship. While I have noted that electronic discourse is putting enormous pressure on the autonomous, proprietary author, I have offered no recommendations for the construction of the author in digitized pedagogy. The omission is intentional. I publish online, I teach online, and I am fascinated by cyberspace. I have read some of the plethora of scholarly works on the topic of digitized authorship. I recognize that many people believe that the current shift in authorship theory is caused by the electronic environment.

But I am more persuaded that critical theory of the author and digitized composition are constituent discourses. The argument that I am advancing about the pedagogical construction of authors and plagiarists is as valid online as it is offline, but it is not precipitated by the electronic environment. I have avoided detailed attention to digitized discourse because I do not want my argument to be misunderstood as a discussion of how authorship is different online. The electronic medium contributes to and participates in the shift in authorship that is presently underway. But that shift is taking place in all media. Authorship is different now than it was a century ago, and pedagogy—in both print and electronic media—must reflect that difference.

NOTES

[1] A typical statement, and one whose isolated presentation here does no injustice to the overall purport of the *Genealogy* (Nietzsche, 1887/1967a):

> The well-being of the majority and the well-being of the few are opposite viewpoints of value: to consider the former *a priori* of higher value may be left to the naiveté of English biologists. (p. 56)

[2] Samples of some of McGann's deformative criticism are available on his website at http://jefferson.village.virginia.edu/~jjm2f/home.html

[3] Social constructionist perspectives have substantially enriched the discourse of composition studies, but they are not without their shortcomings. Linda Flower (1996), for example, says that social constructionism theory fails to account for conversational complexity. It postulates a single outcome of conversation, whereas each participant actually goes away with different meanings. Suzanne Clark (1994) charges that accounts of social construction "fail...to include feminists in the conversation" (p. 104). My own difficulty is the agency assumed by most social constructionist accounts of writing. Subjects are possessed of free will, self-determination, and an equal shot at affecting the outcome of the construction. The determinism of Bourdieu and Foucault is also difficult to accept, but its recognition of the unequal distribution of power and the hidden linguistic mechanisms of maintaining that power are much closer to the mark.

[4] I should reiterate that I use the words *lay* and *laity* to refer to all nonspecialists. In this case, those words refer both to the general public and to members of other academic disciplines.

[5] Bradford (1997) offers a contrasting description of textualist stylistics:

> [Textualist theories of style] share a common assumption: that the stylistic character of a literary text defines it as literature and distinguishes it from the linguistic rules and conventions of non-literary discourse. The theories are textualist in that they perceive the literary text as a cohesive unity of pat-

terns, structures and effects. Textualists record the ways in which literature borrows features from non-literary language but maintain that these borrowings are transformed by the literary stylistics of the text." (p. 73)

[6]In composition studies, a growing number of textbook readers address these issues. See, for example, Dock (1996) and Vitanza (1996).

9

Reforming Plagiarism Policies

Authorship...may have less to do with the act of writing than with processes of negotiation by which recognition is allocated. It is a fluid and potentially contested social status that is determined concretely at particular conjunctures of laboratory life in science.

John Trimbur and Lundy A. Braun (1992)

The task of explicating the cultural notions that sustain current pedagogy and in searching for alternatives bears some resemblance to the restructuring metaphor invoked by Anne Ruggles Gere (1993) in her introduction to *Into the Field: Sites of Composition Studies*. She privileges restructuring over the more familiar bridge-building metaphor that leaves existing structures intact. Restructuring, Gere says, works in terms of both theory and application, and it works in three dimensions: "reconceptualizing the discipline," "deconstructing received boundaries," and "repairing...relations between theory and application" (pp. 3–4). Gere's task in *Into the Field* is one of wide scope, whereas mine focuses specifically on representations of student authorship. Both, however, bid to change how our discipline operates, and I invoke Gere's metaphor by way of describing my objective here.

By imagining nonjuridical and even positive definitions of and responses to strategies of writer-text collaboration that have long been depicted in the criminal terms of plagiarism, the reports and recommendations of scholars such as Charney and Carlson (1995), Corbett (1971), Drum (1986), Hull and Rose (1989), and Minock (1995) render impossible a unitary representation of autonomous student authorship. These challenges and revisions are, however, insufficient as long as the autonomous author continues to prevail as a regulatory fiction in academic prohibitions against plagiarism. Colleges' uniformly juridical policies against plagiarism restrict the extent to which pedagogy can respond to revised cultural representations of authorship.

Without specifying how they might be made, Andrea A. Lunsford and Lisa Ede (1994) as well as Keith Miller (1993) recommend changes in colleges' plagiarism policies. Significant changes must indeed be made; otherwise, the pedagogical possibilities described in the previous chapter can bear little fruit. Jaszi and Woodmansee (1994) say that the pressures on the established economy of authorship have not yet caused revision of juridical installations regarding copyright and plagiarism; if anything, these have become even more strident in defense of textual purity. Observing the chasm between theory and the law, we must recognize that pedagogical applications of contemporary theory have gone as far as they can within the limits of now-outdated law. Therefore, it is time to revise the law so that it acknowledges rather than obscures the complexities of authorship.

Composition teachers' classroom revisions of the modern economy of authorship are plausible only if a college's regulations permit them. Teachers who treat patchwriting not as plagiarism, a transgression to be disciplined or punished, but as writer-text collaboration, a normal part of the writing process, might find themselves professionally compromised if their institution's regulations provide only for discipline and punishment.[1] Teachers may therefore be forced into counter-pedagogical responses; as Jaszi and Woodmansee (1994) point out, it is the students who suffer and pay for intractable policies that are at variance with widely endorsed theories of authorship.

Undergraduate student Todd Kehley (1994) says, "The plagiarism rules presently in place are too strict. A great thinker such as Dr. King learned through the use of others' work. Why can't young people do the same?" Though I do not concur with Kehley's assumption that the issue is one of strictness or leniency, I do agree that plagiarism policies need to be changed so that they provide for rather than hinder learning. College plagiarism policies need to account for the terms of contemporary intellectual life, including its electronic media, its historical contingency and cultural diversity, and its attention to the social dynamics of composing. The changes I suggest affirm the possibility of a policy on plagiarism. The policy I propose would represent the contingent nature of authorship and its constituent discourses; account for the collaborative nature of writing, allowing authorial intention as a factor not just in the adjudication but the definition of plagiarism; and attribute positive value to patchwriting, a textual strategy that is too often classified as plagiarism, regarded as immoral, and punished by "Fs" and even expulsion.

Whatever changes we make in plagiarism policies, as long as we imagine the possibility of autonomous, originary writing, we will still suffer the anxiety of authorship, and we will still be unable to adjudicate it sanely. What I recommend will not "fix" the situation, because our culture will continue to sustain the figure of the autonomous, originary writer. The question is whether that figure will function as part of the general discourse or as a regulatory fiction. In either case, the autonomous, originary writer should not continue to stand alone. Instead, we need to recognize and authorize pedagogical possibilities that have previously been obscured by overdetermined policies on plagiarism, policies that have resulted from the representational exclusivity of the autonomous, originary author and that have attempted to assuage an anxiety of authorship that cannot be comforted.

The revision of plagiarism policy will not stabilize the indeterminacy of authorship in the academy. But it can acknowledge the conflicted terms of contemporary authorship, rather than clinging to an ideal that has been demonstrated unworkable in academic life and contradictory to much of contemporary theory. The epistemological desire that propels us to attempt plagiarism regulations that would accomplish neat definitions to be cleanly applied to all cases cannot be fulfilled. Textuality and authorship can never be fully articulated—much less regulated. They can only be enacted.

ESTABLISHED PLAGIARISM POLICIES

Peter Jaszi and Martha Woodmansee (1994) cite Barthes, Foucault, and Derrida as demonstration that representations of authorship are changing radically in literary theory, but they note that the law (which includes institutions' policies on plagiarism) is slow to change. This is especially problematic, they say, in the case of students:

> The stakes are high in disciplinary actions against students accused of intramural offenses against authorship. Indeed, our institutions underline the seriousness of these proceedings by giving them the form, as well as some of the content, of legal actions for violations of copyright law. (p. 9)

At present, institutions' juridical installations against plagiarism reify the formalist definitions in which plagiarism is a unified category that includes patchwriting, the purchase of term papers, and the absence of citation. The only responses to this unified category are to teach citation or to punish the infraction. These options are regarded as lenient and harsh choices, respectively. Authors' intentions are excluded from the definition of plagiarism and often from the response to it, as well, and readers and contexts are ignored as potential factors. Complexity is elided; plagiarism, categorized as "academic dishonesty," is represented not only as a unified category, but as a transparent, simple one. Hence the "Academic and Disciplinary Policies" handbook of The Bishop's School, in La Jolla, California, reported by Watson Branch (1994):

> In writing your paper you could easily end up sewing together with the thread of your own words the patches of material taken from other people—as if those patches had originally come from you. The finished product might appear to be all your own work (because ideas do not display their origins as obviously as pieces of material in a patchwork quilt do theirs), but in fact such a paper is plagiarized.
>
> The message is clear: never pretend that words or ideas taken from another person are your own; always give that person credit. To do otherwise is dishonest and dishonorable. (p. 10)

Just as the commission of patchwriting (here called "plagiarism") is described as "easy," so is its prevention: "You can *easily* avoid plagiarism by giving credit to the person whose words or ideas you use in your written work" (emphasis added, Branch, 1994, p. 10). Frank McCormick (1989), however, doesn't think the matter is this easy. Neither does undergraduate Jennifer Markson (1994): "In my case the plagiarism was unintentional. It was just what you've described: I didn't understand the text. From a student's point of view the handbook seems harsh and the policy not logical."

Something is clearly missing from the standard account of student plagiarism. Something is very wrong when teachers cannot communicate to students the importance and methods of attributed writing from sources. That "something," I believe, is missing because the juridical lexicon and formalist criteria for textual purity obscure it from us: There are very good reasons for students to patchwrite, and these reasons have nothing to do with ethical codes or knowledge of citation conventions. These good reasons are already being acknowledged and discussed in some scholarly treatments of student plagiarism. These can take a prominent place in the discourse of student authorship, however, only when plagiarism policies allow not only text but reader, writer, and context to play a role in determinations of plagiarism.

Rutgers University takes an apparently positive step by instituting a two-level punishment system for cheating:

[W]e would allow students to accept faculty-imposed penalties—such as being forced to rewrite a paper or retake an exam, receiving a failing grade on an assignment or in the course itself.... More serious offenses, such as purchasing a term paper, stealing a test, or having a substitute take an examination, would be subject to a disciplinary hearing. (see Fishbein, 1993, p. A52)

This distinction is positive in that it allows teacher and student to determine the outcome of textual infractions without the intervention of judicial boards. It also implies a differentiation among types of "cheating" (a category in which Rutgers, following received practice, groups patchwriting), with commensurably varying degrees of punishment. But it is still insufficient, for it does not challenge the inclusion of patchwriting in the category of plagiarism—and hence it defines patchwriting in juridical terms.

DISCIPLINE AND PUNISH

Even when a plagiarism policy recommends that teachers rather than institutional boards punish plagiarism and even when it offers differential punishment for various types of plagiarism, it can still participate in the hierarchical textual formation that accords authorial status to published writers, but not to students; that represents authorship as the natural product of the unteachable gift of genius; that, by postulating an autonomous author, denies to students means whereby they might attain authorial status; and that defines students' writer-text collaboration as an ethical transgression or an ignorance of citation conventions. As long as the writer-text collaboration of patchwriting is regarded as an ethical issue susceptible to punishment, response to it participates in the reproduction of established power relations rather than in the fostering of intellectual growth to which most teachers believe themselves committed. In Foucault's (1979) terms, the discipline and punishment of patchwriting differentiates in order to control and manipulate. Establishing a range of punishments only contributes to the reproduction of the hierarchical system, for it provides apparent escapes from the punitive force of that system—escapes in the form of teacher-controlled discipline—without challenging the definition of writer-text collaboration as an unethical behavior. Thus, such avenues of apparent amelioration forestall significant change in the textual status quo in whose terms teachers are expected to conduct their classes.

Plagiarism, especially when it includes patchwriting, is couched in juridical terms in order to support distinctions between high and low culture, insiders and outsiders. In being converted to this economy, the sub-ject acknowledges his or her place in it—the place of the rejected—and also acknowledges that he or she has earned this place by making immoral (or, at best, ignorant) choices. To locate plagiarism in an ethical realm is to describe it as a choice behavior; hence those who plagiarize can be punished and numbered among the rejected—consigned to dwell in the shadows of giants—for they have chosen to transgress against fun-damental morals.

The plagiarism policy that I suggest would not dismiss ethical interpre-tations of plagiarism. Neither I nor any commentator whom I have encountered would condone the plagiarism that approaches fraud—for example, the purchase of term papers that is ably described by Galles (1987), Hawley (1984), Pemberton (1992), and White (1993). Giles Con-stable (1983) reminds us that Dante takes a particularly dim view of fraud, putting "all types of defrauders in the two lowest circles of Hell, with fal-sifiers at the bottom of the eighth circle" (p. 20). Most commentators today would agree that the submitters of purchased, ghostwritten, stolen, or borrowed term papers should be classified with the perpetrators of fraud. But patchwriting does not belong in this category. Only if the patchwriter is found to have fraudulent intentions should the matter be considered ethically based and hence adjudicable.

REPRESENTATIONAL COMPROMISE

This proposal may adduce responses not unlike those that greeted the publication of *Students' Right to Their Own Language* (Butler, 1974). Lester Faigley (1992) describes that response:

> [T]he moment writing teachers began to recognize language diversity in public ways with the *Students' Right* statement in 1974, *Newsweek* and other periodicals quickly responded with alarms of a "literacy crisis" and accused writing teachers of being an "enemy within." (p. 79)

Given the contested notions of authorship in the academy today, the Romantic originator can no longer function as the sole model of the author on which colleges' plagiarism policies draw. Nor can a revised (or discarded) policy declare the student author a casualty in the postmodern death of the author. We must redefine institutional policies to account for the dialectic. In that dialectic, we may discover phenomena of authorship that were obscured by overdetermined definitions of and legislation against plagiarism.

AUTHORIAL INTENTION

A considerable quantity of contemporary pedagogy already recognizes the writers and readers of plagiarism. The April 1994 *Council Chronicle* offers "Techniques for Preventing Plagiarism," which include supervision of students' writing processes and assignment design that considers their capabilities. In a 1970 article, Roger Palmer Saalbach advocates instruction in critical thinking—not citation conventions—as a plagiarism preventative. Elaine E. Whitaker (1993) uses collaborative classroom activities to avert plagiarism, and Margaret Kantz (1990) recommends clear representations of the writing task. Engaging students in discussion of cheating, says John P. Houston (1983), reduces transgressions. High school assistant principal Roger Sauer (1983) advocates teachers' discouraging plagiarists by making it known that they maintain their own files of students' papers. David W. Smit (1990) discourages plagiarism by having students include drafts in their portfolios.

Some of those who describe means for preventing plagiarism are, like Sauer (1983) and Smit (1990), simply trying to discourage the unethical; others, like Houston (1983), are trying to raise students' moral character; but others, like Saalbach (1970), Whitaker (1993), and Kantz (1990), raise the possibility that the teacher and the context may be factors in plagiarism. Those who describe anything but a hegemonic, monolithic punishment for plagiarism are admitting emotional, interpersonal considerations into the equation as well: the emotions of the unjustly accused, the unjust accuser, the thwarted accuser. Those who advocate differential response to unintentional plagiarism or to patchwriting are admitting slippery human factors into the equation, factors of context and authorial intention. Although plagiarism is commonly depicted as a unitary, stable field, the subject in the adjudication of plagiarism— whether that subject is the plagiarist or the teacher—is not. Hence, William Gribbin (1994):

> [P]lagiarism may be intentional or unintentional, as elegant as some "derivative" forms and as detestable as much sloppy scholarship; but in each case the determining factor does not lie only in the eyes of the beholder. Rather, much of the answer lies in the context created by the writer and her or his circumstances. (p. 14)

Authorial intention, says Marilyn Randall (1991), is integral to issues of plagiarism:

> [Q]uotation and plagiarism surely occupy antipodal positions on the axis of possible repetitions. Their difference, however, has distinguished since clas-

sical times between vile and proper imitation, in other words, not between two different *acts*, but two different *intentions*. The accusation of plagiarism partly depends, for contemporary legal questions as for classical aesthetic ones, not on the *textual fact* of repetition, but on the author's presumed intention to conceal the act and thus to deceive. (original emphasis, p. 527)

That presumed intention, Randall (1994) explains, can establish a wide range of interpretations of plagiarism; the determination of authorial intention can variously identify plagiarism as fraudulent, aesthetic, or subversive.

The exclusion of authorial intent from questions of textuality has, of course, a context much larger than the adjudication of plagiarism. Reflecting on one aspect of that larger context, Foucault (1977b) observes that one of the themes that purportedly replaces authorial privilege is that of the work, whose examination excludes questions of authorial intent, looking instead at self-contained architectonics. But how, then, is "work" to be understood? Is it only when we conceive of a person as an author that pieces of paper containing prose become a "work"? And just what do we include in our definition of an author's "work"—his laundry lists? The question, Foucault tells us, is even more difficult with a deceased author. It is that focus on the "work" that formalist policies on plagiarism undertake; but the issue of authorial intent is, as in Foucault's context, inescapable. The issue is difficult with a deceased author; it is difficult, too, with a very-much-alive student author.

A major underlying issue in acknowledging authorial intent as a factor in defining and adjudicating plagiarism is whether we will accord authorial status to the student writer. To focus solely on the student's text is not to accord her the status of author-function; it is to consign her to subauthorial status. But students' "plagiarism," bereft of authorial intention, is interpreted only as fraudulent, that fraudulence deriving from either the student's lack of ethics or from a lack of understanding of citation conventions.

The denial of authorial intention in the adjudication of plagiarism contradicts, of course, the origin and development of the concept, as Giles Constable (1983) suggests:

To plagiarize...derives from the Latin word for a kidnapper or seducer, and refers to taking some one else's ideas or words and passing them off as one's own.... [T]he intention to deceive is as central as the actual deception. (p. 3)

What revised policies on student plagiarism might acknowledge is the possibility that intentions of writers other than poets and writers of fiction might justify acts of plagiarism. With Lunsford and Ede (1994), I am proposing that student writing be accorded the same respect as professional writing—that it be treated as a subject rather than object formation:

> The concepts of author and authorship, so radically destabilized in contemporary literary theory—and in current discursive practice in fields as far removed as engineering and law—have also been problematized in the field of rhetoric and composition studies, where scholars have challenged the traditional exclusion of student writing from claims to "real writing" and "authorship," explored the ways in which *authority* is experienced by student writers, and increasingly sought to map various models of composing processes. (original emphasis, p. 417)

That we might consider any other course of action is indeed remarkable, given that composition studies so thoroughly subscribes to the notion of authorial agency—which includes, of course, authorial intention. David Bleich (1988) expresses it succinctly: "The writer's motive is the most important element in the activity of writing" (p. 371).

In order to make judgments about a writer's morality, one must turn to the writer, not his or her text. A revised policy on plagiarism needs to ask the same questions about students' motivation that Eliot (1932), McCracken (1991), Meltzer (1994), Randall (1991), and Stewart (1991) ask of their professional writers. In reading students' prose, we need to know whether the writer intended to plagiarize. If the plagiarism was intentional, we then need to know motivations.

On the final examination in an authorship theory class at Colgate University, undergraduate Ki O (1994) examines an example of patchwriting and makes his case for the importance of real writers' intentions:

> To determine the extent to which these notes may be plagiarism, one must consider intent. (The word "intent" will haunt me till I die.) If the intent of these notes was to blatantly copy word for word to a finished paper, then, of course, this is not acceptable. However, if the intent of these notes is to organize, collect, and help formulate ideas—ideas that can build a thesis— then these notes should be acceptable.
>
> As always, the punishment to plagiarists can only follow if the actual intent is known. This is one of the hardest reasons why we cannot define "plagiarism" or subject students to correct and just punishment. (n.p.)

Addressing the same issue on the same final examination, Patrick Peto (1994) warns of the perils of taking writers' intent into account:

> A student pressed for time could use the patchwriting excuse to simply plagiarize with the thought that he/she will be allowed to rewrite the paper for a better grade and more time. It will inevitably be very difficult to deter-

mine when such a case occurs, but this must be examined individually, and students subsequently punished for this action. (n.p.)

Concerns of this very sort make educators eager to embrace text-only criteria for defining and responding to plagiarism. But after a century of adjudicating student plagiarism, the academy has not yet been able to adduce unified, stable criteria for defining and responding to plagiarism, even while limiting its quest to the most arid of formalist textual features. That same academy has all the while been plagued by the slippery motives of plagiarists, despite its attempts to exclude their real "intentions." It would seem, therefore, that the academy has little to lose by abandoning the text-only hunt for determinacy and instead allowing the full panoply of factors—text, writer, reader, and context—into the discussion. In the matter of student plagiarism, it is real people who are at issue. These are not author-functions; these are human beings sitting in one's class, one's office. And it is not their texts that are punished, but their persons. Their persons, therefore, must be integral to the definition of their plagiarism. For plagiarism, finally, is not a feature of a text. It is an action that involves both reader and writer.

It *must* involve both reader and writer; and it must involve context, as well; for actions do not take place in some atemporal ether. We must ask questions such as these: Is the student experienced with the discourse of the discipline in which he is writing? Has she been introduced to the textual conventions of the discipline? (Some disciplines, for example, have a considerably higher tolerance for and expectation of students' recapitulating their sources—whether in paraphrase, summary, quotation, or patchwriting—than do others.) Is the student writing from sources that were assigned by the reader, the instructor? (In such cases, it is highly unlikely that she intended to deceive.) Different answers to these questions should elicit different responses from the questioner. And this raises another inescapable component of plagiarism: the reader. Textual purity does not, in fact, reside in the text, but in the interplay of text, intertext(s), writer, social context—and reader. Linda Hutcheon (1986) points out that plagiarism occurs only in the reader's interpretation, when "visible sources become signs of plagiarism, and influences yield to 'intertextual' echoes" (p. 230).

CONTEXT AND READER

The possibility of the reader as a defining factor in plagiarism is, in fact, already present in the literature, expounded upon in theory and also scattered in chance remarks. Critics such as Hutcheon (1986), McCracken

(1991), Meltzer (1994), and Stewart (1991) use plagiarism as a wedge to destabilize the notion of authorship as solitary, autonomous, originary labor that produces the literary capital of words and ideas whose ownership can be ascertained, assaulted, and defended. They postulate authors whose identity is always in process, always contingent, always entwined with others, always already located in language; texts that are a pastiche of sources of which the author may be largely unaware; and meaning that proceeds from readers' participation. Such notions of authorship inevitably call into question text-based notions of plagiarism, as Hutcheon explains: "...perhaps only in a Romantic (and capitalist?) context where individuality and originality define art can the 'borrowing' from other texts be considered plagiarism—or 'stealing'" (p. 234). In Hutcheon's account, a writer produces a text that acquires meaning—including the "meaning" of plagiarism—only when the reader places the text in interaction with his or her own intertexts. Françoise Meltzer, too, believes that plagiarism is an action by the reader rather than a property of the text.

We cannot eliminate the role of the reader in the issue of plagiarism, nor should we ignore it; the professorial reader will respond with emotion because he or she will feel personally affronted, his or her intelligence insulted, his or her values degraded. D. Kay Johnston (1991) describes the emotion that cheating precipitates. She learned that students had cheated on an unproctored midterm exam. "My initial reaction to the discovery...was fury. How could 'they' do this to me" (p. 285)? We need to recognize the role of that outraged reader, and we need to agree that it must not be hidden behind the facade of text-only criteria alleged to be so dispassionate that they can even be mechanized in plagiarism-checking software. Moreover, we must realize that the established categories of "intentional" and "unintentional" plagiarism may, despite the apparent writer-orientation of the labels, also be supporting a formalist approach to authorship, an approach that obscures writers' actual intentions rather than taking them into account.

TOWARD A REVISED POLICY

A workable plagiarism policy must recognize the Foucauldian assertion that the text is a contested site. Instead of fruitlessly trying to solve all ambiguities involved with plagiarism, it must acknowledge the complexities of the issue and offer guidelines for negotiating what will continue to be contested terrain. It must acknowledge the terms of that contest and urge all participants—writers and readers—to engage it as openly as possible.

In a recent attempt to sketch an equitable plagiarism policy (Howard, 1995b), I left patchwriting in the category of plagiarism but advocated differential response to it, depending on authorial intention. I am now concerned, however, that, like the Rutgers plagiarism policy (see Fishbein, 1993), such an arrangement does not go far enough. It is an improvement upon standard policies, but it leaves patchwriting in the transgressive category. I would therefore now propose removing patchwriting from the category of plagiarism altogether, except in cases where there is evidence that the writer engaged in patchwriting for the purpose of defrauding. Let the word *plagiarism* describe the intentional representation of others' words and ideas as one's own,[2] and let it continue to be classified as a subset of academic dishonesty. Let "failure to cite" describe the act of ignorance committed by students who do not know academic citation conventions, and let us cease to terrorize students who do not know those conventions. Instead, let us respond pedagogically to ignorance of citation systems, just as we do to the presence of comma splices or the absence of a thesis statement. Let us recognize, as does Jennifer Markson (1994), the limitations and ultimate inefficacy of such systems. Reading a draft of a proposed policy on plagiarism (which I eventually published as "Plagiarisms, Authorships, and the Academic Death Penalty"; see Howard, 1995b), she observes,

> You say, "When in doubt, cite"; but that would mean the student would cite everything! There comes a point where everything you say comes from someplace else. A friend of mine who was told by a professor to cite everything felt as if the work wasn't her own. (n.p.)

Finally, let "patchwriting" describe the act of enthusiasm in which students collaborate with their source texts for the purposes of understanding them and entering their discourse. Let us respond pedagogically to that phenomenon, too. That pedagogical response can regard the patchwriting as a transitional stage toward full comprehension of the text or toward full membership in a discourse community, or it can celebrate patchwriting as (re)formative composition. But let us, at last, quit telling our students and ourselves that writer-text collaboration is a crime.

NOTES

[1]A word here about the definition of *discipline:* sometimes I use the word to refer to academic disciplines. Heather Murray (1991) quotes rhetorician Stephen Toulmin: "We can think of it as a discipline, comprising a communal tradition of procedures and techniques for dealing with theoretical or practical problems; or

we can think of it as a profession, comprising the organized set of institutions, roles, and men whose task it is to apply and improve those procedures and techniques" (p. 204). Trickling beneath the surface of this innocuous definition of *discipline,* however, is another way in which I use the word: the Foucaudian definition that conjoins *discipline* with *punishment:* Discipline does not blend people into a mass; it differentiates them so that they may be controlled and manipulated. "Discipline 'makes' individuals; it is the specific technique of a power that regards individuals both as objects and as instruments of its exercise" (Foucault, 1979, p. 170). The two definitions are not fully separable.

[2] I use the phrase "one's own" in full awareness of its irony.

Afterword

One is never installed within transgression, one never lives elsewhere. Transgression implies that the limit is always at work.

Ernst Behler (1991)

C ontemporary theorists—including me—take a great deal of satisfaction in declaring, with certainty, that writing is by nature collaborative—a position associated with, though by no means identical to, the mimetic culture of authorship that prevailed in the Middle Ages. Even as I make such declarations, I recognize that I am expressing values consonant with my culture. With the writing of this book, I have not "established" the always-true, foundational, enduring definition of authorship; rather, I have articulated a theory of authorship that has, in various manifestations, contributed to Western letters since the Classical period.

The competing theories have always been there, and presumably they always will. I believe that they are actually necessary. Even though I am committed to collaborative authorship, I believe that the figure of the solitary author makes a significant contribution to our understanding of writing. However, the figure of the solitary author cannot and should not be sustained as the organizing principle of composition's representations of authorship.

References

Aarsleff, H. (1982). *From Locke to Saussure: Essays on the study of language and intellectual history*. Minneapolis, MN: University of Minnesota Press.

Abrams, M. H. (1958). *The mirror and the lamp: Romantic theory and critical tradition*. New York: Norton.

Acoff-Rose Music, Inc. v. Campbell, F.2d 972 (1992).

Adams, H. (1973). *The education of Henry Adams* (E. Samuels, Ed.). Boston: Houghton Mifflin. (Original work published 1918)

Allen, C. (1994). Their cheating hearts. *Lingua Franca*, 61–65.

Anson, C. M., & Schwegler, R. A. (1996). *The Longman handbook for writers and readers*. New York: Longman.

Appell, G. N. (1988). Introduction. In G. N. Appell & T. Maden (Eds.), *Choice and morality in anthropological perspective* (pp. 31–40). Albany, NY: State University of New York Press.

Atlas, J. (1991, July 28). When an original idea sounds really familiar. *New York Times*, p. 2.

Atwood, J. W. (1992). Collaborative writing: The "other" game in town. *The Writing Instructor, 12*, 13–26.

Bakhtin, M. M. (1981). *The dialogic imagination* (M. Holquist & C. Emerson, Eds. & Trans.). Austin, TX: University of Texas Press.

Baron, D. (1994). *Guide to home language repair*. Urbana, IL: National Council of Teachers of English.

Barthes, R. (1977). The death of the author. In S. Heath (Trans.), *Image, music, text*. New York: Hill and Wang.

Basic Books, Inc. v. Kinko's Graphics Corp. 758 F. Supp. 1522–1547 (1991).

Bauer, D. M. (1998). Indecent proposals: Teachers in the movies. *College English, 60*, 301–317.

Behler, E. (1991). *Confrontations: Derrida/Heidegger/Nietzsche* (S. Taubeneck, Trans.). Stanford, CA: Stanford University Press.

Bender, H. (1994, September). Letter. *The Council Chronicle*, p. 11.

Bergmann, L.S. (1994, June). Letter. *The Council Chronicle*, p. 15.

Bercovitch, S. (1974). The American Puritan imagination: An introduction. In S. Bercovitch (Ed.), *The American Puritan imagination: Essays in revaluation* (pp. 1–18). New York: Cambridge University Press.

Berlin, J. A. (1984). *Writing instruction in nineteenth-century American colleges*. Carbondale, IL: Southern Illinois University Press.

Berlin, J. A. (1987). *Rhetoric and reality: Writing instruction in American colleges, 1900–1985*. Carbondale, IL: Southern Illinois University Press.

Berlin, J. A. (1996). *Rhetorics, poetics, and cultures: Refiguring college English studies*. Urbana, IL: National Council of Teachers of English.

Bizzell, P. (1982). Cognition, convention, and certainty: What we need to know about writing. *Pre/Text*, 3, 213–244.

Blackstone, W. (1979). *Commentaries on the laws of England* (Vols. 1-4). Chicago: University of Chicago Press. (Original work published 1765–1769)

Bleich, D. (1988). *The double perspective: Language, literacy, and social relations*. New York: Oxford University Press.

Bloom, A. (1990). *Giants and dwarfs: Essays 1960–1990*. New York: Simon & Schuster.

Bloom, H. (1973). *The anxiety of influence: A theory of poetry*. New York: Oxford University Press.

Bolter, J. D. (1990). *Writing space: The computer, hypertext, and the history of writing*. Hillsdale, NJ: Lawrence Erlbaum.

Bourdieu, P. (1986). The forms of capital. In J. G. Richardson (Ed.) & R. Nice (Trans.), *Handbook of theory and research for the sociology of education* (pp. 241–260). New York: Greenwood Press. (Reprinted from *Soziale Ungleichheiten*, pp. 183–198, by R. Kreckel, Ed., 1983, Goettingen, Germany: Otto Schartz)

Bourdieu, P., & Passeron, J.-C. (1990). *Reproduction in education, society and culture*. Newbury Park, CA: Sage. (Original work published 1977)

Bradford, R. (1997). *Stylistics*. New York: Routledge.

Branch, W. (1994, September). Letter. *The Council Chronicle*, p. 10.

Brereton, J. C. (Ed.). (1995). *The origins of composition studies in the American college, 1875–1925: A documentary history*. Pittsburgh, PA: University of Pittsburgh Press.

Brodkey, L. (1987). Modernism and the scene(s) of writing. *College English*, 49, 396–418.

Brody, M. (1993). *Manly writing: Gender, rhetoric, and the rise of composition*. Carbondale, IL: Southern Illinois University Press.

Brooke, R., Levin, J., & Ritchie, J. (1994). Teaching composition and reading Lacan: An exploration in wild analysis. In J. Clifford & J. Schilb (Eds.), *Writing theory and critical theory* (pp. 159–178). New York: Modern Language Association.

Brooks, G. H. (1989). Exploring plagiarism in the composition classroom. *Freshman English News*, 17, 31–35.

Bruffee, K. A. (1984). Collaborative learning and the "conversation of mankind." *College English*, 46, 635–652.

Burckhardt, J. (1945). *The civilization of the Renaissance in Italy* (S. G. C. Middlemore, Trans.; 2nd ed.). New York: Oxford University Press.

Burke, K. (1941). The rhetoric of Hitler's "battle." In *The philosophy of literary form: Studies in symbolic action* (pp. 191–220). Baton Rouge, LA: Louisiana State University Press.

Burke, S. (1992). *The death and return of the author: Criticism and subjectivity in Barthes, Foucault and Derrida.* Edinburgh, Scotland: Edinburgh University Press.

Burke, S. (Ed.). (1995). *Authorship: From Plato to the postmodern.* Edinburgh, Scotland: Edinburgh University Press.

Butler, J. (1990). *Gender trouble: Feminism and the subversion of identity.* New York: Routledge.

Butler, M. (Ed.). (1974). *Students' right to their own language.* Urbana, IL: National Council of Teachers of English.

Campbell, C. (1987). *Writing with others' words: Native and non-native university students' use of information from a background reading text in academic compositions.* Washington, DC: Office of Educational Research and Improvement (ED). (ERIC Document Reproduction Service No. ED 287 315)

Carey, J. (1992). *The intellectuals and the masses: Pride and prejudice among the literary intelligentsia, 1880–1939.* New York: St. Martin's Press.

Caucus on Intellectual Property of the Conference on College Composition and Communication [Online]. (1996). Available: http://tempest.english.purdue.edu/cccc-ip/welcome.html

Chalmers, A. (1990). *Science and its fabrication.* Minneapolis, MN: University of Minnesota Press.

Chaney, J., & Duncan, T. (1985). Editors, teachers disagree about definition of plagiarism. *The Journalism Educator, 40*(2), 13–16.

Charney, D. H., & Carlson, R. A. (1995). Learning to write in a genre: What student writers take from model texts. *Research in the Teaching of English, 29,* 88–125.

Chartier, R. (1994). Figures of the author. In B. Sherman & A. Strowell (Eds.), *Of authors and origins: Essays on copyright law* (pp. 7–22). New York: Oxford University Press.

Cicero. (1968). *On invention* (H. M. Hubbell, Trans.). Cambridge, MA: Harvard University Press.

Cixous, H. (1991). Coming to writing. In D. Jenson (Ed.) & S. Cornell (Trans.), *Coming to writing and other essays* (pp. 1–59). Cambridge, MA: Harvard University Press.

Clark, I. L. (1988). Collaboration and ethics in writing center pedagogy. *Writing Center Journal, 9*(1), 3–12.

Clark, I. L. (1993). Portfolio evaluation, collaboration, and writing centers. *College Composition and Communication, 44,* 515–524.

Clark, S. (1994). Rhetoric, social construction, and gender: Is it bad to be sentimental? In J. Clifford & J. Schilb (Eds.), *Writing theory and critical theory* (pp. 96–108). New York: Modern Language Association.

Clark, S., & Ede, L. (1990). Collaboration, resistance, and the teaching of writing. In A. A. Lunsford, H. Moglen, & J. Slevin (Eds.), *The right to literacy* (pp. 276–285). New York: Modern Language Association.

Cohen, H. F. (1994). *The scientific revolution*. Chicago: University of Chicago Press.

Condon, W., & Hamp-Lyons, L. (1991). Introducing a portfolio-based writing assessment. In P. Belanoff & M. Dickson (Eds.), *Portfolios: Process and product* (pp. 231–247). Portsmouth, NH: Boynton/Cook.

Connors, R. J. (1991). Writing the history of our discipline. In E. Lindemann (Ed.), *An introduction to composition studies* (pp. 49–71). New York: Oxford University Press.

Constable, G. (1983). Forgery and plagiarism in the Middle Ages. *Archiv für Diplomatik, Schriftgeschichte, Siegel-und Wappenkunde, 29*, 1–41.

Cooper, M. M. (1989). Why are we talking about discourse communities? Or, foundationalism rears its ugly head once more. In M. M. Cooper & M. Holzman (Eds.), *Writing as social action* (pp. 202–220). Portsmouth, NH: Boynton/Cook.

Corbett, E. P. J. (1971). The theory and practice of imitation in classical rhetoric. *College Composition and Communication, 22*, 243–250.

Corngold, S., & Giersing, I. (1991). *Borrowed lives*. Albany, NY: State University of New York Press.

Critical Art Ensemble. (1996). Utopian plagiarism, hypertextuality, and electronic cultural production. In V. J. Vitanza (Ed.), *Cyberreader* (pp. 320–330). Boston: Allyn and Bacon.

Crowley, S. (1984). Neo-Romanticism and the history of rhetoric. *Pre/Text, 5*, 19–38.

Crowley, S. (1990). *The methodical memory: Invention in current-traditional rhetoric*. Carbondale, IL: Southern Illinois University Press.

Crowley, S. (1994). *Ancient rhetorics for contemporary students*. New York: MacMillan.

D'Angelo, F. J. (1979). The art of paraphrase. *College Composition and Communication, 30*, 255–259.

Dant, D. R. (1986). Plagiarism in high school: A survey. *English Journal, 75*, 81–84.

Davidson, R. L. (1973). *Genesis 1-11*. Cambridge, MA: Cambridge University Press.

Dean, T. (1994). Bodies that mutter: Rhetoric and sexuality. *Pre/Text, 15*, 80–117.

Descartes, R. (1965). *Discourse on method, optics, geometry, and meteorology* (P. J. Olscamp, Trans.). Indianapolis, IN: Bobbs-Merrill. (Original work published 1637)

DiBacco, D. (1994). *Untitled*. Unpublished manuscript, Colgate University, Hamilton, NY.

Dillon, G. L. (1988). My words of an other. *College English, 50*, 63–73.

Dock, J. B. (1996). *The press of ideas: Readings for writers on print culture and the Information Age*. Boston: Bedford Books.

Drum, A. (1986). Responding to plagiarism. *College Composition and Communication, 37*, 241–243.

Dunkle, A. (1994). *Untitled*. Unpublished manuscript, Colgate University, Hamilton, NY.

Ebert, T. L. (1991). The "difference" of postmodern feminism. *College English, 53*, 886–904.

Ede, L., & Lunsford, A. A. (1983). Why write...together? *Rhetoric Review, 1*, 150–157.

Edelman, M. (1988). *Constructing the political spectacle*. Chicago: University of Chicago Press.

Eisenstein, E. (1979). *The printing press as an agent of change* (Vols. 1-2). Cambridge, MA: Cambridge University Press.

Elbow, P. (1983). Embracing contraries in the teaching process. *College English, 45,* 327–339.

Elbow, P. (1986). *Embracing contraries: Explorations in learning and teaching*. New York: Oxford University Press.

Eliot, T. S. (1932). Philip Massinger. In *Essays on Elizabethan drama* (pp. 141–161). New York: Harcourt, Brace, & World.

Emerson, R. W. (1950a). *Nature*. In B. Atkinson (Ed.), *Selected writings of Emerson* (pp. 3–44). New York: Modern Library.

Emerson, R. W. (1950b). Self-reliance. In B. Atkinson (Ed.), *Selected writings of Emerson* (pp. 145–169). New York: Modern Library.

Engels, F. (1986). *The origin of the family, private property and the State*. New York: Penguin. (Original work published 1884)

Enos, R. L. (1993). *Greek rhetoric before Aristotle*. Prospect Heights, IL: Waveland Press.

Fahnestock, J., & Secor, M. (1990). *A rhetoric of argument* (2nd ed.). New York: McGraw-Hill.

Farrell, T. J. (1983). IQ and standard English. *College Composition and Communication, 34,* 470–484.

Faigley, L. (1992). *Fragments of rationality: Postmodernity and the subject of composition*. Pittsburgh, PA: University of Pittsburgh Press.

Fass, R. A. (1986). By honor bound: Encouraging academic honesty. *Educational Record, 67,* 32–36.

Fishbein, L. (1993, December 1). Curbing cheating and restoring academic integrity. *Chronicle of Higher Education*, p. A52.

Fisher, W. R. (1992). Narration, reason, and community. In R. H. Brown (Ed.), *Writing the social text: Poetics and politics in social science discourse* (pp. 199–218). New York: Aldine de Gruyter.

Flanagan, A. (1994, February). Experts agree plagiarism hard to define, hard to stop. *The Council Chronicle*, p. 6.

Flannery, K. T. (1991). Composing and the question of agency. *College English, 53,* 701–713.

Flower, L. (1979). Writer-based prose: A cognitive basis for problems in writing. *College English, 41,* 19–37.

Flower, L. (1996). Negotiating the meaning of difference. *Written Communication, 13,* 44–92.

Flower, L., & Hayes, J. R. (1981). A cognitive process theory of writing. *College Composition and Communication, 32,* 365–387.

Foucault, M. (1973). *The order of things: An archaeology of the human sciences*. New York: Vintage Books.

Foucault, M. (1977a). Nietzsche, genealogy, history. In D. F. Bouchard (Ed.) & D.F. Bouchard & S. Simon (Trans.), *Language, counter-memory, practice: Selected essays and interviews* (pp. 139–164). Ithaca, NY: Cornell University Press. (Reprinted from *Hommage à Jean Hyppolite*, pp. 145–172, by M. Foucault, 1971, Paris: Presses Universitaires de France)

Foucault, M. (1977b). What is an author? In D. F. Bouchard (Ed.) & D. F. Bouchard & S. Simon (Trans.), *Language, counter-memory, practice: Selected essays and interviews* (pp. 113–138). Ithaca, NY: Cornell University Press.

Foucault, M. (1979). *Discipline and punish: The birth of the prison* (A. Sheridan, Trans.). New York: Vintage Books.

Freire, P. (1968). *Pedagogy of the oppressed* (M. B. Ramos, Trans.). New York: Seabury.

Freud, S. (1963). *Dora: An analysis of a case of hysteria*. New York: Collier.

Fruman, N. (1971). *Coleridge: The damaged archangel*. New York: Braziller.

Galles, G. M. (1987, October 28). Professors are woefully ignorant of a well-organized market inimical to learning: The big business in research papers. *Chronicle of Higher Education*, pp. B1, B3.

Garis, L. (1990, October 7). Through West Indian eyes. *New York Times Magazine*, 78.

Garrow, D. J. (1991). King's plagiarism: Imitation, insecurity, and transformation. *Journal of American History, 78*, 86–92.

Gates, H. L., Jr. (1986). Writing "race" and the difference it makes. In H. L. Gates, Jr. (Ed.), *Race, writing, and difference* (pp. 1–20). Chicago: University of Chicago Press.

Gay, P. (1966). *The Enlightenment: An interpretation*. New York: Vintage Books.

Geertz, C. (1983). *Local knowledge*. New York: Basic Books.

Geosits, M. S., & Kirk, W. R. (1983). Sowing the seeds of plagiarism. *Principal, 62*, 35–38.

Gere, A. R. (1987). *Writing groups: History, theory, and implications*. Carbondale, IL: Southern Illinois University Press.

Gere, A. R. (1993). Introduction. In A. R. Gere (Ed.), *Into the field: Sites of composition studies* (pp. 1–8). New York: Modern Language Association.

Gere, A. R. (1994). Common properties of pleasure: Texts in nineteenth century women's clubs. In M. Woodmansee & P. Jaszi (Eds.), *The construction of authorship: Textual appropriation in law and literature* (pp. 383–400). Durham, NC: Duke University Press.

Gilbert, S. M., & Gubar, S. (1986). Tradition and the female talent. In N. K. Miller (Ed.), *The poetics of gender* (pp. 183–207). New York: Columbia University Press.

Gilbert, S. M., & Gubar, S. (1991). Infection in the sentence: The woman writer and the anxiety of authorship. In R. R. Warhol & D. P. Herndl (Eds.), *Feminisms: An anthology of literary theory and criticism* (pp. 289–300). New Brunswick, NJ: Rutgers University Press. (Reprinted from *The madwoman in the attic: The woman writer and the nineteenth-century literary imagination*, 1979, New Haven, CT: Yale University Press)

Gilmore, M. T. (1985). *American Romanticism and the marketplace*. Chicago: University of Chicago Press.

Giroux, H. A. (1991). Modernism, postmodernism, and feminism: Rethinking the boundaries of educational discourse. In H. A. Giroux (Ed.), *Postmodernism, feminism, and cultural politics: Redrawing educational boundaries* (pp. 1–59). Albany, NY: State University of New York Press.

The Glatt Plagiarism Teaching Program [Computer software]. (1988). Sacramento, CA: Glatt Plagiarism Services.

Gray, A. (1981). *Lanark*. New York: Harper & Row.

Gray, P. (1993, April 26). The Purloined Letters. *Time*, 59–60.

Gray, W. L. (1994, June). Letter. *The Council Chronicle*, p. 14.

Greene, S. (1995). Making sense of my own ideas: The problems of authorship in a beginning writing classroom. *Written Communication, 12,* 186–218.

Greene, T. (1982). *The light in Troy: Imitation and discovery in Renaissance poetry.* New Haven, CT: Yale University Press.

Gribbin, W. G. (1994, June). Letter. *The Council Chronicle*, pp. 14–15.

Gumperz, J. J., & Cook-Gumperz, J. (1981). Ethnic differences in communicative style. In C. Ferguson & S. B. Heath (Eds.), *Language in the USA* (pp. 430–445). New York: Cambridge University Press.

Hacker, D. (1998). *The Bedford handbook* (5th ed.). Boston: Bedford Books.

Hairston, M. (1982). The winds of change: Thomas Kuhn and the revolution in the teaching of writing. *College Composition and Communication, 33,* 76–88.

Hammersley, M., & Atkinson, P. (1983). *Ethnography: Principles in practice.* New York: Tavistock.

Harkin, P. (1989). Bringing lore to light. *Pre/Text, 10,* 55–67.

Harris, J. (1989). The idea of community in the study of writing. *College Composition and Communication, 40,* 11–22.

Harris, J. (1990). *Expressive discourse.* Dallas, TX: Southern Methodist University Press.

Havelock, E. (1995). The coming of literate communication to Western culture. In W. A. Covino & D. A. Jolliffe (Eds.), *Rhetoric: Concepts, definitions, boundaries* (pp. 690–698). Boston: Allyn and Bacon.

Hawley, C. S. (1984). The thieves of academe: Plagiarism in the university system. *Improving College and University Teaching, 32,* 35–39.

Haynes-Burton, C. (1995). Intellectual (proper)ty in writing centers: Retro texts and positive plagiarism. In B. L. Stay, C. Murphy, & E. H. Hobson (Eds.), *Writing center perspectives* (pp. 84–93). Emmitsburg, MD: National Writing Center Association Press.

Hecht, M. L., Collier, M. J., & Ribeau, S. A. (1993). *African American communication: Ethnic identity and cultural interpretation.* Newbury Park, CA: Sage.

Herrington, A. J. (1992). Composing one's self in a discipline: Students' and teachers' negotiations. In M. Secor & D. Charney (Eds.), *Constructing rhetorical education* (pp. 91–115). Carbondale, IL: Southern Illinois University Press.

Hertz, N. (1982). Two extravagant teachings. *Yale French Studies, 63,* 59–71.

Hesiod. (1993). *Works and days* and *Theogony* (S. Lombardo, Trans.). Indianapolis, IN: Hackett.

Hilts, P. J. (1993, March 29). When does duplication of words become theft? *New York Times*, p. A10.

Hobbes, T. (1988). *Leviathan.* Buffalo, NY: Prometheus Books.

Holland, P. (1993). Authorship and collaboration: The problem of editing Shakespeare. In W. Chernaik, C. Davis, & M. Deegan (Eds.), *The politics of the electronic text* (pp. 17–24). Oxford, England: Office for Humanities Communication.

Homer. (1967). *The odyssey* (R. Lattimore, Trans.). New York: HarperCollins.

Houston, J. P. (1983). Kohlberg-type moral instruction and cheating behavior. *College Student Journal, 172*, 196–204.

Horner, B. (1997). Students, authorship, and the work of composition. *College English, 59*, 505–529.

Howard, R. M. (1993). A plagiarism *pentimento. Journal of Teaching Writing, 11*, 233–246.

Howard, R. M. (1995a). Cryoauthorship: The mummy walks! *Pre/Text, 16*, 38–53.

Howard, R. M. (1995b). Plagiarisms, authorships, and the academic death penalty. *College English, 57*, 708–736.

Howard, R. M., & Jamieson, S. (1995). *The Bedford guide to yeaching writing in the disciplines.* Boston: Bedford Books.

Howells, W. D. (1879). *The lady of the Aroostook.* Boston: Houghton, Osgood.

Howells, W. D. (1968). The psychology of plagiarism. In *Literature and life* (pp. 273–227). Port Washington, NY: Kennikat Press. (Original work published 1902)

Hull, G., & Rose, M. (1989). Rethinking remediation: Toward a social-cognitive understanding of problematic reading and writing. *Written Communication, 6*, 139–154.

Humphries, J. (1987). The origin of the family: Born out of scarcity not wealth. In J. Sayers, M. Evans, & N. Redclift (Eds.), *Engels revisited: New feminist essays* (pp. 11–36). New York: Tavistock.

Hutcheon, L. (1986). Literary borrowing...and stealing: Plagiarism, sources, influences, and intertexts. *English Studies in Canada, 12*, 229–239.

(In)Citers$_1$. (1998). The citation functions: Literary production and reception. *Kairos* [Online], *3*. Available: http://english.ttu.edu/kairos/3.1

Ison, D. L. (1994, September). Letter. *The Council Chronicle*, pp. 10–11.

Jamieson, K. H. (1988). *Eloquence in an electronic age: The transformation of political speechmaking.* New York: Oxford University Press.

Jaszi, P., & Woodmansee, M. (1994). Introduction. In M. Woodmansee & P. Jaszi (Eds.), *The construction of authorship: Textual appropriation in law and literature* (pp. 1–13). Durham, NC: Duke University Press.

Jaszi, P., & Woodmansee, M. (1996). The ethical reaches of authorship. *South Atlantic Quarterly, 95*, 947–977.

Jauss, H. R. (1979). The alterity and modernity of medieval literature. *New Literary History, 10*, 181–229.

Johnston, D. K. (1991). Cheating: Reflections on a moral dilemma. *Journal of Moral Education, 20*, 283–291.

Jones, D. C. (1996). Beyond the postmodern impasse of agency: The resounding relevance of John Dewey's tacit tradition. *JAC: A Journal of Composition Theory, 16*, 81–102.

Joseph, G. (1994). Charles Dickens, international copyright, and the discretionary silence of *Martin Chuzzlewit.* In M. Woodmansee & P. Jaszi (Eds.), *The construction of authorship: Textual appropriation in law and literature* (pp. 259–270). Durham, NC: Duke University Press.

Kantz, M. (1990). Helping students use textual sources persuasively. *College English, 52*, 74–91.

Kaufman, W. (1995). Nietzsche's attitude toward Socrates. In P. Sedgwick (Ed.), *Nietzsche: A critical reader* (pp. 123–143). Cambridge, MA: Basil Blackwell. (Reprinted from *Nietzsche: Philosopher, psychologist, antichrist*, 4th ed., pp. 391–411, by W. Kaufman, 1974, Princeton, NJ: Princeton University Press)

Kehley, T. (1994, May 5). *Untitled*. Unpublished manuscript, Colgate University, Hamilton, NY.

Kennedy, G. A. (1980). *Classical rhetoric and its Christian and secular tradition from ancient to modern times*. Chapel Hill, NC: University of North Carolina Press.

Knoblauch, C. H., & Brannon, L. (1983). Writing as learning through the curriculum. *College English, 45*, 465–474.

Kolich, A. M. (1983). Plagiarism: The worm of reason. *College English, 45*, 141–148.

Kopff, E. C. (1993, September). Mimesis and perjury. *Chronicles*, 19–20.

Kroll, B. M. (1988). How college freshmen view plagiarism. *Written Communication, 5*, 203–221.

Lanham, R. (1994). *The electronic word: Democracy, technology, and the arts*. Chicago: University of Chicago Press.

LeFevre, K. B. (1987). *Invention as a social act*. Carbondale, IL: Southern Illinois University Press.

Leggett, G., Mead, C. D., & Kramer, M. G. (1991). *Prentice Hall handbook for writers* (11th ed.). Englewood Cliffs, NJ: Prentice Hall.

Levy, D. (1994, March 30). Two scientific watchdogs are leashed. *USA Today*, p. 5D.

Lewis, D. L. (1991). Failing to know Martin Luther King, Jr. *Journal of American History, 78*, 81–85.

Lindey, A. (1952). *Plagiarism and originality*. New York: Harper.

Locke, J. (1960). *Two treatises of government* (P. Laslett, Ed.). Cambridge, England: Cambridge University Press.

Locke, J. (1979). *Essay concerning human understanding* (P. H. Nidditch, Ed.). Oxford, England: Clarendon.

Loveless, E. M. (1994, September). Letter. *The Council Chronicle*, p. 10.

Lunsford, A. A., & Connors, R. (1992). *The St. Martin's handbook* (2nd ed.). New York: St. Martin's Press.

Lunsford, A. A., & Ede, L. (1990). *Singular texts/Plural authors: Perspectives on collaborative writing*. Carbondale, IL: Southern Illinois University Press.

Lunsford, A. A., & Ede, L. (1994). Collaborative authorship and the teaching of writing. In M. Woodmansee & P. Jaszi (Eds.), *The construction of authorship: Textual appropriation in law and literature* (pp. 417–438). Durham, NC: Duke University Press.

Lunsford, A. A., & West, S. (1996). Intellectual property and composition studies. *College Composition and Communication, 47*, 383–411.

Magner, D. K. (1993, April 14). Historian who was accused of plagiarism faces new complaint. *Chronicle of Higher Education*, pp. A19–A20.

Magner, D. K. (1994, January 5). Verdict in a plagiarism case. *Chronicle of Higher Education*, pp. A17, A20.

Mallon, T. (1989). *Stolen words: Forays into the origins and ravages of plagiarism*. New York: Ticknor and Fields.

Markson, J. (1994, May 5). *Untitled*. Unpublished manuscript, Colgate University, Hamilton, NY.

Matalene, C. (1985). Contrastive rhetoric: An American writing teacher in China. *College English, 47*, 789–808.

McCormick, F. J. (1989). The *plagiario* and the professor in our peculiar institution. *Journal of Teaching Writing, 8*, 133–145.

McCormick, F. J. (1994, April). Quizzing the suspected plagiarist. *Composition Chronicle*, 4–6.

McCracken, E. (1991). Metaplagiarism and the critic's role as detective: Ricardo Piglia's reinvention of Roberto Arlt. *PMLA, 106*, 1071–1082.

McFarland, T. (1985). *Originality and imagination*. Baltimore: Johns Hopkins University Press.

McGann, J. (1998, March 6). *The dawn of the dead: Dante Gabriel Rossetti at the end of the twentieth century*. Paper presented at the conference The Sociomaterial Turn: Excavating Modernism, University of Tulsa, OK.

McLeod, S. H. (1992). Responding to plagiarism: The role of the WPA. *WPA: Writing Program Administration, 15*, 7–16.

Meltzer, F. (1994). *Hot property: The stakes and claims of literary originality*. Chicago: University of Chicago Press.

Merton, R. K. (1965). *On the shoulders of giants: A Shandean postscript*. New York: Free Press.

Metz, R. (1994, February 1). *Untitled*. Unpublished manuscript, Colgate University, Hamilton, NY.

Miller, K. D. (1990). Composing Martin Luther King, Jr. *PMLA, 105*, 70–82.

Miller, K. D. (1992). *Voice of deliverance: The language of Martin Luther King, Jr. and its sources*. New York: Free Press.

Miller, K. D. (1993, January 20). Redefining plagiarism: Martin Luther King's use of an oral tradition. *Chronicle of Higher Education*, p. A60.

Miller, S. (1989). *Rescuing the subject: A critical introduction to rhetoric and the writer*. Carbondale, IL: Southern Illinois University Press.

Miller, S. (1991). *Textual carnivals: The politics of composition*. Carbondale, IL: Southern Illinois University Press.

Minnis, A. J. (1987). *Medieval theory of authorship: Scholastic literary attitudes in the later Middle Ages* (2nd ed.). Philadelphia: University of Pennsylvania Press.

Minock, M. (1995). Toward a postmodern pedagogy of imitation. *JAC: A Journal of Composition Theory, 15*, 489–510.

Mooney, C. J. (1992a, February 12). Critics question higher education's commitment and effectiveness in dealing with plagiarism. *Chronicle of Higher Education*, pp. A13, A16.

Murphy, R. (1990). Anorexia: The cheating disorder. *College English, 52*, 898–903.

Murray, H. (1991). Close reading, closed writing. *College English, 53*, 195–208.

Navrozov, A. (1993, October 2). The age of plagiarism. *The New York Times Magazine*, 40.

Nietzsche, F. (1967a). *On the genealogy of morals* (W. Kaufmann & R. J. Hollingdale, Trans.). New York: Vintage Books. (Original work published 1887)

Nietzsche, F. (1967b). *The will to power* (W. Kaufmann & R. J. Hollingdale, Trans.). New York: Random House.

Nuss, E. M. (1984). Academic integrity: Comparing faculty and student attitudes. *Improving College and University Teaching, 32,* 140–143.

O, K. (1994, May 5). *Untitled.* Unpublished manuscript, Colgate University, Hamilton, NY.

Ohmann, R. (1976). *English in America: A radical view of the profession.* New York: Oxford University Press.

O'Neill, M. T. (1980). Plagiarism: Writing responsibly. *The ABCA Bulletin, 43,* 34–36.

Palmer, B. (1994, September). Letter. *The Council Chronicle,* p. 11.

Pappas, T. (1993, September). Truth or consequences: Redefining plagiarism. *Chronicles,* 41–42.

Pemberton, M. (1992). Threshold of desperation: Winning the fight against term paper mills. *The Writing Instructor,* 11, 143–152.

Perl, S., & Egendorf, A. (1986). The process of creative discovery: Theory, research, and implications for teaching. In D. McQuade (Ed.), *The territory of language: Linguistics, stylistics, and the teaching of composition* (pp. 251–268). Carbondale, IL: Southern Illinois University Press.

Peterson, L. (1986). *Teaching academic integrity: A cognitive developmental model based on Kohlberg's theory of moral development.* (ERIC Document Reproduction Service No. ED 270 052)

Peterson, L. (1997, November 10). *Margaret Oliphant's* Autobiography *as professional artist's life.* Paper presented at the Lorraine Sherley Graduate Lecture Series, Texas Christian University, Fort Worth.

Peto, P. (1994, May 5). *Untitled.* Unpublished manuscript, Colgate University, Hamilton, NY.

Pfau, T. (1994). The pragmatics of genre: Moral theory and lyric authorship in Hegel and Wordsworth. In M. Woodmansee & P. Jaszi (Eds.), *The construction of authorship: Textual appropriation in law and literature* (pp. 133–158). Durham, NC: Duke University Press.

Phillips, P. (1984). *The adventurous muse: Theories of originality in English poetics, 1650–1760.* Uppsala, Sweden: Studia Anglistica Upsaliensia.

Plagiarism is rampant, a survey finds. (1990, April 1). *New York Times,* pp. 36–37.

Plato. (1916). *Republic.* In E. Hamilton & H. Cairns (Eds.), *The collected dialogues of Plato.* Princeton, NJ: Princeton University Press.

Plato. (1981). *Phaedo.* In G. M. A. Grube (Trans.), *Five dialogues of Plato* (pp. 93–155). Indianapolis, IN: Hackett.

Plato. (1990). *Phaedrus.* In P. Bizzell & B. Herzberg (Eds.), *The rhetorical tradition: Readings from classical times to the present* (pp. 113–143). Boston: Bedford Books. (Reprinted from *Gorgias,* H. N. Fowler, Trans., 1914, Loeb Classical Library)

Plato. (1994). *Crito.* In N. M. Bradbury & A. Quinn, *Audiences and intentions: A book of arguments* (2nd ed.; pp. 327–337). New York: MacMillan. (Reprinted from *The Last Days of Socrates,* 2nd Rev. ed., H. Tredennick, Trans., 1969, New York: Penguin)

Plato. (1995). *Ion.* In S. Burke (Ed.), *Authorship: From Plato to the postmodern* (pp. 13–16). Edinburgh, Scotland: Edinburgh University Press.

Pope, A. (1962). *Essay on criticism.* St. Louis, MO: Washington University Press. (Original work published 1709

Porter, J. E. (1986). Intertextuality and the discourse community. *Rhetoric Review, 5,* 34–47.

Porter, J. E. (1993). Selected bibliography: The concept of "author" in rhetoric/composition and literary theory. *Rhetoric Society Quarterly, 23,* 71–75.

Porter, J. E. (1996). Author. In T. Enos (Ed.), *Encyclopedia of rhetoric and composition: Communication from ancient times to the Information Age* (pp. 54–56). New York: Garland.

Pound, E. (1935). How to read. In T. S. Eliot (Ed.), *Literary essays of Ezra Pound* (pp. 19–31). New York: New Directions.

Pratt, M. L. (1991). Arts of the contact zone. *Profession,* 33–40.

Quintilian. (1987). *Institutio Oratoria.* In J. J. Murphy (Ed.), *Quintilian on the teaching of speaking and writing: Translations from Books One, Two, and Ten of the* Institutio Oratoria. Carbondale, IL: Southern Illinois University Press.

Randall, M. (1991). Appropriate(d) discourse: Plagiarism and decolonization. *New Literary History, 22,* 525–541.

Randall, M. (1994, December 28). Plagiarism and postmodern appropriation. Paper presented at the annual meeting of the Modern Language Association, San Diego, CA.

Rankin, E. (1994). *Seeing yourself as a teacher: Conversations with five new teachers in a university writing program.* Urbana, IL: National Council of Teachers of English.

Raymond, C. (1990, November 21). Discovery of early plagiarism by Martin Luther King raises troubling questions for scholars and admirers. *Chronicle of Higher Education,* pp. A1, A8.

Raymond, C. (1991, July 10). Allegations of plagiarism alter historians' views of civil-rights leader. *Chronicle of Higher Education,* pp. A5, A9.

Rose, M. (1993). *Authors and owners: The invention of copyright.* Cambridge, MA: Harvard University Press.

Rowe, G. E. (1988). *Distinguishing Jonson: Imitation, rivalry, and the direction of a dramatic career.* Lincoln, NE: University of Nebraska Press.

Russell, D. R. (1988). Romantics on writing: Liberal culture and the abolition of composition courses. *Rhetoric Review, 6,* 132–148.

Russell, D. R. (1993). Vygotsky, Dewey, and externalism: Beyond the student/discipline dichotomy. *Journal of Advanced Composition, 13,* 173–198.

Saalbach, R. P. (1970). Critical thinking and the problem of plagiarism. *College Composition and Communication, 21,* 45–47.

Sauer, R. (1983). Coping with copiers. *English Journal, 72,* 50–52.

Schab, F. (1980). Cheating among college and non-college bound pupils, 1969–1979. *The Clearing House, 53,* 379–380.

Schilb, J. (1988). Ideology and composition scholarship. *Journal of Advanced Composition, 8,* 22–29.

Schilb, J. (1992). The sociological imagination and the ethics of collaboration. In J. Forman (Ed.), *New visions of collaborative writing* (pp. 105–119). Portsmouth, NH: Boynton/Cook.

Schroeder, P. (1996). A comment on "The Law of Texts: Copyright in the Academy" and "Plagiarisms, Authorships, and the Academic Death Penalty." *College English, 58*, 853–855.

Shaw, P. (1982). Plagiary. *The American Scholar, 51*, 325–337.

Shea, J. (1987). When borrowing becomes burglary. *Currents, 13*, 38–42.

Shen, F. (1989). The classroom and the wider culture: Identity as a key to learning English composition. *College Composition and Communication, 40*, 459–466.

Sidney, P. (1995). An apology for poetry. In S. Burke, Ed., *Authorship: From Plato to the postmodern* (pp. 31–36). Edinburgh, Scotland: Edinburgh University Press.

Simpson-Esper, M. K. (1988). Monitoring individual progress in revision groups. In J. Golub (Ed.), *Focus on collaborative learning: Classroom practices in teaching English, 1988* (pp. 93–98). Urbana, IL: National Council of Teachers of English.

Skom, E. (1986, October). Plagiarism: Quite a rather bad little crime. *AAHE Bulletin*, 3–7.

Smit, D. W. (1990). Evaluating a portfolio system. *WPA: Writing Program Administration, 14*, 51–62.

Smith, H. N. (1974). The scribbling women and the cosmic success story. *Critical Inquiry, 1*, 47–70.

Sosnoski, J. J. (1991). A mindless man-driven theory machine: Intellectuality, sexuality, and the institution of criticism. In R. R. Warhol & D. P. Herndl (Eds.), *Feminisms: An anthology of literary theory and criticism* (pp. 40–57). New Brunswick, NJ: Rutgers University Press.

Spanos, W. (1993). *The end of education: Toward posthumanism.* Minneapolis, MN: University of Minnesota Press.

Stallybrass, P., & White, A. (1986). *The politics and poetics of transgression.* Ithaca, NY: Cornell University Press.

Stanley, W. B. (1992). *Curriculum for utopia: Social reconstructionism and critical pedagogy in the postmodern era.* Albany, NY: State University of New York Press.

Steinberg, E. R. (1995). Imaginative literature in composition classrooms? *College English, 57*, 266–280.

Stevens, M. J. (1994, May 5). *Untitled.* Unpublished manuscript, Colgate University, Hamilton, NY.

Stewart, S. (1991). *Crimes of writing: Problems in the containment of representation.* New York: Oxford University Press.

Stieglitz, A. (1899). Pictorial photography. *Scribners Magazine, 26*, 528–537.

Swearingen, C. J. (1991). *Rhetoric and irony: Western literacy and Western lies.* New York: Oxford University Press.

Techniques for preventing plagiarism. (1994, April). *Council Chronicle*, 5–6.

Thelen, D. (Ed.). (1991). Becoming Martin Luther King, Jr.—Plagiarism and originality: A round table [Special issue]. *Journal of American History, 78*(1).

Thomas, D. M. (1993). *The white hotel.* New York: Penguin. (Original work published 1981)

Thoreau, H. D. (1950). *Walden* (B. Atkinson, Ed.). New York: Modern Library.

Thralls, C. (1992). Bakhtin, collaborative partners, and published discourse: A collaborative view of composing. In J. Forman (Ed.), *New visions of collaborative writing* (pp. 63–81). Portsmouth, NH: Boynton/Cook.

Ticknor, C. (1913). *Hawthorne and his publishers.* Boston: Houghton Mifflin.

Trimbur, J., & Braun, L. A. (1992). Laboratory life and the determination of authorship. In J. Forman (Ed.), *New visions of collaborative writing* (pp. 19–36). Portsmouth, NH: Boynton/Cook.

Troyka, L. Q. (1996). *Simon & Schuster handbook for writers* (4th ed.). Upper Saddle River, NJ: Prentice Hall.

Tsujimoto, S. E. (1988). Partners in the writing process. In J. Golub (Ed.), *Focus on collaborative learning: Classroom practices in teaching English, 1988* (pp. 85–92). Urbana, IL: National Council of Teachers of English.

Tuman, M. C. (1992). First thoughts. In M. C. Tuman (Ed.), *Literacy online: The promise (and peril) of reading and writing with computers* (pp. 3–15). Pittsburgh, PA: University of Pittsburgh Press.

Tyler, S. A. (1986). Post-modern ethnography: From document of the occult to occult document. In J. Clifford & G. E. Marcus (Eds.), *Writing culture: The poetics and politics of ethnography* (pp. 122–141). Berkeley, CA: University of California Press.

United States Department of Commerce. (1994, July). *Intellectual property and the national information infrastructure: A preliminary draft of the report of the Working Group on Intellectual Property Rights.* Washington, DC: Author.

University of Illinois international students learn about plagiarism in class. (1994, February). *The Council Chronicle,* p. 6.

Verbitsky, P. (1994, May 5). *Untitled.* Unpublished manuscript, Colgate University, Hamilton, NY.

Vitanza, V. J. (Ed.). (1996). *Cyberreader.* Boston: Allyn and Bacon.

Wall, W. (1993). *The imprint of gender: Authorship and publication in the English Renaissance.* Ithaca, NY: Cornell University Press.

We want to know: How do you define plagiarism? (1993). *The Council Chronicle,* pp. 3, 8.

Weeks, K. M. (1994). Interrogatories: Plagiarism and negligent scholarship. *Lex Collegii, 18,* 7–8.

Welch, B. (1996). A comment on "Plagiarisms, Authorships, and the Academic Death Penalty." *College English, 58,* 855–858.

Wells, D. (1993). Causes of unintentional plagiarism. *WPA: Writing Program Administration, 16,* 59–71.

Whitaker, E. E. (1993). A pedagogy to address plagiarism. *College Composition and Communication, 44,* 509–514.

White, E. M. (1989). *Developing successful college writing programs.* San Francisco: Jossey-Bass.

White, E. M. (1993, February 24). Too many campuses want to sweep student plagiarism under the rug. *Chronicle of Higher Education,* p. A44.

White, H. O. (1935). *Plagiarism and imitation during the English Renaissance: A study of critical distinctions.* Cambridge, MA: Harvard University Press.

Wittgenstein, L. (1972). *Lectures and conversations on aesthetics, psychology and religious belief* (C. Barrett, Ed.). Berkeley, CA: University of California Press.

Wood, R. G. (1994, June). Letter. *The Council Chronicle*, p. 14.

Woodmansee, M. (1984). The genius and the copyright: Economic and legal conditions of the emergence of the "author." *Eighteenth-Century Studies, 17,* 425–448.

Woodmansee, M. (1994a). *The author, art, and the market: Rereading the history of aesthetics.* New York: Columbia University Press.

Woodmansee, M. (1994b). On the author effect: Recovering collectivity. In M. Woodmansee & P. Jaszi (Eds.), *The construction of authorship: Textual appropriation in law and literature* (pp. 15–28). Durham, NC: Duke University Press.

Woodmansee, M., & Jaszi, P. (Eds.). (1994a). *The construction of authorship: Textual appropriation in law and literature.* Durham, NC: Duke University Press.

Woodmansee, M., & Jaszi, P. (1994b, December 28). *Plagiarism and copyright infringement: Bad borrowings between academia and the law.* Paper presented at the annual meeting of the Modern Language Association, San Diego, CA.

Woodmansee, M., & Jaszi, P. (1995). The law of texts: Copyright in the academy. *College English, 57,* 769–787.

Woolf, V. (1923). *Jacob's room.* New York: Harcourt, Brace, & World.

Wordsworth, W. (1974). Essay, supplementary to the Preface. In W. J. B. Owen & J. W. Smyser (Eds.), *The prose works of William Wordsworth* (Vol. 3). Oxford, England: Clarendon Press. (Original work published 1798)

Worsham, L. (1991). Writing against writing: The predicament of *Écriture Féminine* in composition studies. In P. Harkin & J. Schilb (Eds.), *Contending with words: Composition and rhetoric in a postmodern age* (pp. 82–104). New York: Modern Language Association.

Young, E. (1966). *Conjectures on original composition.* Leeds, England: Scolar Press. (Original work published 1759)

Author Index

Subject Index